Managing Modern Healthcare

Until now, research has given us only a limited understanding of how managers make sense of and apply management knowledge; how networks of interaction amongst managers help or hinder processes of knowledge diffusion and the sharing of best practice; and how these processes are all influenced both by the organizations in which managers act and by the professional communities of practice to which they belong. *Managing Modern Healthcare* fills these important gaps in our understanding by drawing upon an in-depth study of management networks and practice in three healthcare organizations in the UK. It draws from that research a number of important and grounded lessons about the sources of knowledge managers rely upon; how management networks influence the spread of management knowledge and practice; how the challenging and changing conditions managers face are shaping the nature of management work, identity and development in healthcare.

This book reveals how managers in practice are responding to the many contemporary challenges facing healthcare (and the NHS in particular) and how they are able or not to effectively exploit sources of knowledge and best practice through the networks of practice they engage in to improve healthcare delivery and healthcare organizational performance.

Managing Modern Healthcare draws upon and makes important theoretical and empirical contributions to wider work on networks and networking, management knowledge, situated learning/communities of practice, professionalization/professional identity and healthcare management more generally. Practical contributions are also made through recommendations for healthcare management practitioners and policy-makers that are intended to help improve healthcare management delivery and performance.

Mike Bresnen is Professor of Organization Studies at Alliance Manchester Business School, University of Manchester, UK.

Damian Hodgson is Professor of Organizational Analysis at Alliance Manchester Business School, University of Manchester, UK.

Simon Bailey is a Research Fellow at Alliance Manchester Business School, University of Manchester, UK.

Paula Hyde is Professor of Organization Studies at Alliance Manchester Business School, University of Manchester, UK.

John Hassard is Professor of Organizational Analysis at Alliance Manchester Business School, University of Manchester, UK.

Routledge Studies in Health Management

Edited by Ewan Ferlie

The health care sector is now of major significance, economically, scientifically and societally. In many countries, health care organizations are experiencing major pressures to change and restructure, while cost containment efforts have been accentuated by global economic crisis. Users are demanding higher service quality, and health care professions are experiencing significant reorganization whilst operating under increased demands from an ageing population.

Critically analytic, politically informed, discursive and theoretically grounded, rather than narrowly technical or positivistic, the series seeks to analyse current health care organizations. Reflecting the intense focus of policy and academic interest, it moves beyond the day to day debate to consider the broader implications of international organizational and management research and different theoretical framings.

1   **Analysing Health Care Organizations**
    A Personal Anthology
    Ewan Ferlie

2   **Managing Modern Healthcare**
    Knowledge, Networks and Practice
    *Mike Bresnen, Damian Hodgson, Simon Bailey,
    Paula Hyde and John Hassard*

Managing Modern Healthcare
Knowledge, Networks and Practice

Mike Bresnen, Damian Hodgson,
Simon Bailey, Paula Hyde and
John Hassard

Routledge
Taylor & Francis Group
New York London

First published 2017
by Routledge

711 Third Avenue, New York, NY 10017
2 Park Square, Milton Park, Abingdon, Oxfordshire OX14 4RN

Routledge is an imprint of the Taylor & Francis Group,
an informa business

First issued in paperback 2018

Library of Congress Cataloging-in-Publication Data
Names: Bresnen, Mike, 1957– author.
Title: Managing modern healthcare : knowledge, networks and practice /
   by Mike Bresnen [and four others].
Description: New York : Routledge, 2017. | Series: Routledge studies in
   health management ; 2 | Includes bibliographical references and index.
Identifi ers: LCCN 2016042058 | ISBN 9781138998780 (hardback :
   alk. paper) | ISBN 9781315658506 (ebook)
Subjects: LCSH: Health services administration. | Health care teams—
   Management.
Classification:LCCRA971.B742017|DDC362.1—dc23
LC record available at https://lccn.loc.gov/2016042058

ISBN: 978-1-138-99878-0 (hbk)
ISBN: 978-0-367-02657-8 (pbk)

Typeset in Sabon
by Apex CoVantage, LLC

Contents

List of Figures and Tables   vi
Acknowledgements   vii
About the Authors   viii

1   Managing Healthcare: Themes and Issues   1

2   Contextualizing Healthcare Management   10

3   Studying Management in Healthcare   25

4   Being a Manager   53

5   Becoming a Manager   78

6   Managers Knowing   101

7   Managers Networking   130

8   Managing Healthcare: Tensions and Prospects   157

Bibliography   184
Index   202

Figures and Tables

Figures

3.1 Identifying Managerial Cohorts   34
3.2 Levels of Formal Training by Trust   37
3.3 Levels of Formal Training by Management Group   38

Tables

2.1 Charting Management Changes in the NHS   12
2.2 Summary of Key NHS Management and Leadership
    Training Programmes   18
3.1 Comparison of Trust Characteristics   32
3.2 Full Sample of Managers by Group and by Trust   35
3.3 Gender Distribution by Trust and Management Group   36
3.4 Age Distribution by Trust   36
3.5 Years Spent in Post, in Trust and in NHS   36
3.6 Data Collected   40
3.7 Comparison of Trusts   41
4.1 Contrasting Portrayals of Management and Leadership   70
5.1 Clinical Backgrounds and Qualifications   85
5.2 Non-clinical Educational Qualifications   86
7.1 Typology of Networks   134
7.2 Dimensions of Networks   134

Acknowledgements

This book would not have been possible without the time that each of the managers we interviewed were generously willing to give to our research and without the gracious help and support of our contacts at each of the trusts who participated in the study. Of course, they remain anonymous out of the need to ensure confidentiality. But we would like to express our heart-felt thanks to them for their huge contributions to the research on which this book is based. Important contributions were made too by members of our project advisory group, and we would like to thank Dean Royles, Maxine Robertson and Ruth Boaden, as well as the representatives from each trust, for their valuable input to the research as it progressed. We would also like to thank Naomi Chambers, who helped sharpen up our discussion of the healthcare sector. Any inaccuracies, omissions or inadequacies in the work remain, of course, the responsibility of the authors. At Routledge, David Varley has been a wonderful source of encouragement and support in developing and progressing the book, and Brianna Ascher and Denise File have provided excellent assistance in moving it through to publication. Last but not least, writing a book asks a lot of our families, and so we would like to give a special mention to Carole, Kay, Sarah, Johnny and Roisin for their constant support and understanding. We would also like to thank Alex, Fiona, Jude, Madeleine, Charlotte, Abigail, Georgina, Imogen, Rob, Cath, Lizzy and Ruth for having to put up with seeing a little less of their parents than usual during its production!

The research reported here was funded by the National Institute for Health Research (NIHR) Service Delivery and Organization Programme (project number 09/1002/29), and the authors would also like to thank the NIHR for their support. The views and opinions expressed herein are those of the authors and do not necessarily reflect those of the NIHR, NHS or Department of Health.

About the Authors

Mike Bresnen is Professor of Organization Studies at Alliance Manchester Business School, University of Manchester. His research interests lie in the organization and management of healthcare and project forms of organization.

Damian Hodgson is Professor of Organizational Analysis at Alliance Manchester Business School, University of Manchester. His research focuses on the organization and management of healthcare.

Simon Bailey is a Research Fellow at Alliance Manchester Business School, University of Manchester. His research interests are in the sociology of organization and public policy and administration.

Paula Hyde is Professor of Organization Studies at Alliance Manchester Business School, University of Manchester. Her research interests lie in the sociology of work and critical explorations of how care is organized.

John Hassard is Professor of Organizational Analysis at Alliance Manchester Business School, University of Manchester. His main research interests lie in organization theory, management history and corporate change.

1 Managing Healthcare
Themes and Issues

Introduction

What does it mean to manage modern healthcare organizations? At first sight, the question does not appear complicated. We might assume the task requires individuals to be equipped with the skills and knowledge they need to be able to cope with the demands on them to help provide effective healthcare; that they need to combine efficient service delivery with a continuous search for performance improvement and best practice; and that they need to be recruited, managed, trained, and developed in such a way that they can rise to the many challenges of managing as complex a set of operations as our contemporary system of healthcare.

While such a job description provides a reasonably good general indication of what is expected of healthcare managers, it says very little about how these expectations might be achieved. It also provides little insight into the particular skill sets and forms of knowledge and expertise that managers need in order to perform their roles. It says even less perhaps about how those expectations square with the reality of managerial work in healthcare organizations, faced by complex conditions and subject to frequent and unpredictable changes (Hyde et al., 2016). Arguably, management in healthcare organizations is sufficiently similar to management in other types of organizations to make more widely adopted principles and practices of management of some generic relevance and use (in leading and motivating staff, for example). However, the particular institutional requirements, strategic imperatives and operational demands that continue to shape management action are markedly different in this sector. These factors pose particular challenges that managers need to respond to if they are to mobilize knowledge effectively to contribute to the delivery of safe and effective healthcare services (Dopson et al., 2008).

This book is centrally concerned with an exploration of the critical issues that these distinctive features raise and of the circumstances surrounding them. Understanding how healthcare managers access and use management knowledge to help improve organizational processes and so promote better service delivery is of pressing importance to policy-makers, practitioners and healthcare researchers (Walshe and Rundall, 2001; Swan et al., 2012; Ferlie, 2016). Nevertheless, health systems internationally are increasingly shaped by a growing range of stakeholder interests, which creates contestation over the features deemed most important to service delivery and the means according to which improvement might be achieved. This in turn raises important questions about the kinds of things managers *ought* to know, where this knowledge *ought* to come from, and how best its translation into the variegated operational front-line of service delivery *ought* to be achieved. When the policies of governments and organizations emphasize the importance of 'cutting edge' managerial thinking, there is an assumed equivocality of meaning, not only of the kind of knowledge required but of its effective transmission to practice (Ferlie et al., 2015; Fischer et al., 2015). Similarly, there is a tendency within official guidance to homogenize both 'management' and the institutional context of the health systems within which they operate. We believe this represents a poor characterization of the diversity of both managers and organizational settings in modern healthcare, and a key objective of this account is to explore this diversity and its implications for management knowledge and knowing.

The over-arching message that emanates from both current research and practical experience is that there continue to be major problems in the mobilization of management knowledge in healthcare settings (Ferlie et al., 2012; Swan et al., 2016). Not only do managers in healthcare face organizationally complex and challenging conditions as well as the distraction of often overwhelming operational demands and pressures (Buchanan et al., 2013); they have also been subject in recent years to waves of institutional reform that have had major effects on managerial capacity and capabilities, as well as induced significant organizational change (Hyde et al., 2016). Rather than experiencing coherence and stability, managers in healthcare instead face conditions of fragmentation and fluidity that, as will be seen, continue to make the generation, application and sharing of a coherent body of knowledge—let alone the development around it of a coherent professional community of practice—a constant challenge and a somewhat distant goal.

Managing in a Modern Healthcare Context

While models of healthcare delivery may differ markedly across different countries and pose distinct challenges for healthcare provision based upon how healthcare in each country is funded, structured and governed, questions of managerial capability and effectiveness in this sector are clearly of wider international relevance (WHO, 2000; OECD, 2002). Since any healthcare organization needs to figure out how to combine clinical and managerial requirements in the interest of delivering effective and efficient healthcare, dealing with the resultant tensions is an inevitable and common problem in any 'professional bureaucracy' (Mintzberg, 1979), such as that found in most forms of healthcare organization. Resolving these tensions and making the best use of management capacity and expertise is a challenge for policy-makers and practitioners, whatever the national healthcare system and context (Buttigieg et al., 2015).

The economic conditions experienced in the wake of the financial crisis of 2008 have been similarly global in character, and this has had a substantial impact on management in both the public and the private sphere. Managers have not only faced increasing threats to their jobs but have also had to cope with additional pressures associated with greater workloads and heightened performance expectations (Hassard et al., 2009). Financial cuts and associated organizational restructuring have had a particularly pronounced effect in the public sector of many advanced economies (Stuckler et al., 2009). Where public provision extends to healthcare, as it does in the case of the UK where the National Health Service (NHS) provides around 90 percent of healthcare, there have been particularly dramatic effects on those employed in middle management positions (Morris and Farrell, 2007; Gabriel et al., 2010). Significant cuts in managerial capacity have led to an intensification of work for remaining managers (Hassard et al., 2009; McCann et al., 2015; Hyde et al., 2016); and pressures on managers have been added to by the increasing complexity of managers' work due to frequent organizational change (Marchington et al., 2004; Ezzamel et al., 2005; Boaden et al., 2008) and the close public scrutiny that has emanated from some well-publicized failings within the sector (e.g. Francis, 2013). While such problems may be particularly pronounced in the UK healthcare sector, the challenges they pose for modern healthcare managers faced with challenging and changing political, economic and social conditions have a much wider global resonance (Reeves et al., 2014; Appleby et al., 2015).

Coping with and excelling within such conditions requires the capacity of healthcare managers to engage with, interpret, adapt and support the implementation of innovations and other advances in research (Fitzgerald et al., 2002; Currie, 2006). Improving this capacity relies then upon a clear understanding of the dynamics of knowledge flow at an individual and collective level, as well as the social, political and professional landscape within which knowledge flows associated with management learning and development take place.

However, despite a good deal of research that looks in depth at healthcare managers, it is only comparatively recently that we have begun to explore how managers access management knowledge, how they interpret and make sense of it and how they apply or adapt it in their own healthcare settings (Ferlie et al., 2012; Fischer et al., 2015). A renewed interest in how healthcare organizations manage or mobilize knowledge has developed in recent years in the wake of debates about the value of 'evidence-based medicine' (EBM) and the corresponding relevance of 'evidence-based management' (EBMgt) (Walshe and Rundall, 2001; Pfeffer and Sutton, 2006). This research agenda has gained impetus in the UK via the Cooksey review of publicly funded research into healthcare, which identified substantial "cultural, institutional and financial barriers to translating research into practice" (Cooksey, 2006: 4). However, important questions remain as to the tensions that exist between the attempt to recognize cultural and institutional particularity alongside the scientific rationalism underscoring the evidence-based movements, with the former emphasizing the subjective and practice-based nature of knowledge; while the latter requires an objective standard to be separate from and applied to practice (Gabbay and Le May, 2004; Learmonth and Harding, 2006; Morrell and Learmonth, 2015).

Similarly, while a significant amount of research has also been conducted into how policy initiatives have helped (or hindered) clinical innovations (Fitzgerald et al, 2002; Swan et al., 2012), there has been less attention directed at exploring the uptake of management research and innovative management practice by healthcare managers (Ferlie et al., 2012). A number of researchers have explored the various distinct epistemic communities in healthcare management and their impact upon the implementation of cross-cutting management initiatives (Ferlie et al., 2005; Swan et al., 2007; Currie et al., 2008). Nonetheless, there has so far been little attempt made to understand the reproduction of knowledge and transmission of learning through and between the various communities of practice found within NHS management. So, for instance, important questions remain unanswered about how networks of interaction amongst managers help or hinder processes of knowledge sharing and the diffusion of best practice and how these processes are influenced by the communities of practice to which managers belong (Bate and Robert, 2002; Gabbay and Le May, 2010).

Despite the recognized importance of organizational context in shaping management action (Dopson et al., 2008), we are also only beginning to understand the dynamic interaction between different healthcare settings, the knowledge work of managers and the pathways through which they learn, adapt and develop their professional/occupational orientations. How, for example, are managers' knowledge requirements affected by the organizational context in which they operate? And how do the communities in which they are socialized and through which they develop affect efforts to create any kind of collective identity amongst the diverse group of professionals that constitutes the managerial cadre in any particular healthcare organization (Kirkpatrick et al., 2005; McKee et al., 2008)?

Knowing, Networking and Practicing Management

The research we present in this book explores how managers in practice are responding to the many contemporary challenges they face in a changing healthcare context. It examines what this means for their ability to harness appropriate sources and types of knowledge and learning through the work they do in particular types of healthcare organization and through their networks of practice. It sets out to trace the effects on managers of changing institutional conditions and shifting managerial discourses, as well as the influence of organizational settings and the impact of managers' own occupational experiences and professional career development. The research therefore emphasizes the importance of understanding flows of management knowledge and learning from the perspective of managers themselves, influenced by the social and organizational context in which they are embedded (Brown and Duguid, 2001; Dopson et al., 2008).

Importantly, the book takes a critical approach to its subject matter that recognizes that many of the key concepts that are germane to an understanding of management in healthcare—such as knowledge, networks, professional identity, leadership and management itself—are not simply objective phenomena that are definitive, abstract and uncontested; but instead are social constructions that are much more fluid, contested and emergent through practice. Management knowledge itself is highly contested—not simply due to its origins in very different contexts such as manufacturing; but also when one considers long-standing debates about the validity of different forms of management knowledge (e.g. Clegg and Palmer, 1996; Barley and Kunda, 2001). Concepts such as leadership and professionalization, when related to management, are no less indeterminate and contested. Indeed, debates have long raged over how leadership relates to management (e.g. Bryman, 1986) and whether management can be considered in any way a 'profession' (e.g. Reed and Anthony, 1992; Khurana, 2010).

Taking a more constructionist line applies also to the approach taken to understanding the nature of (management) knowledge and the networks of interaction through which it flows. We take as problematic the idea that management knowledge can effectively be conceived of as a commodity that is readily transferable into and across healthcare contexts; as well as the presumption that management networks and communities of practice can be comparatively easily rendered through policy initiatives and practical action and then simply mobilized for the purposes of knowledge sharing or learning (cf. Ferlie et al., 2012). Instead, the approach taken here emphasizes the importance of understanding processes of knowledge generation, sharing, transformation and learning as intrinsically linked to (management) practice—an approach that shifts the focus from understanding the supposedly objective qualities of (management) knowledge, to emphasizing instead the socially situated nature of processes of (managerial) knowing (e.g. Cook and Brown, 1999; Brown and Duguid, 2001; Carlile, 2004; Nicolini, 2011).

As such, the approach adopted is one that is not only sensitive to the complexities (and contested nature) of the knowledge base used by managers but also to the socially constituted and situated processes of knowing and learning connected with that knowledge base. Particular attention is therefore paid to the ways in which the translation of managerial knowledge into practice is strongly influenced by both management practice and by the context of management (Cook and Brown, 1999; Newell et al., 2003; Dopson and Fitzgerald, 2006). In doing so, space is also created for highlighting how differences in perspective, interests and power might have profound influences upon the flows of knowledge and learning occurring within and between managerial groups (Contu and Willmott, 2003; Carlile, 2004; Roberts, 2006).

Importantly too, the starting point for understanding management in healthcare is taken to be managers themselves—how they see their managerial work and expectations placed on them to demonstrate leadership; what forms of knowledge and learning and which types of network they engage with to do their work; and what sort of managers they see themselves as being and becoming through their professional career development in healthcare. While our approach recognizes that the institutional and organizational contexts they work in can have powerful effects on shaping and constraining managerial choice and action, getting a good sense of what it means to be a manager in a modern healthcare organization inevitably points to the need to fully explore managers' perspectives on their own roles, knowledge bases, networking opportunities and career moves. Only by doing so is it possible to examine the manner in which individuals attempt to make sense of their professional role and identity and how this relates to how they mobilize knowledge in the contexts in which they act (cf. Watson, 1994, 2008; Weick, 1995).

At the same time, in practical terms there is a need to locate what we mean by managers in this particular context. What do we mean by 'management' or more specifically, 'middle management' in healthcare? The question is particularly important given the tendency in research to focus on management as a role, as opposed to management as a (distributed) function in healthcare organizations, undertaken across a wide range of clinical and non-clinical groups (Buchanan, 2013). Middle managers are traditionally a difficult cadre to define, as the demarcations between hierarchical levels in contemporary organizations are often unclear (Currie and Procter, 2005; McConville, 2006; Hassard et al., 2009). As we shall see, the research reported in this book relies upon McConville's (2006: 639) definition of middle managers as being those who are located at least two levels up and two levels down the managerial hierarchy. It also includes within its scope not just those who could be described as 'general managers'; but also those clinicians as well as other specialists (e.g. financial managers) whose remit is managerial and who thus have responsibility for the performance of their clinical or other, specialist teams.

To capture the diversity in management, we develop a framework based upon differences in managers' clinical and managerial experience. The aim is to capture samples of different managerial cohorts who had their own quite diverse needs and perspectives and who naturally draw upon different types of management knowledge (e.g. medical, operational, financial). Such an approach allowed for a more contextualized understanding of management in the organizations studied and acknowledges the highly distributed nature of the management and leadership function in healthcare (Buchanan et al., 2007).

Contextual influences—particularly the organizations in which managers are based and the communities to which they belong—are also expected to have an important bearing on how managers access management knowledge and apply it to their management practice. As will be seen, the research explored the perspectives of middle managers across three types of NHS trust (located in England). The three trusts were selected to represent quite different types of healthcare organization that provided diverse forms of service. This would mean a good deal of variation in managers' role expectations and knowledge requirements and in the networks available to them. By drilling down into an exploration of management in three quite dissimilar healthcare trusts, it was intended that insights would be generated that were sensitive to differences in healthcare setting and that grounded lessons would be produced that were generalizable to equivalent types of healthcare setting and context—both nationally and internationally. To develop this comparative case study analysis, qualitative methods involving a combination of interviews and observation were chosen to capture the subtleties of how different groups of managers went about mobilizing and using management knowledge in their everyday work (Yin, 1984; Eisenhardt and Graebner, 2007).

Contributions to Theory, Research, Policy and Practice

The main intention of this book is to contribute to the development of a critical mass of research on healthcare management that recognizes the importance of understanding managers' perspectives on their evolving work, roles and professional identity (cf. Watson, 2008). In particular, the research reported here sets out to contribute theoretically and empirically to understanding how management practice in healthcare relates to wider discourses of leadership within the sector (cf. O'Reilly and Reed, 2011); how managers mobilize management knowledge and apply it to their everyday management practice (cf. Ferlie et al., 2015; Swan et al., 2016); how managers make use of the professional and occupational networks in which they are embedded; and what this all means for management learning within healthcare and the development of a distinct professional/occupational identity (cf. von Knorring et al., 2016).

A distinctive contribution of the book is that it recognizes—and attempts to capture—the diverse nature of management in healthcare, by examining management experiences in three distinct, archetypal forms of healthcare organization and by developing a novel framework that differentiates between very different types of manager—in order to highlight the distinct practices in which they engage and the diverse challenges they face. As such, the research develops a nuanced account of management in healthcare that recognizes not only its diverse and fragmented nature (Buchanan et al., 2013) but also the influence of organizational context on managerial action (cf. Dopson et al., 2008). Moreover, it presents an analysis that interprets how wider changes within the sector are shaping and constraining managerial action and management development. In so doing, it highlights the many tensions and contradictions that emerge when one compares the dynamics of change within the sector with the orientations of practicing healthcare managers charged with exercising leadership, mobilizing 'cutting edge' knowledge, exploiting networks of interaction and aspiring to develop professional careers.

These more critical aims distinguish it from other, more prescriptive 'textbook' accounts of how management in healthcare might be enhanced or improved. Indeed, it should come as no surprise that our account suggests that there are major challenges facing the healthcare sector if best use is to be made of its managerial capacity and capabilities. In particular, it brings into question the extent to which changes occurring in healthcare organization have beneficial effects on management practice, and it draws out some of the unintended consequences of actions taken to improve managerial capabilities and performance. It also highlights the precariousness of management in healthcare (cf. Collinson, 2003) and the tremendous efforts managers themselves are making to cope with the effects of change and to maintain a sense of continuity, coherence and control in conditions of institutional complexity and political and economic uncertainty.

Nevertheless, the approach adopted does produce a number of important and grounded lessons about how forms of management knowledge and networks in healthcare influence management practice; how management learning, training and development relate to the needs of managers facing challenging conditions; and what the prospects are for leadership development and the professionalization of healthcare management. Practical contributions come in the form of recommendations and suggestions for how healthcare management practitioners and policy-makers might take steps that help enhance healthcare management delivery and performance—particularly with regard to understanding the challenges in promoting more effective leadership and the barriers and enablers to the uptake of management knowledge and networking opportunities.

The Structure of the Book

In Chapter 2 that follows, we set the scene for the main empirical chapters by presenting an overview of the institutional context of healthcare management and of the changes that have occurred in recent years as a result of policy initiatives. The focus is on the English context, its principal characteristics and how healthcare management has been shaped by successive waves of leadership and management training and development initiatives that reflect often contradictory discourses of healthcare management.

Chapter 3 introduces the empirical research and outlines the perspective used to explore what managing means for managers 'on the ground', what processes of knowing, learning and networking managers engage with and how this relates to their evolving sense of professional/occupational identity. The frameworks used to select case study trusts and managerial cohorts are introduced, as are the methods used to conduct the research and produce the cases themselves. The rest of this book then follows a structure that relates to each of the four main empirical themes explored through the research.

In Chapter 4, we examine what *being* a manager in healthcare means to those we interviewed. The chapter explores managers' perceptions of their roles and responsibilities in the current context. It examines, in particular, how management background and local conditions shape managerial roles and thinking, the different strategies used for managing the clinical-managerial divide and how aspirations of leadership mesh with day-to-day management experience.

Chapter 5 builds upon the theme of managerial identity that emerges towards the end of the previous chapter by considering what it means to *become* a manager in healthcare. The backgrounds and career trajectories of the managers we interviewed are examined, as are their experiences and orientations towards management. Particular attention is directed towards the nature of managerial identity associated with the proliferation in healthcare of so-called 'hybrid' managers (e.g. Currie and White, 2012; Buchanan, 2014).

Chapter 6 is concerned with managerial *knowing* and considers how managers access and use management knowledge and the possibilities, constraints and limitations for translating more general management knowledge into a healthcare setting. Different forms and sources of knowledge available to the distinct groups of managers interviewed are explored, and a particular accent is put on the juxtaposition of local and situated forms of knowledge with knowledge that is more abstract and codified.

Chapter 7 builds upon the theme of exploring sources of knowledge by examining managers' *networking* activities. Based upon managerial perceptions of networking (rather than formal network mapping), the range and nature of networks engaged with by managers are explored, as too are the motives for, and perceived benefits from, networking. Barriers and constraints to the development of networks within and among different types of healthcare organization and management groups are also assessed.

In the concluding Chapter 8, we draw together the threads of analysis in the preceding four chapters to revisit the challenges facing management in healthcare in the current context and to draw out the implications for theory and practice that emerge from this research.

2 Contextualizing Healthcare Management

Introduction

Established in 1948, the NHS represented a radical attempt to provide nationalized healthcare free at the point of need. Despite many reorganizations, the NHS continues to operate under severe pressures as it faces increasing patient demand, decreasing resources and a rise in external competition. More than ever before, it relies on the knowledge and efforts of its workforce. Over and above these on-going pressures, shortages of trained workers and financial restraints present several challenges for managers. This chapter provides a two-part overview; first, of changes to healthcare policy in England and how these changes have affected managers; and second, of changes to arrangements for management and leadership development in the NHS. The first part charts the changes that have occurred in recent years that have shaped the landscape of healthcare management and defined the challenges faced by leaders and managers in healthcare. The analysis of the present state of play is set within the national and international context of healthcare management. Particular attention is focused on changes to current institutional conditions in the UK as a result of policy initiatives and developments in practice within the sector. Important and on-going policy and academic debates about the nature of change in healthcare and its future trajectory are examined. The second part of the chapter focuses specifically on the nature of management in healthcare and examines the structure of healthcare organizations and the place of managers within them. The many initiatives that have shaped the identity of managers in healthcare over several years are examined, including the shift in emphasis from management to leadership. The various leadership and management training and development initiatives across the sector are also examined.

Managing Healthcare Organizations

Managers matter in the vast and complex web of organizations that make up the NHS (Kings Fund, 2011). In 2015, the NHS employed 1.3 million people,[1] making it the fifth-largest employer in the world (Alexander, 2012).

The wage bill alone for the NHS is £45 billion (DDRB, 2016), and for NHS providers in England, staffing accounts for 'about two thirds' of total expenditure (Lafond, 2015). Moreover, the NHS contains over 300 different occupations and over 1000 employing organizations, all of which present an unenviable management challenge (Hyde and Exworthy, 2016).

Nevertheless, there have been a swathe of recent reforms intended to reduce the number of managers in the NHS, most notably through the abolition of particular layers of hierarchy (including 151 Primary Care Trusts and 10 over-arching Strategic Health Authorities) following the implementation of the *Health and Social Care Act* from 2012 onwards. The policy direction informing this is summarized in the White Paper *Equity and Excellence: Liberating the NHS*:

> The Government will reduce NHS management costs by more than 45% over the next four years, freeing up further resources for front-line care.
>
> (2010: 5)

Managers, and middle managers in particular, play a vital role in large organizations, co-ordinating activity between the upper and lower organizational reaches and across various departments, translating broader policy/strategy into operational outcomes and frequently serving as a key repository of organizational memory (Huy, 2001). However, managers also represent one of the least contentious targets of restructuring, particularly reductions in headcount that attempt to avoid impacting the 'front-line' of operations (Cascio, 2002; Hassard et al., 2009). In this context, it is unsurprising that 'management' represents an identity few find desirable, and even those with the responsibility of 'managing' repudiate the 'management' part of their role (Brocklehurst et al., 2009)—with, we argue, significant repercussions for managerial work.

It may be argued that these wider tensions have impinged even more acutely upon managers in the NHS in recent years (McConville, 2006). As noted, reforms instigated by the coalition government from 2012 specifically targeted a huge reduction in management costs as the primary means of improving NHS efficiency. Although many aspects of the reforms have been subject to intense debate, there was remarkably little negative reaction to the proposed cuts in management costs. This lack of public outcry can be accounted for as resulting from negative characterizations of NHS middle managers, casting them as petty bureaucrats and descriptions of the NHS as a whole as burdened by a growing, unproductive and even obstructive management cadre (Merali, 2003; Kings Fund, 2011; Buchanan et al., 2013). To understand the nature of management in the current NHS, then, it is essential to situate NHS management as an activity and a formal role in some historical context.

Reforming and Restructuring the NHS

The NHS has undergone regular, radical reform over the last forty years. These reforms have involved structural changes, reorganization and adjustments to management arrangements. There have been general moves towards marketization and business-like functioning. These changes have had striking effects on management practice, professional values and service organization and delivery in the NHS as a whole and in the English context in particular (which is the focus of this research). This section provides an overview of government policy as it affects NHS management and presents the changes as a series of stages or phases to illustrate how the direction of travel has been towards a more entrepreneurial service (for fuller accounts of NHS policy, see Harrison and McDonald (2008), and Klein (2010)).

Table 2.1 indicates several periods of change mapped against major policy initiatives. In the period 1948–1982, administrative arrangements for

Table 2.1 Charting Management Changes in the NHS

Period	Management changes	Major policy initiatives
1948–1982	Public administration and 'consensus management'	Nationalization of health 1974 NHS Reorganization
1983–1997	General management and gradual adoption of New Public Management philosophy from boards down	Griffiths Report (1983)
	Quasi-markets	NHS and Community Care Act (1990)
1997–2007	Business management	New NHS: Modern, Dependable (1997)
	Overhaul of career structures and performance related pay	Agenda for Change (1999; implemented nationally in 2004)
	Regulatory reform and increased investment	NHS Plan (2000)
	Foundation trusts, quality commission and independent regulator	Community Health and Standards Act (2003)
2008–2012	Leadership	Darzi Review (2008)
	Structural reform	Liberating the NHS (2010)
2012–2016	Entrepreneurship Competitive market Efficiency savings (the £20bn 'Nicholson challenge') High turnover of senior management, driving demand for highly lucrative interim appointments	Health and Social Care Act (2012)

the NHS remained relatively stable from nationalization up until the introduction of general management following the Griffiths Report. The period 1983–1997 saw government health policy that emphasized the importance of specific managerial roles to improve efficiencies as part of a number of NHS reorganizations. The *NHS Management Inquiry* (1983) by Roy Griffiths, chairman of the supermarket chain Sainsbury's, effectively abolished 'consensus' management in favour of 'general management' and provided the structural arrangement for a rational management system (Exworthy et al., 2009). As a result of Griffiths' recommendations, the following management reforms took place: appointment of general managers, introduction of management budgets, value for money reforms and management training and education. General managers from inside and outside the NHS were to be in place in hospitals and health authorities by the end of 1985. Management budgets were to be introduced alongside greater financial controls. Savings arising from these reforms were to be returned to improving services for patients; and the NHS Training Authority was established in order to extend management training, especially for doctors (Griffiths, 1983). Doctors were to become more closely involved in financial matters and budgeting. Although many clinicians did not identify themselves as managers at all, they found themselves having to balance patient care and concerns for resource management and the like (Anthony and Reed, 1990: 22).

The period 1983–1997 involved early attempts to prepare the NHS for market competition and consequently demanded business skills and knowledge from NHS managers. The 1989 white paper *Working for Patients* passed into law as the *NHS and Community Care Act* in 1990. This act introduced an (internal) quasi-market for healthcare by encouraging services to split along 'purchaser' (Health Authority and some GPs) and 'provider' (acute, mental health, ambulance and community) lines. Purchasers were given budgets to buy healthcare from providers. Providers became NHS trusts (independent organizations with their own management teams). These trusts would then compete with each other to provide services to the purchasers. Between 1991 and 1995 all providers became NHS trusts. GPs could hold budgets (GP fund holding) to purchase care for their patients from the NHS or private providers. Some GP fund-holders were able to accelerate care for their patients, leading to accusations of a two-tier health system emerging (Klein, 2010). As well as attempting to increase managerial control of services, these changes were also designed to introduce competition and a business culture.

Although these quasi-market institutions were originally abandoned by the new Labour government of 1997, these early experiences may have paved the way for a later return to market-oriented reforms. The period between 1997 and 2007 saw unprecedented change involving the formation and dissolution and rearrangement of structures and responsibilities of NHS authorities and trusts. Importantly, this was accompanied by the devolution of responsibility for healthcare within the UK from 1999 onwards to the newly established administrations in Scotland, Wales and later Northern Ireland, who as a whole placed less emphasis on patient choice and competition than did England. As a consequence, much of what follows focuses primarily on the NHS in England.[2]

The white paper *The New NHS: Modern, Dependable* (Department of Health, 1997) saw the abolition of the internal market and dismantling of GP fund holding. This was an era of centralized management of the NHS as if it were one organization. It involved national target-setting intended to reduce waiting times and improve access to services and the introduction of a star rating system for NHS organizations. Organizations were rated by the newly established Commission for Health Improvement (CHI). Although national targets were subsequently abandoned, along with the star rating system, priorities continued to be indicated through the annual Operating Framework for the NHS published each year. The National Institute for Clinical Excellence (NICE) was created in 1999 to make decisions on the adoption of treatments.[3] These two institutions (CHI and NICE) took control of areas previously controlled by the medical profession. Decisions about efficacy and cost-effectiveness of treatments were now being made by NICE, and clinical governance was being carried out by the CHI. Research at the time found enmities between clinicians and managers to the extent that Dopson (1994: 7) claimed that "general managers have been singularly unsuccessful in involving clinicians in managing their services." Nevertheless, front-line managers emerged as nurse-managers, and doctors were managed by clinical directors. The various reforms meant that increasingly managers had to engage with marketization and to acquire business knowledge.

The *NHS Plan* (Department of Health, 2000)—a ten-year plan for the NHS and National Service Frameworks—described service standards for areas such as mental health and cardiac care. Decades of under-spending on healthcare meant that England had notably poor health outcomes compared to other developed nations. In 2000, the government promised to increase health spending to European levels. This meant a rise from 6.6 percent (1999/2000) to 9 percent of GDP (2005/6). Although the targets and associated penalties were initially successful in reducing waiting times, increasingly disturbing behaviours linked to intense centralized control preceded a radical change in direction towards decentralization and the re-adoption of market-based reforms. These included the promotion of patient choice and competition between providers as well as allowing for organizations based on not-for-profit structures—NHS Foundation Trusts. The first wave of Foundation Trusts came into being in 2004. At the same time, the previous system of block contracts to service providers was replaced by a new funding system called *Payment by Results*. This system was aimed at reducing waiting times by targeting payments towards specific treatments and thus providing a powerful incentive for trusts to direct activity towards areas of greatest need. In addition it allowed for private providers to claim payments for services provided in new, privately-owned Independent Treatment Centres. GP incentives to provide more services outside of hospital were provided for through the Quality Outcomes Framework.

The period 2008–2012 began with the Darzi review (2008), which set out a second ten-year plan for the NHS, although this was soon displaced by the unfolding financial crisis and the change of government in 2009. The immediate impact of the financial crisis in 2007–08 and the subsequent debt crisis faced by the UK was to place NHS finances under severe pressure. While the NHS budget was officially 'protected' from the level of cuts faced by other public services, faced with increasing demand, a growing and ageing population and spiralling treatment costs, significant savings were necessary simply to maintain the same level of service. From 2009, the NHS was tasked with making efficiency savings of £20 billion over five years in line with what was named the *Nicholson Challenge* (after the NHS Chief Executive at the time, Sir David Nicholson). This was then superseded in 2014 by the *Five Year Forward View* (NHS England, 2014), which proposed £22 billion of efficiency savings by 2020. While similar fiscal pressures were experienced in the healthcare systems of countries across the world following the financial crisis, the direct budgetary challenges in the UK impacted directly on almost every aspect of healthcare during the period of time covered by this study.

Equally significant for the UK healthcare sector were the major structural reforms enacted in this period—in particular, the *Health and Social Care Act (2012)*, the impact of which was felt from 2010 onwards as the bill progressed through the British parliament. The first white paper of the Conservative-Liberal Democrat coalition government in 2010, *Equity and Excellence: Liberating the NHS*, advocated what were said to be the most significant changes to the NHS since it began (Whitehead et al., 2010). As already mentioned, it proposed reducing management costs by 45 percent over four years and delayering the NHS by removing Primary Care Trusts and Strategic Health Authorities, the local and regional tiers of commissioning and strategic planning. However, many of the responsibilities of these layers were to be replaced by various new agencies focused on commissioning services, with much of the commissioning role to be taken up by entirely new local organizations known as Clinical Commissioning Groups (CCGs). *The Health and Social Care Act (2012)* also sought to 'liberate' the healthcare economy, encouraging the provision of healthcare services from new public or private providers "in a competitive consumer market" (Hyde et al., 2016: 27). Requiring commissioners to consider bids from 'any qualified provider' opened up the sector to new private or third sector organizations to an unprecedented degree. The view was to intensify competition between providers, with public and private bodies notionally on a 'level playing field'. To compete to retain contracts, managers of provider services were therefore required to become increasingly entrepreneurial. In a similar vein, Foundation Trusts were now allowed to generate up to 49 percent of their revenue from private sources, again encouraging increased entrepreneurial zeal among their management staffs.

A third major event—in a tumultuous period for the NHS—was the publication of the Francis Report (2013), following an official enquiry into the poor quality of care at Mid Staffordshire NHS Foundation Trust. The report criticized senior management for prioritizing finance targets while neglecting concerns over the quality of care delivered to patients, with this being reinforced by a culture which sought to silence the concerns of staff, patients and families. One year after publication, a continuing tendency for top-down targets and performance management systems to produce a bullying culture was reported, described by Robert Francis QC as "a persistence of somewhat oppressive reactions to reports of problems in meeting financial and other corporate requirements" (Dayan, 2014: 5). The report led to a number of policy changes, including those in inspection regimes, roles and standards, and with a greater focus on patient care. Although many welcomed its impact in re-prioritizing care, the tension between meeting demanding financial targets and maintaining an acceptable quality of care was not resolved by the report (Dayan, 2014). The combined effects of major reorganization and extreme financial pressures in this decade placed even more intense pressure on healthcare managers in light of Francis's recommendations.

As can be seen, the substantial institutional changes affecting healthcare in the UK in recent decades have if anything accelerated in both pace and magnitude through the course of the period of our study, with far-reaching consequences on management practice, professional values and service organization in the NHS as a whole. Moves towards the decentralized control of NHS organizations, with increasing numbers of hospitals becoming Foundation Trusts, and efforts to increase patient choice and competition between health provider organizations, have relied upon NHS management for delivery. Increasing institutional regulation of health and care providers, through national bodies such as NICE, and Monitor and the Care Quality Commission (CQC) in England, have increased scrutiny on the performance of those charged with managing these organizations, as well as maintaining a bureaucratic burden on healthcare administrators. Managers have thus been given increasing responsibility for implementing health service reforms, providing the links between planning and organizing activities and those providing services to patients. At the same time, they have borne the brunt of the efficiencies required by the reforms—a theme to which the discussion now turns.

Consequences for Managers and Management

Between 2000 and 2009, amidst these changes, the NHS workforce grew by around 30 percent. Across this period, as NHS expenditure almost doubled (Walshe and Smith, 2011), the number of managers and senior managers rose from 2.7 percent (full-time equivalent) in 2000 (n=24,253) to

3.4 percent in 2009 (n=40,094) (NHSIC, 2010), remaining broadly in line with figures for most other developed countries (WHO, 2006). Since 2010, however, employment in the NHS has been falling and recent reductions in overall NHS staffing numbers have been more than matched by reductions in the total numbers of managers. Figures from 2012 show the proportion of managers at 3.2 percent, suggesting that policy reforms targeted at reducing management costs were beginning to bite (NHSIC, 2012). Notwithstanding definitional difficulties (Kings Fund, 2011: 4), managers appear to account for over one-fifth of the total number of redundancies between 2011 and 2014. As Street and Grasic (2015) argue: "[Health service] managers now account for just 3 percent of the NHS workforce, a much lower proportion than the 15 percent in the workforce generally." Reductions in managerial staffing appear to have been followed by re-employment of some managers (Hyde and Exworthy, 2016), but this has not compensated for the more substantial loss of managerial capacity. In parallel, it can be observed that NHS spending on management consultants rose from £313m in 2010 to £640m in 2014 (Campbell, 2014).

In all likelihood, managerial numbers will continue to decrease in subsequent years as middle managers continue to be targeted in health reforms aimed at reducing management costs in a period of austerity. This comes at a time when effective organizational co-ordination will be central to maintaining safety and quality of care during a period of reduced investment.

As well as the increased demands for management resulting from higher staffing levels, other recent institutional changes which have generated additional management workloads include:

- moving to service line management
- applying for Foundation Trust status
- achieving national performance standards
- payment by results, changing to tariffs, fines
- Quality, Innovation, Productivity and Prevention (QIPP) agenda
- creation of clinical commissioning groups
- changing regulatory, auditing and accreditation regimes
- making £20 billion savings by 2015. (Buchanan et al., 2013)

The impact of recent changes across the NHS, in particular the *Health and Social Care Act (2012)*, is still being felt. Throughout the period of our study, the immediate consequences were of widespread uncertainty exacerbated by the on-going and substantial pressures to reduce costs significantly, year on year, while at the same time maintaining service quality. Achieving this with often-reduced staff numbers, particularly reduced number of managers as attempts were made to avoid reductions in 'front-line' staffing levels (i.e. doctors and nurses), led to a widespread experience of severe work intensification among NHS managers, described elsewhere as 'normalized intensity' (McCann et al., 2008). Furthermore, as trusts reached the limits of savings achievable through relatively minor efficiency savings (such as minor reductions in staffing levels), management was increasingly charged with devising and enacting more substantial and sweeping service redesign to achieve the scale of savings demanded.

In this section we have charted political change—influential government policies and consequent institutional and cultural changes—involving management of the NHS from its inception to date. In the next section, we explore the professional development challenges facing managers in the sector and the initiatives taken to develop managerial and leadership capabilities.

Initiatives for Management Change and Leadership Development

Since the first intake of the NHS Management Training Scheme in September 1956, the content, location and impact of management and later leadership development in the NHS has undergone regular transformation (see table 2.2 below). While terminology has changed, the core aim of these

Table 2.2 Summary of Key NHS Management and Leadership Training Programmes

Year	Management Training Programme	Agency Responsible
1956-	National Administrative Training Scheme	Regional Staffing Officers (RSO) National Staff Committee for Administrative and Clerical Staff (NSCA&C) Standing Committee on Management Education and Training (SCMET)
1983-	National Management Training Scheme	NHS Training Authority
1986-	Graduate Management Training Scheme	
1993-	National Management Training Scheme National Management Development programme	NHS Training Directorate
2002-	Graduate Management Training Scheme Breaking Through Gateway to Leadership	NHS Leadership Centre
2009-	Top Leaders Emerging Leaders Inclusion Clinical Leadership Board Development	NHS Leadership Council
2012-	Foundation programme • (award: post-graduate diploma) Mid-career programme • (award: Masters degree) Executive/senior leadership programme • (peer assessed)	NHS Leadership Academy

programmes remains consistent: in 1955, the aim was to provide the NHS with "well-trained administrators who would be competent to fill senior administrative posts in years to come" (Powell et al., 2012: 37); while in 2012, the newly formed NHS Leadership Academy set out as its aim "to create, for the first time, a cadre of leaders who, irrespective of professional background, are comprehensively equipped to lead and develop high performing organizations with behaviours that are congruent with NHS values and uphold the NHS Constitution."[4]

While the core aims have remained, the discursive shifts reflecting the policy shifts described above are notable. In particular, we note here the acknowledgement of hybridization, the shift towards leadership and the stitching together of the needs for both 'equity *and* excellence' for which leaders will be held to account. Notable too are the contrasts between the stability and predictability of the 1955 version, which reads as 'a job for life for competent people', and the absence of such values in the later version, replaced with the dynamic, yet unstable, language of the leader. These themes, noted only in brief here, will be picked up at later points in this book.

In the period between 1955 and 2012, the responsibility for producing these administrators, managers and latterly, leaders has oscillated between the regions and more central NHS bodies. There has also been a notable shift in the basis of professionalization of NHS managers represented by the shift in terminology from administration, to management and to leadership (Learmonth, 2005; O'Reilly and Reed, 2011).

The NHS Graduate Management Training Scheme (GMTS) broadly retains the structure set up in 1986, combining formal education (leading to a MSc) with a series of rotatory placements and internships in NHS organizations that give prospective managers direct experience of a range of healthcare management situations together with formalized education and training. Following the introduction of the GMTS, several other management/leadership development programmes were established as part of the *Modernization Agenda* in the early 2000s, including initiatives promoting diversity in management, including *Breaking Through* (for Black and Minority Ethnic employees), *Gateway to Leadership* (to develop senior managers from outside the NHS) and the *Athena Programme for Executive Women*. Such initiatives were underpinned by the creation of the *Leadership Qualities Framework* (LQF) in 2004 by the NHS Leadership Centre.

In 2009, the Department of Health published *Inspiring Leaders*. Reflecting strategy set out in *The Operating Framework for the NHS in England 2008/09*, the *Inspiring Leaders* report explicitly devolved responsibility for leadership development to regional employers, requiring SHAs to produce talent and leadership plans by the end of July 2009. In line with the principle of 'subsidiarity', these plans were to be cascaded down to the local and individual level, guided by the over-arching activities of the newly formed NHS Leadership Council.

Any potential impact of this was, however, curtailed by the change of government and the *Health and Social Care Bill (2012)* which set in train the abolition of the bodies charged with overseeing leadership development. With the abolition of SHAs, PCTs and various other organizations:

> Planned changes for the NHS mean that many of the organizations and structures in place that host and/or deliver national leadership activities will no longer be in a position to continue this work and this poses a threat to the continued success of leadership development across the NHS, without other arrangements being in place.[5]

The new arrangement to ensure continuity in this area took the form of the replacement of the short-lived NHS Leadership Council with a new NHS Leadership Academy (formed in April 2012). The principle of 'subsidiarity', whereby responsibility for leadership development would be cascaded down to regional and local organizations, was rejected. Instead, the NHS Leadership Academy was formed: (1) to ensure a more centralized strategy, reducing duplication, fragmentation and discontinuity by providing a single national structure for leadership development; and (2) to set in place a more bottom-up approach to development by giving employers "greater autonomy and accountability for planning and developing the workforce" (Department of Health, 2010: 40). The intention was to ensure that "the integrated national approach proposed enables the more efficient use of resources by reducing variable and fragmented locally defined provision of basic leadership training as well as enabling shared experiences and the development of a common language for leaders across the service."[6] The academy also received unprecedented levels of investment, as part of the attempt to systematise management and leadership development in the NHS in England.

The NHS Leadership Academy sets as one of its primary tasks the "professionalization of healthcare leadership" so as to:

> raise the profile, performance and impact of leaders in health and create an environment where leaders at all levels are required and supported to demonstrate their fit and proper readiness to fulfil the role they occupy. This will elevate leadership as a profession.

Citing recent research reports (Nicolson et al., 2011), wider academic research and widely cited instances from the private sector (e.g. General Electric), the NHSLA briefing makes strong claims about the ability of leadership to make a significant difference to organizations' performance and outcomes. The Leadership Academy initially set out three core programmes that were to be established:

1   Foundation programme (Mary Seacole): aimed at aspiring leaders with some experience of managing people and leading to a post-graduate certificate

2   Mid-career programme (Elizabeth Garrett Anderson): aimed at those who manage team leaders, for example, and who seek a broader leadership role. This programme leads to a master's degree

3   Senior leadership programme (Nye Bevan): as preparation for an executive, national or other senior leadership role. The programme is unusual as, while it is not academic award-bearing, it does lead to an Academy Award which not everyone passes and which is only gained following rigorous peer assessment

These programmes are delivered in collaboration with an increasing number of public and private sector partners—the Elizabeth Garratt Anderson Programme, for example, is certified by an MSc but also involves business consultancies such as KPMG, and the patient group, National Voices. Just as shifts towards a discourse of 'leaderism' are consistent with broader shifts towards market logics in healthcare (O'Reilly and Reed, 2011), so too we see traces of this logic in the diversification of available leadership programmes, offering the aspiring leader choices tailored to their developmental needs, delivered by 'market experts' and 'held to account' by consumer groups.

The establishment of the Leadership Academy itself, and the centralization of development resources and standardization of curriculum which it brought with it, also demonstrates the growing influence of corporate logics. The shift to leaderism provides a language which in its apparent dynamism can be applied with greater ease to a greater number of different groups than the somewhat denigrated language of management—not just managers can be converted into leaders, but so too clinicians, patients and the public. As Martin and Learmonth (2012) argue, the notion of 'dispersed' or 'distributed' leadership that this shift enacts stands in stark contrast to the increasingly centralized control of public healthcare. The existence of the Academy is one example of such centralization. However, there is a double shift at work here, whereby leadership roles are understood to be dispersed, but the major responsibility for the formal creation and distribution of leadership 'texts' is placed in a single entity. This creates discursive closure around particular ways of doing leadership, creating an abstracted set of 'evidence-based' or 'best practices', which may be a poor fit for the pragmatic and other interests that face managers/leaders decision-making in practice (Learmonth and Harding, 2006; Morrell and Learmonth, 2015). For example, the *Leadership Qualities Framework*, which was introduced in 2011, is organized around two distinct and potentially conflicted sides to the role of leaders within a centralized and publicly funded bureaucracy: "developing the vision" while also "delivering the strategy."[7] This framework was replaced in 2013 with the *Healthcare Leadership Model*, which is organized around nine dimensions.[8] While this has removed the dualistic opposition between the need for leaders to act with autonomy *and* in consonance with government policy, such a tension still remains, with the central dimension, 'inspiring shared purpose' making the presumption that 'purpose' is universally and uniformly understood by leaders.

Of course, it is not the case that a singular and universal vision of leadership is passed down unmediated from academy to the individual on the ground. Firstly, there are regional bodies, currently called Leadership Delivery Partners, who work as partners with the Leadership Academy and commission and provide programmes for the organizations in their locality. Individual organizations also provide their own development programmes, as do national bodies, such as the Care Quality Commission. This means that while the Leadership Academy is the single biggest provider of development programmes, it does not hold any kind of monopoly, and a tiered system from the national level down to the local level is still in operation.

In conclusion, we might project further the policy trajectory traced above and speculate on the contemporary emergence of alternatives to the current 'leaderism' in the NHS. The direction of travel of recent reforms point towards a reliance on more 'enterprising' and innovative organizations imagined by the *Health and Social Care Act (2012)*, driven by the newly liberated competition laws that allow for service provision from 'any qualified provider'. This competitive challenge might be expected to bring about a shift towards more entrepreneurial management practices in order to capitalize on the opportunities for expansion created by frequent and compulsory competitive tendering, and the increased scope for Foundation Trusts to raise income from private sources. We noted above the potential for conflict between the need for leaders who are both creative and obedient; it could be argued that the ideal of the entrepreneur pushes this tension further, with the potential for the opportunism and risk-taking at the heart of traditional concepts of the entrepreneur to radically alter the nature of healthcare organizations, and with it the 'values' of the system which it is the leaders job to uphold. This articulates core concerns within the current legislative context which seeks to marry 'greater autonomy' with 'increased accountability' (Department of Health, 2010). Standing in contrast to the presumed energy and dynamism of the entrepreneurial spirit (Osborne and Gaebler, 1993) is the current predicament of senior managers in the NHS, faced with widespread and very public criticisms concerning the valuing of financial management over quality and safety (e.g. Francis, 2013), while they are also required to deliver unprecedented efficiency savings, and with reduced expenditure allocated from government spending.[9]

Summary

In this chapter, we have examined evolving healthcare policy in the UK, looking specifically at the impact of this context for healthcare management and leadership. Charting the main policy changes in the NHS since its formation in 1948, we have traced the corresponding changes in what is seen as the appropriate mode of governance: from health administration in the mid-20th century, through general and business management—as quasi-markets were introduced and extended in the 1980s onwards—towards a more recent emphasis on leadership and entrepreneurship in a 'liberated' and fragmented NHS. In defining the contemporary context, we have emphasized three major events that have impacted the NHS through the period of our study: the financial crisis and subsequent daunting 'efficiency challenges'; the accompanying sweeping reforms that occurred via the *Health and Social Care Act (2012)*; and the impact of the scandal at Mid Staffordshire Foundation Trust and the heightened scrutiny of care and managerial culture following the Francis Report. We argue that these financial, structural and regulatory pressures have impacted disproportionately upon the management cadre within the NHS—as they are required to meet financial targets, while simultaneously being charged with delivering the new structure and making huge efficiency savings—yet without compromising the quality of care. Turning then to the kind of managers who might rise to this set of challenges, we discussed the changing programmes of management and leadership development in the NHS as they seek to address the breadth of responsibilities encompassed by healthcare managers. In other words, to reconcile tensions within the role itself—between national standards and local responsiveness, between enterprise and rigorous governance, between management and leadership, and between autonomy and control.

In the next chapter, we start to drill down further into investigating what these changes and tensions at an institutional and organizational level might mean for practicing managers 'on the ground'. We do so by introducing our study of healthcare managers, which was conducted at this time of profound change within the sector, and which was specifically concerned with understanding the processes of knowledge mobilization engaged in by healthcare managers and how that relates to management practice, the background and experiences of managers and their (changing) organizational circumstances. This chapter has highlighted some important contextual themes that will be revisited in the later analysis of managerial work in healthcare and which relate to the pressures and demands facing healthcare managers, the expectations that they should provide effective leadership, and the requirements on managers to make best use of appropriate management knowledge, learning and networking opportunities. Before we turn to a more detailed examination of these issues, however, we proceed first by introducing the empirical work on which that further in-depth analysis is based.

Notes

1 Health Education England, *Workforce planning*, London: NHS Health Education, https://hee.nhs.uk/our-work/planning-commissioning/workforce-planning
2 For a comparison of the healthcare systems of the various regions of the UK, see NAO (2012), Ham et al. (2013), and Bevan et al. (2014).
3 NICE joined with the Health Development Agency in 2005 to form the National Institute for Health and Clinical Excellence, and was in 2012 renamed the

National Institute for Health and Care Excellence. The acronym has remained NICE throughout.
4 NHS Leadership Academy. Why Do We Need the NHS Leadership Academy Core Programmes? www.leadershipacademy.nhs.uk.
5 NHS Institute for Innovation and Improvement. About the NHS Institute. www.institute.nhs.uk/organisation/about_nhsi/about_the_nhs_institute.html.
6 NHS Leadership Academy. Why Do We Need the NHS Leadership Academy Core Programmes? www.leadershipacademy.nhs.uk.
7 http://www.leadershipacademy.nhs.uk/wp-content/uploads/2012/11/NHSLeadership-Framework-LeadershipFramework-Summary.pdf.
8 http://www.leadershipacademy.nhs.uk/wp-content/uploads/dlm_uploads/2014/10/NHSLeadership-LeadershipModel-colour.pdf.
9 For a fuller history of management and leadership in the NHS, see Chambers and Walshe (2010), and Walshe and Smith (2016).

3   Studying Management in Healthcare

The previous chapter charted the policy changes that have occurred in recent decades and which have shaped the institutional landscape of healthcare and defined the challenges facing both healthcare organizations and healthcare managers, especially in terms of organizational change and leadership development. This current chapter develops further the themes outlined in Chapter 1 and then contextualized in Chapter 2 by introducing the empirical research that forms the centrepiece of this book and which was designed to examine in greater depth the practice of healthcare management 'on the ground', using data collected from three archetypal case study healthcare organizations.

Given the changing context of management in healthcare, it is clearly important to examine what that means for the changing nature of managerial work and its effects in practice. What this crucially requires, however, is drilling down further to discover how this impacts upon managers' sense of their own professional/occupational identity; the challenges and opportunities it opens up for them in the performance of their role; the types of knowledge and expertise they depend on, access and use; how that is formed and developed through socialization, learning and development processes (professional and/or organizational); and what part managers' networks of interaction and communities of practice play in enhancing or inhibiting flows of knowledge, learning and support. It is these types of question that the study was specifically designed to address and which the empirical work in later chapters examines. Before saying more about the design of the study and the case study organizations selected, however, this chapter proceeds by first setting out the main aims of the research and the perspective taken on management practice, knowledge, learning and networks that informs the later analysis.

Perspectives on Healthcare Management Practice

The overall aim of the empirical research that forms the basis of this book was to explore the nature of managerial knowledge acquired and used by healthcare managers, focusing in particular upon different types and sources of knowledge and learning available to those acting as middle managers in NHS organizations. The research set out to examine how management knowledge requirements were being shaped and constrained by managerial roles and responsibilities and how management knowledge sharing and learning processes were related to managers' occupational background and careers; organizational learning and management development processes; and wider interactions through professional and other networks and communities of practice. Consequently, the empirical research was centrally concerned with understanding flows of management knowledge and learning as they impact upon management practice and as they are shaped and constrained by the social and organizational context within which managers and their work are embedded (Brown and Duguid, 2001; Dopson et al., 2008). These contextual influences—career background experiences, the organizational settings in which managers operate and the networks and communities to which they belong—were expected to have a crucial bearing on the ways in which managers relate to different forms of management knowledge and learning and apply it to and through their management practice.

The perspective taken to explore these issues was one that recognizes that knowing and learning and associated processes of networking and identity development are highly situated in practice as well as being socially mediated (e.g. Nicolini et al., 2003). Research concerned with understanding flows of knowledge and learning related to management practice has evolved significantly in recent years away from early approaches, which tended to treat knowledge itself (including management knowledge) as effectively a neutral object or commodity that could be abstracted from practice and readily transferred from one setting to another (Gourlay, 2006; Greenhalgh, 2010b). More contemporary approaches emphasize instead the importance of understanding the close, symbiotic relationship between knowledge and practice, where knowledge is made sense of and applied in and through (management) practice. These more process- or practice-based approaches (Newell et al., 2009) consequently reject the idea of treating knowledge as, effectively, a physical entity or possession, going much further than simply seeing the embedding of new knowledge as a problem of transfer or even one of translation of knowledge from one domain of practice to another (Carlile, 2004). Instead of emphasizing the more abstract, individual and formal aspects of knowledge, that encourage the search for ways of converting it into more codified systems that can promote knowledge sharing and creation (e.g. Nonaka and Takeuchi, 1995), they instead place considerable emphasis on understanding the socially mediated, highly situated and provisional nature of knowledge and the importance of practice as the crucial nexus of knowing and learning (e.g. Lave and Wenger, 1991; Blackler, 1995; Cook and Brown, 1999; Brown and Duguid, 2001; Nicolini et al., 2003; Newell et al., 2009).

A typical and well-established view on how these processes coalesce to shape the development of knowledge and learning in particular practical domains is found in the extensive literature on communities and networks of practice (Lave and Wenger, 1991; Wenger, 1998, 2000; Brown and Duguid, 2001). Communities of practice link individuals and groups with shared interests and professions and provide the networks of social and professional relationships within which information and experiences are shared and through which learning and professional identity develop. Lave and Wenger (1991) refer to the socialization processes involved in becoming part of a community of practice as *legitimate peripheral participation*. They demonstrate how, through the situated learning that occurs as individuals engage jointly in practice with other members of the community, over time they progressively become accepted and included within the community of practice. Through this induction and socialization, they develop and refine their occupational or professional identity.

Importantly, communities of practice are not restricted to the boundaries of particular organizations or departmental groups and can encompass the wider networks of occupational and professional relationships within which individuals are embedded (Brown and Duguid, 2001). They also often interact with other communities of practice whose members need to be engaged (or confronted) in order to perform particular activities. In such instances, conditions at the boundary between communities of practice have an important part to play in enabling (or inhibiting) effective communication and co-ordination of effort (Boland and Tenkasi, 1995). In some cases, of course, communities of practice become formalized and institutionalized in what would be clearly recognized as distinct professions. These are able to achieve occupational 'closure' through a more rigid form of legitimate peripheral participation based upon accreditation by professional governing bodies centred around a distinct and accepted professional body of knowledge and accompanying set of professional codes, norms and standards (Larson, 1977; Abbott, 1988; Murphy, 1988).

Understanding how communities of practice—whether institutionalized or not—promote or inhibit the spread of particular types of knowledge and pathways to learning provides a useful starting point for understanding the development and spread of management knowledge in a complex multidisciplinary setting such as healthcare. Such an approach recognizes that barriers and enablers of knowledge sharing and learning reside not simply in the capabilities of individuals or in the cultures of particular organizations (Carlile, 2004), but also in the conditions governing knowledge sharing, diffusion and learning through wider networks of occupational or professional practice (Brown and Duguid, 2001). Moreover, the dynamic interpretation afforded by situated learning theory provides a useful analytical lens for understanding how communities of practice and their constituent elements (social networks, material conditions) may help shape the on-going reproduction or transformation of managerial practice and professional identity (Boland and Tenkasi, 1995; Brown and Duguid, 2001; Wenger et al., 2002; Carlile, 2004). Indeed, similar developments in thinking about the importance of understanding knowledge flows as processes and practices can be found in the growing literature on management knowledge and learning in healthcare (Nicolini et al., 2008; Greenhalgh, 2010b; Nicolini, 2011; Oborn et al., 2013). Included within that tradition are a number of contributions that very explicitly draw upon concepts and ideas from the communities of practice literature to explore management and innovation processes in healthcare contexts (Bate and Robert, 2002; Ferlie et al., 2005).

At the same time, however, it is important to retain some critical distance and avoid too simplified or reified a view of communities of practice when it comes to what they offer for enabling flows of knowledge and learning (cf. Wenger, 2000). As already implied, communities and networks of practice can, through their very cohesion and insularity, effectively hinder flows of certain types of knowledge and learning (Boland and Tenkasi, 1995; Ferlie et al., 2005; Roberts, 2006). Moreover, as the literature on professionalization and the development of professional domains and jurisdictions makes clear, professional communities of practice are often actively engaged in promoting their own values, norms and practices in competition with other nascent professional or quasi-professional groups that seek to occupy similar, practice domains (e.g. Abbott, 1988).

More generally, from a conceptual point of view, it is impossible to disentangle flows of knowledge and processes of learning from the relations of power through which they are constituted (Foucault, 1980). If one takes the line, as this research does, that knowledge and learning processes are situated in practice and socially mediated, then they are also potentially contested (Blackler, 1995). Considering the political dynamics referred to earlier and the discourses of knowledge and learning that they promote, it is not that difficult then to see how knowledge and learning are inevitably shaped by the relations of power within organizations and across wider communities (Alvesson and Karreman, 2001). Critical analyses of the workings of communities of practice have very effectively demonstrated the importance of power relations in inhibiting flows of knowledge and learning within and between managerial groups, requiring them to find ways of transforming common practice (Carlile, 2004; Roberts, 2006). Contu and Willmott's (2003) re-working of Orr's (1996) classic work at Xerox, for example, shows how communities of practice emerged not in the interests of performance improvement, but out of necessity to help maintenance engineers cope with the demands of their employers who exercised power by virtue of their dominant position in the employment relationship.

When one considers management knowledge within a healthcare context, it is not difficult to see how 'management knowledge' itself and associated processes of learning and networked interaction may thus be influenced and shaped by relations of power—both within particular organizations and networks and in the deeper set of social forces and influences driving and inhibiting change within the sector. A particularly good example already flagged up in Chapter 2—and which will be explored further in the next chapter—relates to the discourse of 'leaderism' that has emerged and is actively shaping perceptions of the changing nature of managerial work in healthcare (O'Reilly and Reed, 2011). As already noted, it is having an impact upon what types of knowledge and modes of learning are considered appropriate and legitimate (e.g. King's Fund, 2011).

Added to this, one needs to consider too what constitutes the knowledge base—that is, what is or should be meant by 'management knowledge'. Doing so not only draws attention to the possibilities of alternative conceptions and discourses of management based, for example, upon leadership or entrepreneurship (Learmonth, 2005; O'Reilly and Reed, 2011); it also brings into sharp focus the recognition that the knowledge base of management is itself both highly variegated (Reed and Anthony, 1992) and seriously contested (Clegg and Palmer, 1996). Added to this, one needs to take into account the promotion of particular discourses of management knowledge (and associated learning processes) that occurs through the promotion of management fads and fashions (Abrahamson, 1996) and through the active role of management consultants in promoting and packaging particular conceptions of management (Sturdy, 2011). Consequently, it becomes important to recognize that understanding flows of managerial knowledge and learning processes in a setting as complex as healthcare requires an approach that not only recognizes that the translation of managerial knowledge into practice is strongly influenced by that context (Dopson and Fitzgerald, 2006), but also that one needs to take into account the socially constituted nature of knowing and learning and the complex and highly contested nature of managerial knowledge itself.

As already noted in Chapter 1, within healthcare, flows of management knowledge into practice are also inevitably affected by the socialization associated with induction into, and progression within, the various communities which constitute the managerial cadre (e.g. Buchanan et al., 2007). Indeed, divisions within healthcare management that mirror political and epistemic differences between policy-makers and various professional communities have been well recorded (Bate and Robert, 2002; Hyde, 2009). A number of researchers have applied practice-based perspectives to explore these distinct epistemic communities in healthcare management and their impact upon the development or implementation of cross-cutting management initiatives (Ferlie et al., 2005; Swan, Bresnen et al., 2007; Currie et al., 2008). There has also been a good deal of attention directed towards the impact of managerialism on the medical profession (e.g. Noordegraaf, 2015). Yet, so far there has been little attempt made to focus upon the reproduction of knowledge and transmission of learning through and between the various communities of practice represented within NHS middle management. There is therefore a good deal of scope still for exploring how such differences influence processes of knowledge and learning associated with the translation of management knowledge into practice, via distinct patterns of socialization and learning associated with the immersion of managers in differentiated managerial and professional activity.

The various (cross-cutting) networks of practice within which managers are embedded are likely to affect, in complex ways, their knowledge sharing and learning and through these, their managerial identity and orientations. So, for example, research on the constant interaction between NHS managers and colleagues in various clinical domains frequently highlights significant differences in perspective on the nature of knowledge or 'evidence' informing practice (Walshe and Rundall, 2001; Pfeffer and Sutton, 2006). These professional/occupational boundaries, where two or more professional groups, are engaged in joint practice, and the mechanisms used to translate knowledge at such boundaries have a significant effect on the knowledge base of managers and their ability to influence practice across the organization, and more widely (Boland and Tenkasi, 1995; Carlile, 2004; Ferlie et al., 2005; Swan et al., 2007). They therefore constitute the site of important knowledge and learning processes that can only be properly understood by inductively tracing the effects of such cross-cutting networks and communities of practice on the mobilization of managerial knowledge and by considering how this shapes and in turn, is shaped by the development of managerial identity (Lave and Wenger, 1991; Watson, 1994).

Developing the Research Approach

Given the emphasis on understanding management practice and the effects of context, an approach was required that could capture in some depth the subtleties of how managers go about accessing and using management knowledge in their everyday work. To achieve this, an interpretivist qualitative methodology was adopted, underscored by a broadly constructivist epistemology. Such an approach contends that realities are socially constructed, the product of individual interpretations and meanings, intersubjective relations and the affordances and limitations of particular social and historical conditions. Accordingly, research which seeks to understand particular realities—in this case how middle managers in healthcare acquire and use management knowledge—proceeds from the assumption that terms such as 'knowledge' (and indeed 'middle manager') are socially defined (and thereby contested) and that, while individuals are placed at the centre of the analysis, it is also important to explore the relations, connections and broader social forces within which they are embedded.

Such an approach reflects the broad epistemological perspective of phenomenology. Following Silverman (1970), phenomenology emphasizes the understanding—rather than positivist measurement—of behaviour, as it is the *meanings* ascribed to phenomena that define social reality rather than social reality being self-evident through inspection. Social reality does not reside 'out there' but instead is constituted inter-subjectively. The inference is that people can adjust and even change meanings through social interaction. Explanations of social action therefore need to take account of the meanings which those participating attach to actions. For Silverman (1970), social researchers should build their theories upon foundations that view reality as being socially constructed, sustained and changed. He argues that the social actor should be at the centre of the analytical stage, for it is crucial that researchers understand subjective and inter-subjective meanings if they are to understand the significance of organizational actions. This puts an emphasis on a view of the social world as *processual*, where organizational actors interpret the situation in which they find themselves and act in ways which are meaningful to them. It also requires the use of interpretive and qualitative research methods that can tap into action at the level of meaning.

The overall intention is to produce an analysis that is meaningful to individuals within these types of situations, while also remaining sensitive to changing social and political forces. This last point is particularly relevant here, given the changes occurring in healthcare explored earlier. In remaining cognisant of the changing political context experienced by managers in this study, we understand that participants' reconstructions are embedded within particular policy narratives, which in turn are embedded within a particular social order. Implicit in the understanding of 'management' as a socially constructed phenomenon is the understanding that particular constructions of management promote the reproduction of particular social and economic relations. Fieldwork is therefore important in developing a more holistic interpretation—one that proceeds from the view that external factors are a fundamental part of the internal composition of the local domain and should be recognized as such, even at the most micro or individual level of interaction.

Adopting a Comparative Case Study Method

To understand the effects of organizational and institutional context upon how managers acquire and use managerial knowledge, a research strategy was required that not only allowed sufficient depth of analysis, but which also allowed variation in context (both organizational and institutional) to be captured, in order to generate findings that were in some way generalizable to a wide variety of healthcare settings. This would enhance the breadth of application of research and ensure that findings did not simply pertain to the particular context investigated. A comparative case study approach is able to achieve this through the in-depth examination it permits of important similarities and differences between and within cases, which, in turn, maximizes the *analytical generalizability* of the findings (Yin, 1995). Indeed, a comparative case study approach has proven to be a powerful methodology— particularly for allowing the direct application of research findings to their practical context and also for helping understand the key issues involved in complex organizational settings (Eisenhardt and Graebner, 2007). It is particularly important where, as the previous discussion suggests, it can be difficult to separate out analysis of the phenomenon of interest from its context (Yin, 1995). Research into healthcare organizations has of course made extensive use of the case study method and to great effect to explore complex network-based interactions amongst managers and clinicians.

A comparative case method was therefore adopted and attention was focused on three case studies representing very distinct types of NHS trust. The cases were thus selected as archetypal health service organizations that provided very different ranges of services and that, consequently, influenced the knowledge requirements faced by managers and the professional networks available to them in diverse ways. The organizations studied were all based in the northwest of England and represented three types of NHS Foundation Trust—an Acute Trust (providing the full range of local hospital services); a Care Trust (providing mental health and community services); and a Specialist/Tertiary level Trust (providing specialist services in cancer treatment and care). The three trusts were differentiated according to several key characteristics, including their geographical spread, the number of locations from which services were provided, the diversity of services provided and the number of organizations purchasing services from them (see table 3.1 below).

More specifically:

1 **Acute Trust** offered a wide range of acute services centralized mainly in one location and covering a fairly limited (local) geographical area. Service contracts tended to originate largely with one commissioner. Managers' sources of knowledge and networks of interaction were expected to vary according to the particular clinical domain or professional specialism.

2 **Care Trust** delivered a diverse range of mental health and community services with operations distributed in many locations over a large (regional) geographical area. Multiple purchasers were likely from both health and social care. Managers' sources of knowledge and networks

Table 3.1 Comparison of Trust Characteristics

Type of Trust	Diversity of Services	Area Coverage	Number of Purchasers	Number of Locations	Nature of patient contact	Managerial Knowledge Networks
Acute	High	Low	Low	Low	Mixed	Varied according to specialism
Care	Medium	Medium	Medium	High	Cyclic	Limited specialisms
Specialist	Low	High	High	Low	Episodic	Focused specialism

of interaction were expected to reflect the more limited and distinct range of specialisms (psychology and social care).

3 **Specialist Trust** offered a limited range of advanced specialist services mainly from one central location to patients spread across a very wide (regional and national) geographical area. The trust contracted with multiple purchasers. Managers' sources of knowledge and networks of interaction were expected to tend to be more centred upon professional networks associated with the trust's clinical specialism.

The categorization of each trust in this table is necessarily very broad, highlighting the factors which were identifiable *a priori* as likely to have an impact on issues of relevance to our study. However, a key priority in the research was also to establish empirically which aspects of context— immediate and more historical—impacted most directly upon operational activity and management processes in each trust. This is the focus of the section towards the end of this chapter, where the most pressing current concerns facing managers at each trust are identified.

Identifying Managerial Cohorts

As already noted, management in the NHS is a highly complex phenomenon, consisting of multiple groups with very distinctive professional orientations and knowledge bases (Hyde and McBride, 2011). The dependence upon management and markets to drive healthcare reform has also meant that a range of hybrid managerial roles have emerged in recent years that require combinations of clinical expertise, public administration and business acumen (Kippist and Fitzgerald, 2009). Furthermore, there is little standardization of role titles between and even within trusts, and research indicates that few people with managerial responsibility actually carry the formal title of 'manager' (Hyde et al., 2013). As a consequence, the identification of distinct cohorts of managers is a difficult problem in a setting as complex as the NHS.

The research set out to capture some of this variation and complexity by selecting middle managers across the three trusts on the basis of anticipated differences in the types of managers who work in these organizations and in the particular managerial activities and challenges they face. Importantly, the scope of the research was to include anyone within each trust who could be considered to have middle management responsibilities. That meant not just those who could be described as 'general managers', but also clinicians as well as other specialists (e.g. financial managers) who had a significant managerial role. Our intention was to understand the effects of differences amongst (and similarities between) NHS managers—including managers of clinical and functional teams—in how they acquired and applied their knowledge and learning. It was important therefore to be able to develop a systematic framework for the identification and selection of managers in order to provide as complete a picture as possible.

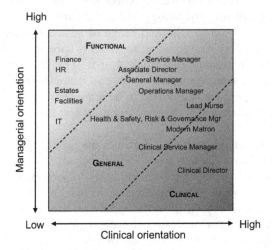

Figure 3.1 Identifying Managerial Cohorts

Figure 3.1 above presents the framework that was developed to help categorize different types of managers and which was then used to help select interviewees. The framework differentiates between managerial groups on the basis of their qualifications and experience, attempting to capture the extent to which they are clinically and/or managerially oriented. It groups managers into three broad categories—Functional, General and Clinical (and locates specific managerial roles found in healthcare within these general categories). However, rather than suggest that managers are simply one thing or the other, the creation of a two-dimensional landscape across which stretches a continuum representing the relative strength of clinical and managerial orientations leaves open the possibility that managerial identity may result from the sedimentation of different layers of (clinical and managerial) expertise and experience. Consequently, not only does this framework allow us to broadly differentiate between types of manager, it also captures the inter-connectedness of managerial and clinical expertise and experience (especially amongst 'general' managers). In so doing, it allows us to appreciate the often blurred boundaries between managerial groups found in healthcare (Buchanan et al., 2007) as well as the importance of hybrid management roles (McGivern et al., 2015).

The framework was arrived at and validated through a literature search and also informed through early stage interviews and discussions with key informants from across the sector (which included representatives of NHS Employers, the NHS Confederation, the King's Fund, the Regional Strategic Health Authority, Regional Leadership Academies and the project Advisory Group). Those interviews and discussions were not only used to help validate our selection frameworks for trusts and managers, but also allowed the research team to gain an overview of the practical challenges facing managers at local, regional and national level in locating, interpreting and applying management knowledge and learning. They therefore allowed a detailed picture to be built up of the background and capabilities of diverse groups of managers, as well as providing further background information and views on the political and practical context of the research.

Using the management selection framework, a sample of interviewees could be constructed in each organization, which served to capture the diversity of 'middle management' in each trust. To achieve this, a purposive, non-random sample of approximately 8 managers was identified for each of the three cohorts of managers in each trust, yielding a total target sample size of around 72 managers who would be interviewed during the main fieldwork phase (in the event, 68 were actually interviewed).

Access to potential participants was arranged through each trust's main point of contact and HR department. Selections were made on the basis of meeting the need to generate sufficient numbers of interviews in each broad group (clinical, general and functional) while allowing some variation in their work position and context (e.g. different clinical/functional specialism or service operation). It also became clear that managerial grade was a useful proxy indicator of middle management status. In the event, most of those managers interviewed had salaries that were in grades 8a–8d (the exceptions were one grade 7 manager, four grade 9 managers and five who were on the consultants' scale). Once potential candidates for interview were identified by the research team and their willingness to participate ascertained, managers were contacted directly and provided with full information about the research, including an Invitation Letter, Participant Information Sheet, Project Summary document and Consent Form (for full details of the procedures employed, see Bresnen et al., 2014).

Sample Characteristics

As noted, the final sample consisted of a total of 68 interviewees across the three trusts. Details of the sample of managers, including their distribution across trusts and management groups as well as information about response rates are presented in table 3.2 below:

Table 3.2 Full Sample of Managers by Group and by Trust

	Clinical Managers	Functional Managers	General Managers	Declined/Did not respond	Total Participants
Acute Trust	5	7	8	4	20
Care Trust	7	6	12	10	25
Specialist Trust	6	8	9	10	23
Total	18	21	29	24	68

There was a relatively even gender spread, apart from a concentration of female general managers in the Care trust. The distribution of managers by age was also relatively even across the trusts, although the age profile of managers in the Care trust was a little higher and of those in the Specialist trust a little lower. The gender and age distribution of the 68 managers interviewed are summarised and compared by trust and managerial group in tables 3.3 and 3.4 below.

Most of those interviewed (64 = 94 percent) were white British, with the remaining 4 (6 percent) being Asian British and all male (2 in the Care trust and 1 each in the other trusts).

Of interest to the study was the career development of managers and table 3.5 below shows the average time managers had spent in their current post, their current organization, in the NHS more generally and also outside the sector.

Table 3.3 Gender Distribution by Trust and Management Group

	Clinical	*Functional*	*General*	*Totals*
Acute	3 Male	4 Male	3 Male	10 Male
	2 Female	3 Female	5 Female	10 Female
Care	3 Male	3 Male	3 Male	9 Male
	4 Female	3 Female	9 Female	16 Female
Specialist	2 Male	3 Male	4 Male	9 Male
	4 Female	5 Female	5 Female	14 Female
Totals	8 Male	10 Male	10 Male	28 Male
	10 Female	11 Female	19 Female	40 Female

Table 3.4 Age Distribution by Trust

Age:	*18–30*	*30–40*	*40–50*	*50–60*	*60+*
Acute	2	4	10	4	–
Care	1	4	13	7	–
Specialist	2	9	9	2	1
Total	5	17	32	13	1

Table 3.5 Years Spent in Post, in Trust and in NHS

Ave time (yrs):	*In post*	*In organization*	*In NHS*	*Outside NHS*
Acute	2.30	4.86	17.25	4.83
Care	3.87	11.71	22.34	3.03
Specialist	3.02	9.09	14.41	6.70

The greatest longevity of employment in both the organization and NHS was found amongst managers in the Care trust (where many had worked for long periods prior to the organization being given trust status and recent reorganizations). Those with considerable experience outside the sector were found mainly in functional management roles and also amongst clinical and general management staff who had worked in private healthcare. Other distinctive and quantifiable features of experience, including educational qualifications, are explored more fully in Chapters 5 and 6.

Managers across the three trusts did have access to a range of local formal training and development opportunities. This encompassed both 'technical' aspects of managerial work (such as health and safety or IT training), as well as interpersonal skills development or leadership training. Based on responses to interview questions about their training, they could be classified as having received: minimal training (i.e. none or only very occasional); some training (sporadic or regular, if not frequent and intense); or substantial training (frequent and intense periods of training). Figures 3.2 and 3.3 below show the numbers of managers in each category (by trust and by managerial group). Most managers (52=76 percent) had received some or a substantial amount of formal management training (including all managers at the Acute trust and most functional managers). General managers at the Care trust and some clinicians at the Care and Specialist trusts were most likely to have received 'minimal' training.

Of course, interviewees were not necessarily 'pure' examples of particular categories of manager but real individuals with complex histories and the precise combination of background experience of each interviewee varied significantly. Indeed, the purpose of the empirical analysis was to explore

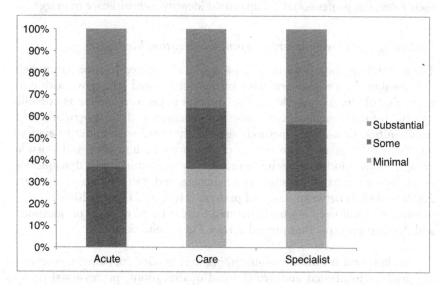

Figure 3.2 Levels of Formal Training by Trust

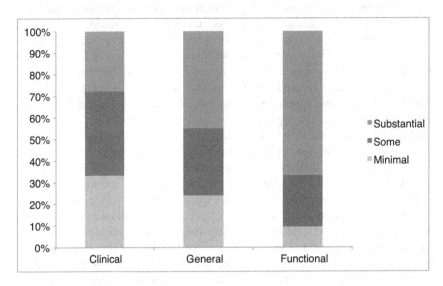

Figure 3.3 Levels of Formal Training by Management Group

these differences in perception—not only to highlight shared experiences and cross-cutting themes (with due allowance being given for contextual influences), but also to be open to the effects of variation and differences in individual as much as group experiences. Later on, in Chapter 5 but also particularly in Chapter 8, we delve more deeply into the nature of individual experiences and explore how this shaped our interviewees' understanding of their emerging professional/occupational identity as healthcare managers.

Collecting Data Using Interviews and Observation Methods

The research methodology involved a qualitative mixed-methods approach that combined a primary emphasis on semi-structured interviews with ethnographic observation methods. The aim was to get as complete as possible a picture of the engagement of cohorts of managers with their networks and communities. Qualitative methods such as these are well suited to exploring the workings of communities of practice—both within and outside organizations—and have been used effectively to illuminate the dynamics of organizational relationships between managers and staff (Hyde and Thomas, 2002) as well as between staff and patients (Hyde and Davies, 2004).

Interviews followed a semi-structured format based on a set of questions and detailed prompts that ranged across 7 key thematic areas:

1   **Background information**—including age, gender, managerial role and grade, educational and professional qualifications, professional background and length of service in the NHS, the trust and the role

2   Occupation/career—including current position and role, educational background and career path and entry into the organization/role
3   Leadership/management—including current managerial responsibilities, leadership aspects of the role and views on the occupational/professional status of management groups
4   Knowledge—including managerial knowledge and skills required, formal and informal sources of knowledge and organizational mechanisms supporting management learning and development
5   Networks—including internal and external networks, their nature, purpose, scope and mode of operation and individual networking activity
6   Organizational context—including factors enabling/hindering knowledge work and barriers and enablers of communication (e.g. structural and spatial aspects of work organization, technology, HR policies and practices)
7   Change—including sector/organizational changes affecting management activities and knowledge and learning processes, the personal impact of change and future career aspirations

Interviews at each trust were carried out by at least two members of the research team. They lasted between 1 and 2 hours (the majority lasting around 1.5 hours) and all were recorded and transcribed. Including 13 earlier key informant interviews, the result was a primary data set that consisted of 139 hours of recorded interviews. Pseudonyms are used throughout the next four chapters when referring to those interviewed.

Where possible and appropriate, meetings and other forms of activity, event or encounter at each trust where managers were involved were also observed (with the explicit agreement of those present). The aim was to underpin the analysis by supplementing interview-based accounts of knowledge processes with observation of how management knowledge was interpreted, accessed, used and shared in practice. It also allowed a more longitudinal element to the research, helping the research team gather more in-depth understanding of how management knowledge and management processes were related and allow the follow up of key themes and issues identified in interviews.

A number of events were observed, including management meetings and leadership training events (for further details see Bresnen et al., 2014). Standard note-taking by members of the research team, structured according to a thematic guide to ensure consistency, formed the main means of capturing action in these meetings and events, and these were transferred to electronic format. In addition, observational elements were included through field note summaries produced by each member of the research team before and after the interviews that aimed to capture general observations and impressions. Table 3.6 below provides an overall summary of data collection across the research, including the time spent in observations.

Table 3.6 Data Collected

	Interviews (formal recorded)	Interviews (informal)	Observations
Key Informants	13	0	3 hours over 3 days
Acute	20	0	18 hours over 6 days
Care	25	13	22 hours over 9 days
Specialist	23	6	11 hours over 2 days
Totals	81	19	54

The rich detail obtained from the observations did not lend itself to coding in the same way as the interview data. This detailed background information was used instead to help contextualize the interview data and/or to provide confirmatory information for points raised or claims made in interviews (for example, about decision-making or management training processes). Consequently, the observation data was used more *implicitly* and *illustratively* to support the analysis and illustrative examples can be found in the chapters that follow.

Coding and Analysing the Data

The data collected were transcribed, collated and stored centrally for coding and analysis using NVivo qualitative data analysis software. The development of the coding framework for the semi-structured interviews (which made up the greater part of the data set) relied on a schema combining open and axial coding methods, which aimed to combine inductive and deductive logics in line with the construction of grounded theory (Strauss and Corbin, 1990). The coding framework was developed through independent coding of a small sample of interview transcripts by members of the research team. This led to the generation of an agreed set of codes that allowed the data to be structured into broad themes (management/leadership, knowledge, networks, organization and personal) and associated subthemes. The coding frame therefore reflected both the research questions that were informed by the literature and the semi-structured format of the interviews described earlier. Coding was undertaken by the members of the research team responsible for data collection in each case study site to capitalize upon the tacit understandings gained through data collection. Inter-rater reliability was maximized through the cross-checking of coding of some transcripts by other members of the research team. Throughout the analysis, the coding framework remained open to the inclusion of additional categories or deletion/combination of nodes.

Themes, rather than cases, are used to organize the presentation of the data, as analysis of the findings at each case clearly indicated that there was a good deal of consistency emerging in responses across the interviews regarding the central themes of management, knowledge and networking. At the same time, important differences between the cases also emerged (for example, in the nature and extent of networking activity). Consequently, while the next section introduces each of the cases, the subsequent chapters are each thematically driven. The steps taken here to strike a balance between thematic analysis and rich case narrative are consistent with those normally associated with qualitative case study research (Eisenhardt and Graebner, 2007).

The Case Study Trusts

Before embarking on that analysis, this section describes each of the case study trusts, highlighting the particularly salient *contextual factors* and *sources of change* affecting the organization. A summary of the key structural, cultural and contextual factors influencing management in each trust is presented in table 3.7 below.

Table 3.7 Comparison of Trusts

	Acute Trust	Care Trust	Specialist Trust
Workforce	5,700	5,500	2,500
Turnover	£275m	£230m	£170m
Spatial/ Geographical	Largely single-site, some off-site community services.	Extremely dispersed geographically.	Largely single-site divided by main road, some outreach.
Cultural	Divided by business group, and between clinicians and management.	Each region has a different culture, substantial effort put in by HQ to coordinate.	Largely unitary culture due to size; some insularity within trust.
Hierarchy	Fairly traditional command and control structure.	Fragmented, efforts by HQ and HR to coordinate/control.	More managerial layers than other trusts.
Clinical-Managerial Relations	Managers attempt to manage clinicians as source of tensions.	Managers typically are clinicians.	Managers attempt to influence clinicians from subordinate role.
Performance Management	Objectives set and clearly communicated by board. Commitment to enact disciplinaries.	Regime seen as inflexible and a little punitive: HR blamed, although most recognize external forces at play.	Increased since acquired FT status.
Competition	Seen as threat, and undermining local collaborative relationships.	Seen as opportunity; strong track record of bidding for contracts and generating income.	Use of outreach to pre-empt takeover threat and some concerns about external providers.

Acute Trust

The largest of the three trusts, Acute, was one of the first Foundation Trusts established and was primarily focused around a large district general hospital originally opened in the early 1900s. It is based in a medium-sized town in Northern England, and with 5700 employees it represents one of the major local employers. The hospital treats around 500,000 patients a year, has over 50 wards and has an annual budget of around £270 million.

During the course of the research, the trust expanded by taking on responsibility for community healthcare services for a local area. Community services now accounted for a third of the trust workforce and a fifth of its income. Apart from its community services provision, the trust is almost entirely located on a single suburban site, with the original buildings the centre of a mesh of expansions and extensions added over nearly a century. Trust senior management is located at the heart of the oldest buildings, while large sections of administration are located in 1960s offices at the outskirts of the grounds.

A strong impression was given in interviews of a highly managed trust, in the sense that there was a strong bureaucratic structure supported by an explicit corporate strategy driving rigorous performance management—which did not necessarily result in harmonious relationships between clinicians and management. Historically, there had been a stable senior management team at the trust, although various changes undermined this throughout the course of the fieldwork. In the same period, Monitor downgraded the financial risk rating for the hospital from 4 to 3, and the governance risk rating increased from amber to red, indicating increased pressures across the trust.

In the view of those interviewed, Acute was seen to have clear strategic direction, thorough systems of governance and a generally formal and 'corporate' style. For example:

> I'd describe Acute as business-like, a lot more business-like. When I came I was like: wow, it's run like a business and that's a cliché. But [my previous trusts] felt amateurish, just bumbling along and "yeah, alright, we spent £2m more than we should do, oh dear" type of thing. But here it's a lot more joined up and a lot more business-like, and a lot more intelligent. I think the trust board, there's a lot of intelligent people on that. A lot of the execs are good people to work with and interesting people to work with, with good ideas.
>
> (Felix, Functional, Acute)

Other accounts, however, challenged this picture of corporate efficiency, pointing to a number of disruptions in the senior management team due to departures and long-term absences and reflected in the changing status

of the trust in the eyes of Monitor. One clinical manager captured well the
growing levels of uncertainty at the trust:

> The trust is in difficulty and the SHA aren't stepping in. Our chief exec's
> on long term sick. Everybody's acting up and shuffling around. Massive
> issues. Monitor are going to step in, this, that and the other. Why aren't
> they doing anything? Are they're waiting for us to fall over and in will
> come somebody else? [laughs] I don't know. Interesting times.
>
> (Bethany, Clinical, Acute)

Compared to the other two trusts, there was very little direct reference
made in the interviews to other particular challenges facing the organization, with the important exception of finance. One explanation for this
might be that the trust was seen as a fairly standard, traditional and typical
DGH (District General Hospital), which, like many others across the NHS,
was facing financial pressures.

Discussions of financial issues pervaded many of the interviews at the
Acute trust. Staff were accustomed to the policy of not replacing colleagues
who left and sharing the work, and it was noticeable how many managers
in the trust, when asked to define their responsibilities, were 'acting up'
or covering two or more positions. The immediate consequence across the
board was a palpable intensification of work:

> It's hard, every day, every week seems harder, it feels like wading through
> treacle . . . It's a lot tighter now. I mean I'm not saying we didn't work
> hard before, but it's really, really pressurized now and there's not a min-
> ute to spare.
>
> (Felix, Functional, Acute)

The process of adapting to demands for more radical change was not
helped by relatively poor relations between management and consultants:

> Most clinicians just want to stick the blinkers on, turn up to their clinic
> and their theatre list and whatever little audit they're doing at the time,
> or whatever service they're trying to develop. They just want to (put)
> blinkers on and do that and be left alone. I think the problem is, there's
> a big ugly truth out there, which is, the NHS can't stay the way it is.
> It's got to change and if you're going to be in a successful hospital, it's
> going to be a hospital that adapts to that change by streamlining ser-
> vices, liaising with others and some services going, some being dropped
> elsewhere, hospitals closing.
>
> (Brian, Clinical, Acute)

The need to share ownership of the financial challenge with clinicians,
although by no means unique to the Acute trust, did pose particular

difficulties, which became more intractable as it became apparent that trimming budgets would not be sufficient and more fundamental rethinking and redesign of clinical services was required. A common theme in interviews was that the trust had saved as much as it could through trimming budgets (e.g. through non-replacement of staff); achieving the scale of savings demanded now required more creative, strategic action. However, the intensity of operational demands often prevented this kind of long-term innovation in service delivery:

> We're too busy staring in the mirror about current problems, and we're not going to deliver 15 million pounds worth of savings to deliver this year. And you can find maybe half of that by working harder and cutting corners and stuff, but at least the other half of that's going to have to come from doing things radically differently. Transformational work.
>
> (Greg, General, Acute)

For others, the scale of the necessary savings led to a kind of fatalism, as expressed well by one clinical manager:

> The amount of cost savings they're expecting, it cannot be done at a business group level, full stop. So I've analysed it and thought about it and from my thinking and understanding. So that actually takes away the pressure completely, because the scale of the financial thing they need can only happen at wide scale organizational changes, i.e. organizations merging or much more transformational change across the health economy.
>
> (Ramesh, Clinical, Acute)

For most, however, maintaining a safe service while delivering savings represented the most immediate and pressing concern, both at the current time and into the foreseeable future.

Apart from finance, a small number of interviewees did point to the impact of Foundation Trust status in the organization, in having led to more stability in strategic direction and leadership when compared to other district general hospitals nearby. Its impact in creating a more professional business culture and clear lines of accountability through the trust was also emphasized:

> Foundation Trusts are so much more business focused and whilst it isn't about profit at any extent above patient care, it is about trying to look at business decisions on things and not just let things go as they always have been. It is about looking at getting the best for your money and about linking it all to quality a lot more and making people think about things.
>
> (Jessica, Functional, Acute)

In the background, the major reorganization implied by the acquisition of new community services and their integration with the trust as a whole and with the existing community services run by Acute was also a pressing issue for some—particularly for those most directly concerned. For those in community services joining the organization, there were complaints about being absorbed by a larger, bureaucratic organization with little interest in their established way of working (through, for instance, multi-professional teams).

> Our business group feel as though we're having to jump through Acute's hoops and we're having to take on things that we actually might feel are a backward step: "Well, we did that ten years ago and we didn't think it was a good idea, and that's why we went through this process and came out here." And an element of frustration: "Why can't Acute see that actually, this is a much better way of doing it?"
>
> (Gloria, General, Acute)

Instead, integration was perceived as simply forcing the new services to comply with procedures that were considered inappropriate or counterproductive for their work. Nonetheless, integration and achieving efficiencies through economies of scale by merging elements of community services were a key element in the cost-savings programme.

Looking ahead, the most pressing concerns for the trust related to the impact of the on-going reforms within the NHS and any resultant internal restructuring and reorganization. Ever-present demands for cost savings, the shift to CCG commissioning and in particular, the drive towards diversity of supply and enhanced supplier competition from 'any qualified provider', exercized the minds of many interviewees at the Acute trust.

Care Trust

The second largest trust studied, Care trust, provides mental health and community services across a mixed urban and rural region. The trust was formed through a merger of various mental health services in the region in the early 2000s and became a Foundation Trust in the late 2000s. It expanded substantially throughout the course of the fieldwork, taking on services in various neighbouring boroughs. By the end of the research, it was providing services to over one million residents across an area covered by several acute trust providers and working in partnership with several local authorities. Although the trust had recently expanded into community services, the research focused upon those parts of the trust dedicated to mental health services. Nevertheless, the impact of this expansion and the reorganization was an important feature of many of the accounts and clearly had an impact across the organization.

Over the previous decade, growth and restructuring had gradually brought together under one organization several different services in different locations. The incorporation of community services, which occurred during the course of the study and almost doubled the organization's size, suggested that this was a pattern that was set to continue. Experiences of restructuring varied in different parts of the trust. One of the most recent restructuring processes had involved integration of four of the main service directorates in one division, under a single services director. This change was perceived to have been successful, partly due to the popularity of the new service director, but also due to the opportunities it afforded for exchange and collaboration within the trust and for heralding a shift to a less directive culture:

> Before the change in management, it was very command and control. It was almost like if you didn't have your deadline met at least three days before, you knew there would be serious trouble . . . and now you meet your deadline, when your deadline comes, you do it the day before. You get reminders but the work still gets done, which I think is interesting. But it gets done without you feeling anxious and therefore I think you produce a better piece of work.
>
> (Heather, General, Care)

Reform was as important at Care as at the other trusts we researched. However, here there was more of an impetus created by the threat of competition from 'any qualified provider'. This threat was felt in the more commercially oriented services in the trust, with their distinctive requirements for commissioning and collaboration. Many in these services feared that private and third sector organizations could take away large parts of their 'business':

> The basic principles [of care are the same] but the actual interventions are different and the commercial world we live in is massively different . . . The first DGH has gone to a private provider, but that's hard getting a DGH off an NHS Trust . . . and it's the same thing with mental health. It's a very specialized, very specific industry. The stuff around the edges, the private providers and the voluntary sector providers are a little bit more geared up, so it makes us very exposed; and things like forensic services, it makes them very exposed as well. So we do have to have quite a different outlook.
>
> (Kerry, General, Care)

Given the distinctive nature and development of Care, it is perhaps not surprising that it faced its own particular challenges and had its own narrative of change. Central to these were the tensions inherent in efforts being made to centralize and standardize processes and rationalize service delivery across an organization that was very fragmented (geographically and structurally) and in which there was little sense of a cohesive culture— notwithstanding efforts by the centre to promote more 'business-like' qualities and a more entrepreneurial approach. Despite there being a quite complex mixture of medical and psychological specialisms, here there was also much less of a structural divide between clinical and managerial groups, as most of those in general management positions were from clinical (especially nursing) backgrounds.

In interviews, managers highlighted a range of contextual factors that were of particular salience in the Care trust. These were largely associated with two prominent features of its recent development, namely: growth through the acquisition of geographically and culturally diverse services; and the attempted integration and centralization of these services. HR was highlighted as a particular issue—in part due to its prominence in these processes of integration and in part due to recent problems within the HR department itself. As a function, HR at Care was organized centrally, with business partners attached to particular service groups and areas. It therefore straddled the central/peripheral divide and found itself responsible for many of the challenges faced in integrating the workforce and developing standard practices. The consensus from both within HR and from other parts of the organization was that it had not coped with recent challenges well. Having also recently lost its director, HR was left with no senior management representation and also had to cope with lower levels of staffing due to downgrading and delayering.

Commercial activity meanwhile was concentrated in specific service areas and was highlighted as having distinctive requirements regarding commissioning and collaboration. Psychological services, rehabilitation services and drug and alcohol services are all external facing and require interaction with a multitude of agencies across different sectors such as social care, the prison service and the third sector. They also have a distinctive commissioning landscape, with regular competitive tendering of services, closer day-to-day relations with commissioners (particularly in drug and alcohol services) and more intense target-focused performance management:

> We are massively visible to our Commissioners in a way that the mental health services aren't . . . My Commissioners know the names of my staff, they are in and out of our buildings . . . It can be quite adversarial.
> (Kerry, General, Care)

As such, these services were quite distinct from what was conventionally seen as the 'main business' of the trust—mental health—which was considered by some to be more localized and insular, less commercially oriented and less involved in external collaborative networks.

Finance was as important an issue here as it was in the other two trusts, for much the same reasons. The recent financial pressures were of great concern across the trust, and in some areas this was more acutely felt than others. The more commercially oriented services were less fearful of financial pressures from the trust—as they were an important part of the trust's business development and central to its growth strategy. However, there was also a threat of increasing external competition.

Foundation Trust status was also seen as an issue. Many of those interviewed had been attached to their local services for a decade or more and memberships of the trust, plus Foundation Trust status, were comparatively recent events. Many spoke of the challenges of integration and assimilation, and when this was attributed specifically to securing Foundation Trust status there was some ambivalence from peripheral services about the more intensified financial accountability and 'business sense' of the trust. This was expressed through a somewhat reluctant recognition of the purpose and benefits of greater rationalization in these areas, combined with a sense of culture shock:

> I think Care's very financially driven but I think that's FT land. That was the biggest change for me culturally . . . Two things are finance and serving effective services—so the regulation and finance. And I guess once you understand that, anything that you're presenting you can present to them in that way. So you've boxed those two key issues off and then you've got the audience there.
>
> (Harriet, General, Care)

Last but not least, the very nature of the patient population and clinical work involved meant that the Care trust came across as distinctly 'therapeutic' in its cultural orientation. Most of the managers interviewed had some kind of clinical background and regularly referred to their dual identity as managers and clinicians. The long-term, cyclical nature of patient interaction at the Care trust also brought a strong relational quality to the activity of management, and many drew upon this in their work-identity narratives:

> I think most people that have been in nursing or other professions and end up in management miss what they went in for, which was speaking to patients, spending time with patients . . . I've had very little clinical time over the past four years so it's been a real shift in that respect. I think sometimes when I'm feeling a bit disillusioned with the job . . . I just go and spend some time on the wards with the patients and then it makes you realise that you're not very hard off really compared to the majority of people on those wards. So that's a good eye-opener. I think most people in the caring profession genuinely want to come in and help people and I don't think that's changed.
>
> (Luke, General, Care)

Similar views were expressed throughout the trust. Not only did this shared orientation go some way to unifying the otherwise somewhat distinct and disparate parts of the organization, but it also fed into the receptivity towards particular forms of management knowledge and development—as will be seen later.

Specialist Trust

Finally, the Specialist trust was the smallest of the three organizations, with around 2,500 staff serving a regional population of around 3 million. The trust is based around a hospital formed at the end of the 19th century and which, from its inception, specialized in cancer treatment and research. It is prominent in its field at national and international levels, a quarter of its patients being referred from outside the local region. Its annual revenue is around £270 million, benefitting from both a successful charity and a substantial amount of research, supported by strong links to a local university. During the period of fieldwork, the trust was undergoing internal restructuring, combining two divisions into one, but otherwise the narrative at the trust was largely one of growth building on success. Monitor ratings for the trust were consistently high throughout the research project and had been so historically.

The Specialist trust was universally described by interviewees as a highly distinctive healthcare organization with elite status, both locally and nationally. Interviewees commonly cited the trust's strong brand, its outstanding clinicians, its world-leading research and its highly effective charity campaigns. As a result, most described the Specialist trust as a rewarding place to work in. For example:

> You would be mental to leave the job here and go and work (elsewhere). And everybody . . . knows the grass is no greener. So we do tend to retain managers and keep people here for quite some time, because it is a nice place to work. Although everybody's faced with financial difficulties, it is a nice place to work: small hospital, friendly hospital, a good ethos and good outcomes. There are things that we can celebrate, there are a lot of successes. Whereas I know that doesn't feel that way at some of the other big acute trusts.
>
> (Becky, General, Specialist)

Indeed, most of those interviewed were fiercely proud about working for such a prestigious institution:

> Go and talk to the people down there. We are the best. We want to be the best. We're going to stay the best. With regards to the NHS overall, I can't really comment because I've only ever worked here. But I think if a lot of the philosophies that are adopted here were adopted elsewhere, possibly the NHS might be in a bit better position.
>
> (Adrian, Functional, Specialist)

Although financial issues were frequently mentioned, and there were clearly pressures to make quite considerable savings, the trust did not face the same financial pressures as Acute and Care. The financial health of the trust was reflected in its physical infrastructure: a substantial new building programme was currently under way, and there was a palpable quality of build in the furniture, décor and surroundings in most parts of the main hospital, including the offices for senior managers and consultants. The administration blocks were of a poorer build standard, with cramped offices and some departments located in prefabricated units. The trust was located on a single site, although there was a clear spatial separation between the management offices and the rest of the hospital, which did lead to some feelings of divisiveness.

Many managers felt that the adoption of Foundation Trust status around five years earlier had resulted in clearer communications and systems of accountability. The organizational culture at the Specialist trust was generally represented as proactive, with a clear strategic direction cascaded effectively through the organization. There was also a good relationship between management and clinicians—with an implicit understanding that both were at the top of their respective fields. A number of general managers at the trust nevertheless mentioned the particular challenge of dealing with the body of consultants, who were less willing to be 'managed' because of their very high clinical status. There was, however, a clear understanding that clinical leadership took precedence, which perhaps accounts for the relative success experienced in securing clinical engagement in difficult areas such as cost-saving through service redesign (in marked contrast to experiences at the Acute trust).

> Over the last 12 to 18 months, the message is out there and now it does feel like it is everyone's responsibility. So when we have a bi-weekly financial review group meeting here, which looks at efficiencies, there is always clinical engagement, medical engagement on there, and they always attend.
>
> (Danielle, Functional, Specialist)

Interestingly, however, discussions of efficiency savings and financial pressure were of a different flavour to those encountered in the other trusts. There was awareness that the trust was relatively affluent and that the savings were largely about protecting the surplus and thus maintaining strong Monitor ratings.

Overall, though, the strength of the culture at the Specialist trust was referred to frequently in interviews, reflected in the pride displayed by many about working for such an organization. It was also reflected in the relatively low turnover of staff. Several respondents did, however, highlight dangers in this internal cohesion—in creating an insularity and complacency at the trust which staff had to deliberately challenge by maintaining external connections.

Managers at the Specialist trust had much less to say on the challenges caused by broader change in the sector than staff in the other two trusts, appearing to face the future with some equanimity. What dominated discussions were possible avenues for growth, including more commercial ventures and partnerships with private or third-sector organizations. There was also some debate about internal organization and the long-term implications of merging two clinical divisions. The challenge of competition was almost entirely disregarded, reflecting the trust's national reputation in its specialist field (apart from some speculation that private sector companies might undercut the trust's basic services provision).

When asked about future challenges, the most threatening scenario most could envisage was the remote possibility that a larger trust might attempt to take it over. Avoiding this had led to the trust 'expanding its footprint', through providing its branded specialist services using facilities based on the premises of neighbouring trusts. This not only helped deter any takeover by increasing the trust's apparent size but also helped its strategy of collaborating with local trusts. In practice, however, competitive tensions and the wider financial landscape often impinged upon such attempts at local cooperation:

> We have got really good relationships with some trusts we [provide specialist services to]; and some of them are very shaky relationships, because they're in a position financially perhaps not as good as we are. So they need to claw an income from whatever they can get, so the negotiation is: "No we're not paying for that, yes we are paying for that and we will provide this service ourselves maybe."
>
> (Hannah, General, Specialist)

Overall, then, a very consistent picture was painted of the trust—one that emphasized its relative financially security due to charity and research income, supplemented by sophisticated commercial operations working effectively to support high quality specialist care.

Summary

In this chapter we have attempted to introduce the main elements of the research process that underpins our investigation. We have introduced the empirical research that forms the focus of this study and which is intended to examine in depth the practice of healthcare management. Our discussion began by first setting out the main aims of the research and the perspective taken on management practice, knowledge, learning and networks that informs the later analysis. In so doing we have taken into consideration the changing context of management in healthcare and what that means for the changing nature of managerial work in practice. The aim has been to open up for further examination how this impacts upon managers' sense of their own professional identity, the types of knowledge and expertise they depend on, and what part managers' communities of practice play in enhancing or inhibiting flows of knowledge, learning and support. It is these questions that the research reported in this book was expressly designed to address and which our empirical work in the following four chapters sets out to examine. In the next chapter, we use the data collected from the three case study healthcare organizations to delve first into what it means to be a manager in the types of healthcare organization studied here.

4   Being a Manager

> I'm tempted to boil it down to three things . . . Some clinical experience,
> some clinical understanding of the work . . . Some ability to understand data
> and number crunching, waiting times and think about capacity and through-
> put . . . [And] managing staff, leadership of staff . . . in a way that combines
> the ability to whip staff up into a passionate frenzy to get them engaged to
> do their job, and also whip them when they don't.
>
> (Laura, General, Care)

Introduction

While the above quote graphically captures one particular way of view-
ing management in healthcare, it starts to highlight some of the ways in
which the managers in our study went about understanding their roles
and responsibilities in practice. It also specifically brings to the fore a
number of key features that had a major bearing upon management
practice—namely, the need to respond to service operational demands
and pressures; the importance of interaction with clinical practice and
practitioners; and the challenges faced in providing leadership and reconciling that with a felt need to exercise control. In doing so, it also hints
at the knowledge base and skills required by managers. As we shall see,
other managers who were interviewed expanded upon, elaborated and
complicated this picture. However, there was still a good deal of consistency in how they viewed their roles and responsibilities and approached
the challenges they faced in responding to operational needs, while at the
same time trying to connect effectively with clinical practice and exercise
leadership.

Drawing upon their accounts, this chapter sets out to explore the nature of
managerial work and practice 'on the ground' in healthcare, focusing upon
three principal themes: how the managers we interviewed viewed their roles
and responsibilities; how they approached their relationships with clinical
practice and clinicians; and what it meant practically to engage in leadership. To move towards understanding what sources of knowledge managers
are inclined to use in their practical day-to-day work and how they mobilize

that knowledge and make use of the networks of practice in which they are engaged, it is first important to understand something about the particular knowledge requirements they face in practice, how these might have developed in the context of recent changes in healthcare, and how this is reflected in the managerial skill sets they see as important. This chapter therefore sets the scene for the later examination of management knowledge and networking by exploring first of all what it means to be a manager in healthcare from the perspective of the managers in our study. Importantly, this takes into consideration any key differences that were associated with the varying organizational conditions (type of trust) they found themselves in or the diverse communities of practice they related to as particular types of manager.

As well as exploring these critical situational influences, this chapter also explores managers' work in the context of the recent changes experienced by and within management that were discussed in Chapter 2. There is an irony, and even contradiction, in the ways in which these wider policy initiatives have impacted upon managers and management practice in healthcare. On the one hand, managers are the supposed beneficiaries of (and likely advocates for) forms of healthcare organization that may be shifting control away from the established medical profession (Osborne and Gaebler, 1993; Kirkpatrick et al., 2005). On the other hand, more recent changes have seen managers put increasingly under pressure to deliver effective healthcare at a time of greater austerity and major cuts in management numbers and capacity. Consequently managers are expected to provide more effective leadership (e.g. King's Fund, 2011; O'Reilly and Reed, 2011) at a time when their capacity to do so is being eroded.

Moreover, as already noted, the delayering of middle management has gone hand-in-hand with its denigration, reinforced by stereotypical portrayals of healthcare middle managers. As one early study of nurse attitudes to management noted, managers were seen as 'aloof', 'smarmy', 'shifty', 'yes-men', who used the 'old boy network', had 'slept or crept their way up', were 'invisible at ward level' and 'hostile to patient care' (McCartney et al., 1993). Similarly, Merali's (2003) study more recently found that most managers were convinced that the general public believed that doctors and nurses were the only professionals in the NHS motivated by a desire to provide public service and patient care. Again, arguably, the lack of any real outcry about the recent cuts to management numbers in healthcare reflects a continued acceptance of the low status of managerial work (cf. Whitehead et al., 2010). In any event, it is difficult to see how such social stigmatization would not feed into the self-concepts of managers and affect their orientations to work (Preston and Loan-Clarke, 2000). An important starting point, therefore, is to recognize that middle managers in healthcare may struggle to establish legitimacy and credibility. Without the influence that senior directors have, and distanced from the clinical front-line, they can find themselves in an ambiguous and fragile occupational space located somewhere between 'board and ward', with only a belief in the NHS or a dedication to public service to provide any kind of guiding ethos. Consequently, the perceived importance of effective management in healthcare may not be matched by the importance and status ascribed to individual managers' roles. However, before we examine in more depth how healthcare managers in our study viewed their management work and responsibilities in the light of these limits to their status and influence, it is useful first to situate this in what we know more generally about the nature of managerial work.

Management Work: Theory and Practice

Healthcare managers are not alone in facing challenges and threats to their security and status. Not only have middle managers generally tended to face greater intensification of work as a result of contemporary organizational changes and associated restructuring and delayering (Grey, 1999; McCann et al., 2008); they have also found it difficult to establish a clear-cut professional status and identity centred around a distinct set of practices and body of knowledge (Reed and Anthony, 1992). Indeed, the activity of management and the skills and knowledge it requires are almost as diffuse as the range of contexts and organizations in which managers act. There is also no obvious common professional body or unifying set of professional requirements that provides a platform for accreditation and a solid enough basis for the 'closure' required around a distinct domain of practice if managers are to achieve professional status (Larson, 1977; Abbott, 1988).

Arguably, circumstances in healthcare heighten this attenuated connection between management practice and professionalization (Currie, 1997). The split of healthcare provision into different parts (primary, secondary and tertiary care) means that healthcare operations are highly differentiated, and high levels of internal departmental differentiation within individual healthcare organizations further shape managerial practice in very different ways (Hartley and Benington, 2006; Willem and Buelens, 2006). Moreover, in any particular healthcare setting, management itself is highly devolved and distributed (Buchanan et al., 2007). It involves not just general managers and administrators but also clinical and nursing staff and extends across multiple clinical specialisms and different modes of delivery. This heterogeneity within healthcare management creates challenges for managers in being able to share a consistent set of management practices and to develop a coherent professional identity.

It also means that any general management initiatives inevitably cut across the interests of a multitude of clinical and other professional/occupational communities of practice (Currie, 1997; Nicolini et al., 2008; Noordegraaf and Van Der Meulen, 2008; Fulop and Mark, 2013). Not only is management practice therefore inevitably shaped by the specific character of healthcare activity; it is also chronically affected by the multiple and distinct professional groupings and communities of practice that managers in healthcare have to relate to and contend with (Ferlie et al., 2005; Currie and White, 2012). Principal amongst these professional groups are clinicians and a good deal of research has, of course, highlighted the challenges associated with the very different logics of action that continue to divide business and clinical managers (Currie, 1997, 2006; Llewellyn, 2001; Hyde, 2010).

Beyond this diversity of practice, for managers generally there are also no clearly defined and agreed upon independent set of standards, norms and practices that they can and should draw upon or adhere to in taking managerial action. There are, of course, well-established prescriptions about what management in any context should entail, and these are commonly articulated as a standard set of management functions (e.g. planning, organizing, staffing, directing and controlling). These putative management functions are based on the legacy of early classical management theorists and can be found in many contemporary management texts. However, their practical application is highly contingent as they are shaped by local circumstances. Moreover, it has long been known that the day-to-day work of managers bears little relation to the image they promote of the rational manager systematically applying management principles to practical management situations (Mintzberg, 1973, 1975; Stewart, 1976, 1983). Instead, the reality of managerial work is known to be much more fragmented, disjointed and fluid, and managers are forced to be much more reactive in how they respond on a day-to-day basis to emerging issues and management problems. As writers in this tradition such as Mintzberg (1975), and Handy (2009) have noted, management is more complex than is conventionally understood and is made up of a diverse set of tasks, responsibilities, competencies, skills and dispositions.

At the same time, important questions have been raised about the extent to which this eclectic mix actually represents a radical departure from the normative prescriptions of classical management theorists. Hales (1986) suggests that there is, in fact, greater consistency with classical management functions than this depiction might imply. Also, the diversity often reflects the different methodologies and categorization schemes used by researchers to understand managerial behaviour. Mintzberg's (1975) influential work on management, for example, suggests that, in practice, management consists of a combination of 10 specific managerial roles grouped into three overarching categories: interpersonal (leader, figurehead, liaison); decisional (monitor, disseminator, spokesperson); and informational (entrepreneur, disturbance-handler, negotiator). Other categorizations (e.g. Stewart, 1976; Kotter, 1982) emphasize instead the activities of managers and/or the performance expectations held of managerial role-holders (Hales, 1986: 108).

Consequently, it is apparent that most classification schemes fail to capture adequately the eclectic nature of managerial work. Nevertheless, focusing on management practice does reveal that managers are as much attenuated from, as driven by, principles of systematic planning, organizing, staffing and the like; that management in practice is much more fragmented and fluid than depicted in classical theories (Hales, 1986: 104); and that management consists of a diverse and often-confusing range of attributes, roles and functions (Thomas and Linstead, 2002). Furthermore, the incorporation of the role of leader in Mintzberg's (1975) typology flags up the somewhat ambiguous position of leadership in relation to management activity—a theme that will be examined in more depth later in this chapter.

More contemporary views on the question of what constitutes management have therefore gone further and suggested that, to understand management, it is insufficient to try to establish some over-arching categorization of roles, tasks, functions or activities. What is important instead is to understand its emergent nature and how managerial practice and identity are shaped through the recursive interplay between wider discursive constructions about what management is meant to be; and the experiences of individuals trying to make sense of their managerial roles and responsibilities in their everyday practice (Watson and Harris, 1999; Thomas and Linstead, 2002; Clarke et al., 2009; Watson, 2009). In other words, the key to understanding what it means to be a manager is to explore how the day-to-day doing of management is shaped not only by the particular organizational contexts in which it occurs; but also by the institutional practices through which managers draw meaning as they construct and maintain particular work-identity narratives (Clarke et al., 2009).

The construction of work-identity narratives is of particular importance to our later examination (in the next chapter) of the career trajectories of the managers in our study, their socialization into healthcare management and their enactment of hybrid management roles (e.g. Llewellyn, 2001). Consequently, a fuller discussion of identity and identity work as it relates to management will not be attempted until then. Nevertheless, it is worth noting at this point how the construction of managerial identity can be conceived of as a practical struggle (Sveningsson and Alvesson, 2003). For managers, the identity work involved in maintaining a clear sense of what it means to manage (Watson, 2008, 2009) is made extremely difficult by the "ambiguity, obscurity and linguistic muddle surrounding the meaning of management itself" (Thomas and Linstead, 2002: 77). Managers are faced with having to strive to create a sense of unity and purpose in their managerial role, while being influenced by the shifting and mutable discursive constructions placed on the managerial role—such as that of 'administrator', 'strategist', 'leader' or 'entrepreneur'. Indeed, as already noted, all of these have, at different times, been used to refer to management in the healthcare context (Learmonth, 2005; O'Reilly and Reed, 2011; Hyde et al., 2016). Such diverse and contradictory meanings create antagonisms in practice, by requiring managers to combine seemingly contradictory logics—such as those of professionalism and commercialism (Harris and Holt, 2013) or patient care and choice (Mol, 2008). The manner in which these antagonisms and logics play out can also vary according to different modes of organization and the different discursive resources available to individual managers. This in turn has important implications for what managers understand to be their primary responsibilities, for how they attempt to engage with clinical practice, and for how they respond to the need to provide effective leadership. In the three sections that follow, we present empirical data from the interviews with managers to explore each of these three themes in turn.

Managers' Roles, Responsibilities and Skills

A good deal of attention was focused in the interviews on how managers interpreted their own roles and responsibilities in their organizations. Responses to questions about managers' day-to-day roles and responsibilities were coded according to several distinct areas of responsibility that emerged inductively. Across the sample of managers, there were four general areas of activity and responsibility that were routinely identified and which were acknowledged as important across the vast bulk of those interviewed, namely: line management, financial, strategic and operational. While they received more or less equal attention in managers' accounts, it was clear that the emphasis on strategy was more aspirational than the others, given the emphasis in managers' accounts on the need to manage staff, manage finance and respond to a multitude of operational demands and pressures. So, for example:

> I think one of the things that happens a lot in the NHS is [that] it is lots of talk and lots of paper and lots of strategy. My view is that anybody can write strategy, it's very easy. We all know what we'd like things to look like. The difficulty and the challenge is how you get that into the real world, so that affects the lived experience . . . I think that's where the magic happens and that's where the challenge is and that's how we have to work.
>
> (Beth, General, Care)

As well as those primary responsibilities, managers flagged up too in their accounts a number of other, secondary responsibilities. These tended to reflect specific roles or context, namely: functional responsibilities (functional managers), research (more common in the Specialist trust), and professional, clinical and educational work (all mostly associated with clinical managers). Comparing management groups, clinical managers experienced the greatest diversity of responsibilities, as they were more likely to be involved in research, clinical work, professional activities and education. Not surprisingly, the responsibilities of functional managers were more narrowly defined, given their more specific roles and more limited operational involvement. General managers as a whole placed a lot of emphasis on their core responsibilities of line management, finance and operational control (and rather less on their strategic influence), and this general picture was repeated across the three types of trust.

Breaking this down further into the particular roles and responsibilities and skill sets required, Mintzberg's managerial role schematic was initially used to code the data. However, while the primary classifications of inter-personal, decisional and informational roles remained relatively robust as a framework to code the data, it was not entirely consistent with the ways in which managers described their pre-occupations in their day to day work of 'just managing'. In particular, making sense of managerial work (cf. Weick, 1995) involved managers combining those role-based accounts of managerial activity with the more substantive, technical and composite aspects of managerial work associated with finance, HR (human resource management), project management (PM) and IT (information technology). Amongst these, finance was given a considerable amount of emphasis in the accounts managers gave. This was indicative not just of the importance attached to managers having the ability to deal with numbers, budgets and balance sheets, but was also symptomatic of the shift to greater marketiza-tion that has emerged in healthcare (e.g. Exworthy et al., 1999). As one manager neatly put it:

> The NHS does not live in a benign helpful background any more [where you're taught] about values and about clinical delivery and about how you set up a ward. That's not what our managers do any more. Our managers have to figure out how to write bids or how to be in meetings with commissioners and come out with a good result or what happens when you get an enormous budget cut that you can do nothing about.
>
> (Kerry, General, Care)

Nevertheless, despite this emphasis on 'hard' business skills, across the data set as a whole, it was the importance of managers' interpersonal role and skills, as well as the communicative aspects of their decisional and informational roles (cf. Mintzberg, 1975), that emerged as a primary way in which they sought to enact their role and make sense of their main respon-sibilities (cf. Silverman, 1970; Weick, 1995). 'Soft' personal and relational skills were consistently seen as of greater importance to managers than the 'hard' technical skills that managers felt were more concrete and tan-gible and that could more easily be developed through formal training (a theme explored further in Chapter 6). Indeed, the 'interpersonal' category of the coding frame was the most used by some considerable way and captured accounts of a wide range of relational skills (including but not restricted to Mintzberg's (1975) leader, figurehead and liaison roles).

The importance of fostering and maintaining relationships was seen as particularly important in strengthening the psychological contract between manager and employee (e.g. Coyle-Shapiro and Parzefall, 2008) in a con-text where there might not always be a formal process to follow or formal contract to back that up:

> There's no contractual relationships, with us, it's purely relationship and commitment and that's one of the unique features . . . A lot of what

we deliver is based on relationships and commitment to having shared vision and to wanting to get that and not, actually, a service-level agreement or a contract . . . I think it requires that commitment to long term maintenance of relationships and constantly keeping them up to date, even if there's nothing happening, even if things are going okay. Just maintaining contact, keeping that dialogue, keeping the vision there.

(Gabrielle, General, Care)

However, it was not necessarily the case that this strong orientation to interpersonal relationships translated into a management style that was simply personally considerate or supportive. In equating her managerial work to parenting, for example, Laura presented a nurturing narrative which may have reflected something of the therapeutic character of the work undertaken at Care, but which was at the same time quite directive:

Managing staff is very much influenced by the need to try and understand where they're at and try and reassure them that I'm on their side as much as I can be, not against them, and will support them as much as I can and I'll roll my sleeves up and do work with them. And I will only whip them [chuckles] if they make me.

(Laura, General, Care)

Moreover, as the two contrasting excerpts below demonstrate, managerial decision-making was approached in very different ways that reflected different stylistic predispositions. For Heather, management was an isolated position where freedom of action was somewhat restricted:

It still feels at times, quite isolating, because I guess the role of a senior manager is that you have to make very difficult decisions. Some quite harsh decisions at times. And people are looking at you to make those decisions for them . . . That's obviously a big challenge, to do that . . . Also, I've got to [encourage] the managers that sit below me . . . to make difficult decisions as well, and actually not to apportion the blame, that it's just my decision.

(Heather, General, Care)

Her response to such feelings of isolation and restriction was to adopt a management style that tried to distribute management decision-making responsibilities amongst her staff (cf. Buchanan et al., 2007).

A contrasting response can be seen in the account below from Harriet, who emphasized instead the opportunities that were potentially created when difficult decisions needed to be made:

I moved into a senior management role and . . . we had two failing residential services, both subject to external reviews . . . It was a case of: "this service is failing we need to put a turnaround team in, will you head that up?" . . . I had a new services manager . . . He'd had a poor experience in the NHS previously in a job that he knew nothing about . . . It was a real tough time for us initially . . . But the good thing is there's only one way to go and you've nothing to lose have you when you take on failing services? So it gave us both quite a lot of opportunities.

(Harriet, General, Care)

Clearly there were important stylistic differences between the approaches of these three general managers at the Care trust that were mirrored at the other two trusts—although perhaps with slightly less emotional investment and attachment than at Care. This was evident too in some important differences between the organizations in how relational skills tended to be viewed and used. Some managers saw the need to develop relationships as an end in itself, as it fostered a working environment that reflected managers' personal values. Others saw it in more instrumental terms, as a means of getting the job done more effectively. Given the nature of work undertaken, it is perhaps not surprising that Care trust provided some of the best examples of individuals striving to develop relationships for their own sake:

I think it's really important for you to know your staff . . . people will say that their personal lives don't matter, but it's totally part and parcel . . . If you're doing a 20-year job, you can't forget that there is an absolute part to people, human beings. You're going to have that. That's so important.

(Hasin, General, Care)

The following account from the Acute trust, still retains some of the quality of Hasin's ideal, although it begins to tie the rationale for developing relationships to implicit purposes or goals:

The one thing I've always tried to do is remember the little things about people. It's the tiny little things that matter. That, even if everything is going really badly and it's really busy, if you just remember some of the small things . . . people will remember them and you'll get people far more on side by doing things like that.

(Jessica, Functional, Acute)

At the other end of the spectrum, the challenges faced in navigating the status barriers that were more in evidence at the Specialist trust put a considerable premium on the instrumental value of relationship building—which was commonly articulated here as knowing the right person in the right place at the right time:

One of the skills you need to build up really quickly is knowing who the important people are and who does what . . . So when you have got a problem, especially in finance, you know who to pick the phone up to. So that's one of the things that I kind of tried to focus on . . . in the first two or three months—is just figure out who was who in the organization, how things worked really.

(Thomas, Functional, Specialist)

The above comment touches upon the importance of networking for managers—a theme that will be explored more fully later in Chapter 7. The point to emphasize here is that, although these differences were not necessarily all-encompassing or indicative of deeply internalized cultural norms, they did nevertheless signal broad cultural differences across the three trusts in how interpersonal relations fitted into conceptions of managerial work and shaped management styles. Moreover, there were echoes of these differences too in the ways in which the relationships between clinical and managerial groups were approached and managed in each case, as will be seen next.

Managing Professionals: Bridging the Clinical-Managerial Divide

Management as a technical practice has long been seen as at odds with the interests of other professional groups who tend to dominate the 'professional bureaucracies' in which they both work (Mintzberg, 1979; Raelin, 1985). Whereas the latter are more able to establish closure around their expertise, the former are not. While closure establishes and maintains high barriers of entry to the profession, it also leads to the development of a distinct community of practice and powerful interest group, with influence that may extend well beyond its own specialist domain. Conventionally this is a model which fits healthcare very well, with the medical profession being one of the oldest and most influential professional groups (Friedson, 1970).

Nevertheless many such studies have noted that what could be depicted as 'professional intransigence' has perhaps only slowed the inevitable encroachment of managerial logics into healthcare organization—most obviously perhaps through the financial rationalization of medical decision-making and the increasing demands placed on healthcare professionals to respond to government targets (Kirkpatrick et al., 2005). This 'hybridization' of work in healthcare has therefore muddied the conventional distinctions between professional and managerial work (Noordegraaf, 2011a, 2011b, 2015). However, it has not only meant the encroachment of managerial responsibilities into clinical work; it has also offered opportunities for some clinical groups—notably nurses—to harness management discourse to further their professionalization project (Brooks, 1999). Consider for example the somewhat contrasting accounts that can be found when one compares the limited responses to targets and performance appraisal available to medical professionals (Hood, 2006; McGivern and Ferlie, 2007) with the prospects available for nurses to expand and transform their roles into 'managerialist professionals' (Brooks, 1999) and exert more strategic influence as 'boundary spanners' (Currie et al., 2008). Indeed, it is somewhat ironic that nurses have been able to use managerial discourse to bolster their own influence when managers themselves have seemingly been unable to do the same. What unites these stories, however, is the remaking of clinical work via managerial responsibilities (see also Llewellyn, 2001)—although it clearly plays out differently for the two different groups of medics and nurses (a theme that will be returned to and explored further in the next chapter).

As noted earlier, the relationship between clinical and managerial groups within the NHS has been extensively researched and written about. Most of this research suggests that it is an inherently problematic relationship. We do not seek to fundamentally displace this assumption, as the majority of interview comments relating to this interface made very explicit reference to continuing problems. For example:

A lot of managers have very poor views of clinicians, they think they're a lazy bunch . . . in the same way as clinicians describe managers as, you know, paper clip counters. It's equally derogatory in both ways.

(Brian, Clinical, Acute)

In fact, the following extract creates an impression of a normalized tension that characterises the relationship between the two—the use of humour signifying a resignation to it as a fact of life:

Consultants hate managers. We don't do anything do we? . . . I am sure some of the staff think I don't do anything. I don't think the junior staff realize the responsibility that we do have certainly. I have joked that I am going on holiday for a week and we'll get one of the Band 5's to step in for me for a week, just to see how it feels.

(Belinda, General, Acute)

Not surprisingly given this context, across all three trusts interpersonal skills were regarded as a crucial element in being able to deal with these inherent and latent tensions between medical and managerial groups—as the following quote suggests:

You're caught in between . . . [With] medics here, I can't go and walk into one and say can you do a clinic tomorrow because I'm telling you. They'll say "on your bike". They'll say "who are you, a manager, coming in to tell me?" . . . It's about how you get across here's what's happening: quite a lot of pressure, what the impact will be, would it be possible for you to look at doing something about it, and then seeing what options come forward. It's taking that approach. So influencing is the key aspect of it.

(Pavak, General, Specialist)

However, the diversity of our sample across different trusts and managerial groups allows us to add some important nuances to understanding the inter-play between these groups, as well as to identify quite different organizational strategies that were used to try to manage relationships between clinicians and managers. Each organization in this study recognized the fundamental tension that could exist between clinicians and managers. However, what arose from the research were a number of important differences in the nature of this relationship across the three trusts and very different means that were developed to try to cope with and manage the interface. While there was some evidence that these were the result of an overt strategy, it was clear too that they had developed as much by accident as by design.

At the Acute trust, the common perception was of a unified and influen-tial body of medical consultants resistant to what was thought to be a 'busi-ness oriented' organization:

> Doctors train to be doctors, they don't train to be managers and actu-ally there's very few of them start aspiring to be managers . . . Unfor-tunately, medical management has been seen as a poisoned chalice that someone has to do their stint . . . and there's not much to draw people into it . . . I think, that's a shame, but . . . most people train to be doc-tors. They don't train to be managers. . . . I don't think we're alone, as a Trust, in that.
>
> (Brian, Clinical, Acute)

Historically this tension had been managed via a combination of charis-matic senior executives and command-and-control management structures. At the time we were researching the trust, there was a period of transition at the top of the organization (as noted in the previous chapter). One of the responses to this period of change was a redesign of the clinical-managerial structure at the sub-board level, which created two new positions of asso-ciate director and associate medical director, who would sit between divi-sional heads and the board. On the clinical side this represented an attempt to try to overcome some of the indifference towards management amongst clinicians by attaching greater status and importance to the medical man-agement role. Brian, the associate medical director at Acute and our key informant about this particular change, takes up the story:

> [We're] trying to draw doctors into the senior management roles, because, in all honesty, up until now, even at clinical director level, there's been a quite serious disengagement from the real mechanics of senior management within the Trust.
>
> (Brian, Clinical, Acute)

By giving medical managers responsibility for groups of consultants out-side their own profession, this redesign could also be seen as an attempt to counter some of the silo effects of professionalism, by drawing doctors away from their core clinical interests and moving them more towards a managerial agenda. One of the unintended effects of this, however, was to create tensions between the new associate medical directors and the consultants they were now asked to manage, since they came from quite distinct professional disciplines and communities of practice:

> We work very closely together and the thought of surgeons being managed by anaesthetists or anaesthetists being managed by a surgeon is a bit abhorrent to a lot of people and it will just be interesting to see how it evolves . . . I had to use all my diplomacy skills managing 32 relatively like-minded anaesthetists. Trying to manage surgeons as an anaesthetist— particularly if I fundamentally disagree with what they're saying, or what they're refusing to do—may prove quite challenging . . . I'll have to support the surgeons, to some extent. I can't just oppose everything they want, otherwise they'll just see me as being the enemy.
>
> (Brian, Clinical, Acute)

In other words, exercising managerial influence across clinical groups could be just as challenging in some respects as representing them in management terms.

Promoting the associate director from a divisional operational remit to this new interface role was also an attempt to create a sense of clinical/ managerial 'synergy':

> With me being associate medical director for surgery and him being associate director for surgery, we should be standing shoulder to shoulder and I should be there to support his ideas, maybe mould him a little bit if I think there are problems. Try and help him find the way forward. But I would see it as really needing to almost act in synergy with each other and I hope that's what I will bring in this new role.
>
> (Brian, Clinical, Acute)

Consequently, the primary mechanisms used at the Acute trust to try to manage the clinical-managerial interface were structural: creating new roles and reconfiguring the organizational structure were seen as the most effective way of realizing the sought-after synergies and benefits of greater clinical-managerial integration. This was not without its political side-effects, however, as Brian's narrative clearly indicates.

At the Care trust, by contrast, there was not the same unified body of consultants. Partly this was due to the narrower range of clinical specialisms and the dominance of psychologists and psychiatric nurses amongst the clinical staff; partly it was due to the diversity of services provided and the wide geographical spread of the organization. Any potential clinical resistance to organizational aims tended to be more associated with the tension between local and central control of operations (and emerged in response to senior management strategies to overcome that), rather than from clinical-managerial interactions at an operational level. As explained in the previous chapter, the trust had grown over time by taking over more and more local services. Whether or not this strategy of expansion led to what was seen as an unwelcome or predatory acquisition (and in some cases problems were clearly experienced), there were many residual tensions that existed between local autonomy and increasing standardization and central control.

One of the ways in which the Care trust presented itself as an organization, however, was through the rhetoric of clinical leadership. In our sample there seemed to be a good deal of reality to this rhetoric: over 90 percent of participants in this trust had a clinical background, and beyond this, many still had some kind of clinical input, even if this was mainly in an advisory capacity. One of the effects of this approach was to create a group of senior managers, who had been promoted through the ranks to become service managers overseeing their locality or operational managers with a wider remit across the whole trust. Indeed, even the trust's finance director (Graham) had a background in nursing (one of only two functional managers across the entire sample with a clinical background; the other was Bridget, a former nurse who was now the head of risk and safety at the Acute trust). This more personal embodiment and internalization of the divide between clinicians and managers was what distinguished the Care trust from the other two, as managers there tended to have more of an explicit dual commitment to both their clinical area and the organization. How this dual orientation shaped managers' ways of bridging the clinical-managerial divide is indicated clearly in the following account:

> I've been in a number of meetings with consultants who've said "well, we can't do that, clinically that wouldn't be viable". But I've done it or other people have done it . . . If I go into a room as a business manager they just see the label. But I've lived and breathed their culture so I understand it.
>
> (Glen, Clinical, Care)

How this embeddedness reflected managerial 'hybridity' and related to the career trajectories and personal development of managers across the sample of managers will be picked up and explored further in the next chapter.

Finally, the Specialist Trust was described as having a powerful and influential body of consultants who were generally recognized as being at the top of their field. However, it also had a strong managerial culture and commercial orientation, which was led from the top and communicated throughout the organization. In this case, therefore, there existed a powerful group of consultants and, when compared with the other two organizations, a powerful countervailing group of commercially minded managers.

With its relatively secure financial position, Specialist managed this potential clash through a multilayered senior clinical and management team structure, which moved beyond what might be called the conventional tri-umvirate of consultant-nurse-manager (Harrison and McDonald, 2008), to introduce an additional layer of middle management between divisional director and service manager. That is, one 'general manager' (at Grade 8d or 9) was to be more externally focused, partnering with the clinical director; and one 'deputy general manager' (at Grade 8b or 8c) was to partner with the lead nurses, be more internally focused in managing day-to-day divisional operations and oversee the work of service managers (at Grade 8a or 8b).

At the Acute trust, these responsibilities had been combined in the single role of the associate director. However, one of the consequences of this had been to create pressure on the hierarchy by drawing the associate director back into sorting out operational problems, thus diverting attention from the more strategic and externally focused aspects of the role. While the dep-uty general manager and the service managers at the Specialist trust did depict their roles as, to some extent, similarly inward-looking, this struc-tural solution nevertheless meant that the overall strategic direction of the trust had both senior management and clinical input. This tended to rein-force the mutual respect in the relations between clinical director and gen-eral manager, and so helped create an organization which more effectively combined clinical and managerial leadership. While the jobs of the deputy general manager and service managers were more akin to the 'conventional' relationship of consultants to managers, this was in an organizational con-text in which there was a considerable degree of job satisfaction among all occupational groups. As one of the deputy general managers put it:

> It's about bringing people with you, especially when they're people that are highly intelligent. I do try to encourage these people to work with me rather than feel they're being told; I don't think they respond too well to that. And certainly the service managers are very good at engag-ing with them.
>
> (Gavin, General, Specialist)

Interviews revealed a shared sense of confidence that, while there were challenges, these were not insurmountable, and that everyone was essen-tially pulling in the same direction. Rather than conflict and mistrust, there was clear recognition of the strategic advantages to be gained from this mutual dependency. Consequently, the structural mechanisms that were adopted by the Specialist trust to bridge the clinical-managerial divide were complemented by a strong sense of mutual dependence and respect between managers and clinicians. Again, making that relationship work put a lot of emphasis on the importance of relational and interpersonal skills. For example:

> I think the key is to build up relationships with clinicians . . . because if you can't approach them in a certain way . . . then you've failed. If you

can't get them on side, you can't do your job; and that takes years to build up that relationship properly.

(Joanna, General, Specialist)

Consequently, managing relations, communicating effectively and dealing with different personalities were seen as the *sine qua non* of management at the Specialist trust. The overall effect was not the eradication of the clinical-management divide or its embodiment in individuals (as tended to be the case at the Care trust), but its more effective management (when compared to the Acute trust).

Management and Leadership

In Chapter 2, it was noted how the discourse of leaderism has taken much more of a hold in policy and practitioner thinking about the management of healthcare (O'Reilly and Reed, 2011; McDonald, 2014). Through its emphasis on individual agency and the supposed (visionary and strategic) transformative capabilities it encapsulates, it clearly appeals to policymakers and practitioners concerned with improving the perceived image and impact of healthcare management, in bridging gaps between aspects of service delivery such as the clinical-managerial divide and in overcoming (structural) barriers to reform (Ford and Harding, 2007). For middle managers, it thus potentially provides a more positive, constructive and even heroic discursive resource to draw upon (Alimo-Metcalfe and Lawler, 2001; King's Fund, 2011). It is also a term that may hold much greater currency with the medical profession, who are perhaps more comfortable providing clinical leadership than clinical management (Spurgeon et al., 2011).

At the same time, however, there remain a number of important questions about what this actually means for managers and managerial work in healthcare and how it translates into managerial practice and affects their evolving sense of managerial identity (cf. Watson, 1994, 2009). So, for example, how does leadership infuse managers' thinking about, talking about and enacting of management? How readily do managers see themselves as leaders, and how does this relate to how leadership translates into management practice? In other words, how do the discursive resources that managers themselves draw upon to make sense of their own situation relate to expectations of leader behaviour? More critically, does the emphasis on leadership in any way threaten further the credibility or legitimacy of middle managers, who may in practice be more engaged in implementing change than in leading it (Dopson and Fitzgerald, 2006)?

Before considering these questions further, it is useful briefly to consider what we know about the concept of leadership more generally with specific reference to how it has figured in accounts of management. As already noted, the distinction between management and leadership has been a topic of investigation in the management literature for some considerable time. The literature on leadership is vast and a review of that literature is well beyond the scope of this chapter.[1] However, it is clear that successive waves of leadership theory and research have tended to depict the relationship in one of three main ways. First, by subsuming leadership within management functions or roles (as implied in Mintzberg's framework and in the depiction of 'leading' as a classical management function (cf. Drucker, 1974)); second, by conflating leadership and management (as is the case with most earlier style and contingency theory approaches to leadership (cf. Bryman, 1986)); third, by proposing a clear conceptual and practical distinction between leadership and management as two quite distinct sets of orientations and practices (e.g. Zaleznik, 1977; Kotter, 1990). It is the third of these approaches that still perhaps best resonates with contemporary discourse and mainstream views about the relationship between leadership and management—notwithstanding the proliferation of alternative perspectives on leadership in recent years.[2] By depicting the relationship between leadership and management as a dualism, attention is directed to what are felt to be inherent differences between them and to the supposed visionary and transformational qualities of individual leaders that distinguish them from 'mere' managers.

While such a distinction may provide a useful way of articulating some basic differences between leadership and management, the questions posed above suggest that it is also important to be critically aware of the ways in which these differences play out in practice and shape managers' sensemaking and evolving sense of identity as managers/leaders (e.g. Carroll and Levy, 2008). Put more simply, do middle managers see themselves as leaders, managers or both? In keeping with the more interpretive, practice-based approach adopted here, such a question highlights the necessity of taking a more critical approach to leadership (and its relationship to management) that is more open than mainstream views to understanding how meanings and understandings of leadership are discursively constructed and situated in practice (Grint, 2005; Ford and Harding, 2007; Carroll and Levy, 2008; Western, 2008; Denis et al., 2010; Ford, 2010; Alvesson and Spicer, 2012). Grint (1997, 2005), for example, emphasizes that leadership itself is a social construction and that situations may be actively framed to require different sorts of leadership action. Such an approach underscores the importance of context in influencing how leadership discourse unfolds in practice. In healthcare specifically, this has led a good many observers to question recent exhortations placed on managers to provide more effective leadership (Wallace and Tomlinson, 2010; O'Reilly and Reed, 2011; Martin and Learmonth, 2012; Tomlinson et al., 2013; McDonald, 2014; Bresnen et al., 2015).

The relative seniority of participants in this study meant that the relationship between management and leadership was important to explore as it was imagined that these skills would be interlinked in practice, and often embodied in the same person. However, the most striking pattern in responses to questions about management and leadership was the conception held by the vast majority of participants that they were best understood as a dualism. Management was seen as more about achieving stability and related to operational skills; leadership was seen as more about change and related to strategic and visionary capabilities. Indeed, the earlier observation in this chapter of varying management styles was very much seen as central to managers' day-to-day responsibilities, as opposed to any real expression of leadership—despite the centrality of style to studies of leadership over time (e.g. Bryman, 1986).

This dualistic separation of management and leadership was made explicit in the following accounts from two general managers at the Acute trust:

> Management is around how you manage the day-to-day operations, the leadership is how you take your team forward and the direction that you want them to go in and how you want your service to develop.
>
> (Hugh, General, Acute)

> I think leadership's more strategic, it's more about vision; having a vision of what's to come and where you want to go and taking people with you. I very much see management more as a day-to-day, more of an operational type concept really. Whereas leadership, I see that as being more strategic and it's making change and delivering change and driving things through people.
>
> (Stewart, General, Acute)

The above views were very typical of those found across management groups at all three trusts. Building upon previous work by Kotter (1990), table 4.1 below represents an attempt to summarize across the sample the key recurrent dichotomies that were used by managers to articulate differences as they saw them between management and leadership:

Table 4.1 Contrasting Portrayals of Management and Leadership

Management	Leadership
Nuts and bolts	Visionary
Following policies, procedures, processes	Make decisions
Day-to-day	Long term
Can read it in a book	Can't be taught
Improved through (standard) training and development experiences	Natural born, charismatic though enhanced through self-awareness training
Sat behind a desk	Being dynamic
Getting people to do their jobs	Helping people see why they do what they do
Holding people to account	Influencing/inspiring people
Safe services from standardization	Improve services by taking risks
Focus on task	Focus on strategy
Bureaucratic	Heroic
Unpleasant	Aspirational
Enacted practices	Embodied qualities

Almost without exception, management was seen as more concerned with the nitty-gritty of day-to-day activity, whereas leadership was seen as more concerned with creating a vision and inspiring others. Although there were also some interesting differences in how leadership and management were related to one another (examined further below), what was remarkable was the surprisingly high degree of consistency across the trusts and across managerial groups in how respondents viewed leadership and management (and the absence of any clear and systematic relationship to factors such as age or training).

Vision, in particular, was one of the primary articulated ways of differentiating between management and leadership.

> I think if you haven't got a vision then other people might struggle to have that vision. At [another trust] where I worked before, the staff knew . . . They knew because I communicated it. The first day I was there I [got] everybody together and [told] them what I'm about.
>
> (Oliver, Clinical, Acute)

At the same time, however, simply having a vision was not enough—there needed to be practical management techniques that could be used to engage people to aspire to and achieve that vision:

> You have to look at what kind of staff you have, you have to look at all your recruitment and how that happens and make sure you get the right people in the right place. I believe very strongly you have to try and engage people with a vision so people know which way they're going.
>
> (Beth, General, Care)

Nevertheless, it was generally felt very strongly that leadership skills were more individual and innate than those associated with management; and that the latter could readily be acquired through experience and training:

> I think managerial stuff, it's something that you can probably be trained and taught. I think that leadership things are something that you maybe either have or you don't have, and it's more difficult to teach people those kinds of things.
>
> (Elena, General, Care)

Similarly:

> I would definitely see management and leadership as different. I think management I see as more of the nuts and bolts, day-to-day, getting tasks done. I see leadership as inspiring people, driving them forward, making them want to come to work, empowering them to use their initiative . . . You can't teach leadership. Management you can read it in a

book and you can teach me how to manage someone . . . But you can't really learn leadership. It's in there somewhere and you have to find it and bring it out.

(Felix, Functional, Acute)

This too was a very common conception across the interviewees. Understanding leadership as a personal, innate set of attributes implies, however, that it is something embodied within individuals and tacit rather than easily codified, shared and developed. This reifies the individual and also creates challenges for developing knowledge about effective leadership—a theme that will be returned to and developed further in the next chapter.

Although many of the characteristics of management undoubtedly fulfil important functions in healthcare—for example paying attention to detail, following policies and procedures exactly and having highly specialized skills—the ways in which management was portrayed by managers showed a clear preference for leadership over management and a corresponding denigration of the latter. Whereas descriptions of leadership qualities emphasized extraordinary powers of vision and influence, management was portrayed as a dull, procedural function that involved implementing policies and procedures and focusing upon the 'nuts and bolts' of the job—despite the importance, noted earlier, of style and interpersonal skills. For example:

I see a manager more as a kind of functional keep the show on the road type job, and I'd say that probably more what I am or how I perceive myself. I think leadership is much more about being out there, being visionary and taking teams with you and less of the kind of mundane day to day stuff.

(Sarah, General, Acute)

For me . . . a leader is someone that is very visionary, innovative . . . they're the people who can sit in a room and come up with something that nobody else can think about . . . As a manager . . . you just tell people what to do . . . I guess managers just manage don't they?

(Ellen, Functional, Specialist)

Furthermore, this denigration of management tended to undermine its importance, reinforcing the view expressed by one participant that the NHS was essentially 'over managed and under-led':

The NHS . . . has got a lot of managers, it's just the way it is . . . Because, you know, everything's in teams and little pockets and things wouldn't be successful if there wasn't someone steering in the right direction . . . But I don't think there's as many leaders in the NHS. I'd say a leader is someone who sticks their head above a bit more and really pushes things forward . . . There's lots of people managing in the NHS.

(Thomas, Functional, Specialist)

Among others, Khurana (2002) has critiqued what he has referred to as the 'quasi-religious belief in the powers of charismatic leaders' arguing that this overlooks more important and essential social and economic determinants of organizational success (see also Bryman, 1992; Western, 2008). Other critics of the 'superleader' concept (e.g. Huy, 2001, 2002) argue that in organizations that face continuous change and reform, middle management is still crucial for achieving the appropriate balance between change and continuity.

Not surprisingly, it was quite clear that the aspiration to exercise leadership was often confounded anyway by the realities of the pressures and demands of everyday work on management. The displacement of energy into more operational matters was apparent in the following account:

[Our] chief exec [is] very keen on [saying] we're going to get together on this Wednesday afternoon for a strategic leadership group or with the clinical directors, and this is going to be our thinking time about where we're headed. But then by the time everybody's put their little bit on the agenda, it's just become another committee.

(Greg, General, Acute)

Observational data from management meetings at all three trusts also tended to confirm that, stylistic differences apart, they were similarly driven by (largely external) reporting requirements that left relatively little time and space for discussions of strategies and missions. Moreover, the question was also raised of whether the organization would be receptive anyway to the more transformative, progressive and democratic ideals associated with this visionary take on leadership:

My total ideal would be if I was working with a whole bunch of managers who actually thought that the hierarchy was upside down and that they were working for their team and that their job was to make their team the best and the most productive and to have the best employment experience they could—not that they're large and in charge and telling people what to do . . . And I don't think that that's necessarily entirely acceptable here by any stretch of the imagination . . . You're expected to get in the front and lead the services.

(Ruth, Functional, Care)

However, having said that, there were some subtle contextual differences between the cases which did have some effect on managerial action. While the more 'hands on' managerial work at the Care and Acute trust did make it more difficult for managers to think and act strategically, there were more opportunities for this at the Specialist trust, where clinical/scientific expertise was the core competence and business development was highly valued. Despite these nuances, however, the actual experience of being a leader-manager at this level tended to contrast with the representation of leadership and management as a simple dualism. The discourse of leadership rapidly dissipated in practice, as local concerns and operational requirements took over and idealized conceptions held of leadership tended to default to the more pressing demands associated with management (Carroll and Levy, 2008).

Furthermore, while there was a surprising uniformity among participants regarding this management/leadership dualism, it was not unanimously held. A small minority of participants were less liable to reify leadership and more inclined to critically reflect upon, and deconstruct, it. A contrasting view was presented instead that emphasized the importance of leaders 'getting their hands dirty':

> Leadership is a very amorphous kind of notion that is very difficult to pin down and therefore very difficult to achieve . . . Leadership is often projected as vision and strategy and actually I think a lot of leadership is about getting your hands dirty with everybody else and not sitting there and going, well you all do it . . . So it is a kind of lead by example, rather than just thinking up a fancy strategy and waiting for everybody who has got a day job to have to do it.
>
> (Kerry, General, Care)

Even when there was not such a conscious self-positioning, some managers would also draw on a very similar conception when reflecting on their own practices:

> I think the way you prove you're a leader in this role is by leading by example, by sorting things out that are quite difficult to sort out, by being on the ward, by being present, by mucking in, by showing that you're able to.
>
> (Luke, General, Care)

Such responses reflect some dissatisfaction with the ambiguity and indeterminacy associated with the concept of leadership (Bresnen, 1995; Carroll and Levy, 2008; Alvesson and Spicer, 2012) and a clear desire to make it more concrete and, literally, 'hands on'.

Taken together, these points reveal a tension between leadership understood as visionary and heroic and what were often felt to be dominant organizational strategies and imperatives. Situated as they were immediately beneath divisional directors and board members, the managers in this study often found themselves as leader-managers having to face simultaneously in two directions:

> It's really important to be a strong leader for your practitioners, so that they know they can discuss issues, that are challenging to them, without it feeling punitive or exposing. They need to feel safe to be able to think about their practice . . . But, equally, you need to be mindful of what the organization is requiring and what the organization might think about some of that practice and some of the changes that the organization tries to impose.
>
> (Gabrielle, General, Care)

Though Gabrielle does refer to the need for active performance management, this is seen to require a softer skill set involving empathy and emotional intelligence—with the intent of reconciling two potentially incongruous perspectives. Regardless of the 'softness' of the approach, the excerpt nevertheless does underline the importance of accountability—an approach more forcefully stated by Kerry:

> I have a couple of phrases I switch between depending on which way the wind is blowing . . . One is, "by any means necessary." So if there is a job to be done, actually we have to get the job done. And the other one [is]: "the job is to get the job done", not some airy fairy idea about . . . my preferred management style.
>
> (Kerry, General, Care)

Again, this echoes the point made earlier about leaders getting their hands dirty. But it also shows some frustration at the emphasis on a 'soft' stylistic approach to management-leadership. As her account continues, Kerry returns to an interrogation of the concept of leadership and the misperceptions it can create further down the hierarchy:

> If you were to go the next layer down, they have this idea of leadership which doesn't involve doing the job that they are doing now . . . My view is you're doing that job that you're doing now and a bit more—it's not a trade-off. When you move up the ladder what you always do is just join at the bottom of the higher food chain . . . I'm at the bottom of a much more senior food chain than my managers . . . And I have much less autonomy than they do.
>
> (Kerry, General, Care)

Her sophisticated take on power and control in organizations and its implications for leadership found an echo in the words of Heather at the Care trust, who commented that "the higher you climb, the less air you breathe".

What is being suggested here is that general managers found it difficult or impossible to realize their expressed leadership ideal. However, for clinicians, the experience was somewhat different. It was interesting to note, in particular, the importance that clinical managers attached to their leadership role:

> I think it's about being seen as a leader, as a clinician that people are in awe of. I don't know how you get that, but it's about being constant and reliable and credible within your organization, credible within the field that you're in. I think it's having the skills to get people to do what you need them to do. Because as a manager you can just say I want you to do that and people will think: "I'm not doing that."
>
> (Thea, Clinical, Care)

This emphasis on the importance of clinical credibility as the basis of influence, expressed through the vehicle of leadership rather than management, was also evident in the following account:

> Most of the clinicians are not in the clinical director roles, or the divisional director roles . . . They want to lead the service, they want to shape the service, they want to set the strategy for their services, they don't want to deal with the operational day to day . . . [They think:] I didn't come into medicine to be a manager. They want to be a leader and they want the kudos! They don't deal with money, they don't deal with targets but, you know! Strategy, yeah, they like strategy.
>
> (Annette, Specialist, General)

The relationship between clinical and managerial orientations will be explored again in the next chapter, when we delve further into the experiences of the 'hybrid' managers in our study. For the moment, observations such as this suggest not only that leadership might have greater traction amongst some managerial groups than others (and perhaps across different types of trust); but also that its discursive power might even help transcend entrenched status differentials between professional/occupational groups. Ironically, it is the indeterminacy in the concept of leadership that again appears to play a significant part in providing a discursive resource for bridging the clinical-managerial divide (Martin and Learmonth, 2012; McDonald, 2014).

Summary

This chapter has set out to explore three main sets of issues pertaining to the experiences of being a healthcare manager: the nature of managerial roles and responsibilities in the context of local operational pressures and wider institutional change; the challenges faced by managers on the ground in overcoming the clinical-managerial divide; and how exhortations to exercise leadership translated into the aspirations and actions of managers. All of this has been set in the context of the profound changes occurring in practice across the sector, as well as long-standing conceptual debates about the nature of management, its professional status and its relationship with the more esoteric concept of leadership.

Despite there being important differences in the responsibilities of management in our sample associated with their diverse managerial roles and organizational contexts, what emerges most strongly perhaps is the consistency in how managerial work is viewed, with a strong emphasis being put upon the importance of interpersonal skills and a downplaying of more 'technical' and administrative skills. While there was some variation in emphasis across the organizations, such differences were more magnified when it came to understanding the ways the three trusts set out to manage the clinical-managerial divide—by relying variously upon structural mechanisms, relational skills or the embodied knowledge and skills of hybrid managers. The idealization of more visionary, transformational approaches to leadership by the vast majority of managers was also apparent. But it stood in stark contrast to the problems managers faced in realizing that ideal due to the pressures created by organizational imperatives and the intrusion of more mundane managerial demands. While this led a small minority to deconstruct such an idealized vision of leadership, it left many others—including many clinical managers—to continue to reify the concept.

Understanding the nature of managerial work in healthcare and the skills required is an essential first step in understanding the types of knowledge that managers require and mobilize. Indeed, at various points in this chapter the relationship between managerial work and management knowledge has been hinted at and further exploration of this will form the main focus of Chapter 6. Before that, however, it is useful to delve deeper into managers' experiences, to try to gain further insights into what the challenges of managing in healthcare mean for managers' emergent sense of professional managerial identity (cf. Watson, 1994). Particularly important here is to explore not only how managers found themselves in their positions as managers; but also whether and how their career transitions involved any clinical-managerial hybridity that has shaped their orientations to management knowledge (cf. Llewellyn, 2001). The next chapter therefore turns to a fuller consideration of managerial careers and managers' evolving sense of their identity, with particular reference to the importance of hybridity in healthcare.

Notes

1 For more complete reviews see, for instance, Bryman (1986), and Grint (1997, 2005).
2 See, for instance, Gronn (2002) on distributed leadership; Gardner et al. (2005) on authentic leadership; and Wu (2010) on substitutes for leadership.

5 Becoming a Manager

> In middle management, you're constantly the meat in between everybody else's sandwich. Everything is about your delivery on this, that and the other thing, and you're constantly having to respond to everybody else's agenda.
>
> (Beth, General, Care)

Introduction

The above quote exemplifies many descriptions of the pressure experienced by healthcare managers in their day-to-day work, resulting in part from their difficult position between senior management and the front-end of healthcare operations; and also as the link between different functional and clinical groups within their organizations. Given these demanding conditions, attention needs to be paid not only to the role and responsibilities of managers and leaders, as discussed in the previous chapter, but also to what it means in practice to strive for and to *become* a manager in healthcare. In this chapter, we look more closely at the backgrounds and career trajectories of the diverse group of managers we interviewed to examine the different types of career and professional development they experienced. We explore the different orientations to management held and the different pathways into management they pursued. Also examined are managers' goals and expectations in the light of changes occurring within their organizations and to managerial work across the sector more generally. Drawing on accounts of career narratives and processes of socialization, we explore in more depth the identity of healthcare managers, paying particular attention to the importance of hybridity among our cohort of managers.

Although the chapter makes reference to the experiences of all types of clinical and general managers in our study, particular attention is therefore directed towards those occupying hybrid manager roles (Fitzgerald and Ferlie, 2000; Currie and White, 2012; McGivern et al., 2015) which typically blend clinical and managerial orientations in different degrees (as reflected in the framework presented earlier as figure 3.1). As already noted, healthcare managers include substantial numbers of doctors, nurses and other allied health professionals who have moved into clinical team leadership positions and/or have switched into more general management roles. Situated at the juncture of clinical and managerial communities of practice and the different discourses that they represent (von Knorring et al., 2016), they occupy important positions as potential mediators of medical and management expertise and, as we have already seen, embody the possibilities for coordinating clinical needs with organizational requirements (Degeling et al., 2001; Llewellyn, 2001).

The previous chapter touched upon the direct implications that managerial hybridity has for managers' work practices and in particular, for helping bridge the clinical-managerial divide. Hybridity also plays an important part in understanding the way individuals make sense of their career development and emerging managerial identity. It is the identity work that results (cf. Watson, 2008, 2009) and the associated sense-making of managers (cf. Weick, 1995) with which the present chapter is principally concerned. In grappling with their hybrid management roles, healthcare managers' struggles for identity are arguably heightened further by the on-going, reflexive work of identification that is needed and through which narratives of self, role, and career are formed and maintained. This will inform later discussions of the implications of managerial hybridity in healthcare on managers' learning, orientations to knowledge and networking with others—for example, in shaping managers' knowledge bases or in influencing their engagement with different networks of practice.

Management Identities and Making Sense of Managerial Careers

Before exploring in more detail managerial hybridity in healthcare, it is useful first to consider briefly what identity theory and, in particular, the concept of identity work, might offer to the exploration of hybrid management roles (Alvesson and Willmott, 2002; Watson, 2008; Alvesson, 2010). It has long been recognized that managerial identities are not clear-cut, stable and unambiguous (Watson, 1994; Sveningsson and Alvesson, 2003; Brown, 2015). Indeed, research has consistently highlighted the fragmented nature of identity (Collinson, 2003) and how managers tend to draw upon a range of organizational discourses, cultural resources, narratives and rhetorical strategies as resources to create a sense of self that helps stabilize their role and identity (e.g. Czarniawska-Joerges, 1994; Down and Reveley, 2009). These, in turn, may help enhance their legitimacy in organizations (cf. Anthony, 1986).

Recent critical work on identity has also gone further by moving away from understanding (managerial) identity as a stable and coherent concept, to emphasizing instead its situated and changing character (Watson, 1994; Collinson, 2003; Sveningsson and Alvesson, 2003; Brown, 2015). This represents a move away from exploring the nature of identities and towards emphasizing instead the processes and practices of *identification*

(Knights and McCabe, 2003). This shift in thinking emphasizes the dynamic interplay between individuals and the organizational and institutional circumstances in which they are situated—which are often characterized by contestation and fluidity (Alvesson et al., 2008; Brown, 2015). This work highlights the multiple forms of 'identity regulation' which impinge upon employees in organizational settings, through the largely deliberate effects of practices such as induction, training, performance appraisal and other, more subtle activities which shape identity in line with organizational goals (Alvesson and Willmott, 2002). This is not to suggest that identity can be easily moulded through such activities, nor that individuals are helpless in the face of such regulation—not least because there are a whole range of forces which inform identity, not all of which relate to work or organizational life (Brown, 2015).

Given the multitude of competing bases of identification that managers are exposed to and can draw upon, with potentially ambiguous and contradictory effects, managers are therefore characterized by some as being constantly engaged in 'identity work' (Sveningsson and Alvesson, 2003; Alvesson, 2010: 8–9). Managerial identity is neither necessarily coherent nor fully stable (Collinson, 2003) and may instead be highly provisional, negotiated and accomplished (Alvesson et al., 2008). The 'struggle' of identification that this creates centres around a combination of 'world-making' and 'sense-making' (cf. Weick, 1995) in an attempt to generate and maintain what Giddens (1991) terms *ontological security*—a sense of order and continuity in terms of oneself and one's place in the world. In this conception of identity work, individual managers therefore draw on the discursive resources available to them within particular situations (Musson and Duberley, 2007) and respond to existing or emerging notions about what constitutes managerial identity in a range of possible ways—for instance, through acceptance, argumentation, resignation or resistance.

Context is therefore fundamentally important. In institutionalized and professionalized environments such as healthcare, one might expect identification to be powerfully influenced or constrained by organizational demands or professional requirements and expectations (e.g. Alvesson and Willmott, 2002). At the same time, however, individual agency is also important and, in as fragmented and changing a landscape as that found in healthcare, there is the ever-present possibility that managers can exert their individual agency and have some freedom of action to respond to, manoeuvre around, and even resist, organizational and other institutional pressures to conform to particular conceptions of their role or identity (Watson, 2008; Brown, 2015: 26). Indeed, many have suggested further how identity work constitutes not only an important part of the active definition and enactment of managerial roles (Järventie-Thesleff and Tienari, 2016) but also an important element in the 'institutional work' associated with the reproduction or change by individual actors of accepted management practice (Creed et al., 2010; Suddaby and Viale, 2011).

Consequently, recent explorations of the identity work that this involves have stressed not just the influence of organizational and extra-organizational sources of meaning which managers may harness; but also how this relates to individuals' own sense of self-identity and how balancing the relationship between the two impacts upon identity construction (Ibarra, 1999; Kreiner et al., 2006). Managers are therefore not only involved directly and actively in the construction of their own identity (Watson, 1994, 2008); they also face the challenge of reconciling their own self-concept with extraneous sources of meaning that circulate through professional and organizational discourses (Kreiner et al., 2006). In characterizing identity work as building a bridge between managers' self-identity and such external, discursive social-identities, Watson (2008), for instance, highlights how identity construction thus involves both 'inward-facing' and 'outward-facing' identity work. He also suggests that the relationship between the two is dialectical in nature. That is, there is potential for some (limited) impact that self-identities might have upon wider shared social-identities through identity work, but that this acts only as a partial counter to the (stronger) impact of social influences in shaping managerial identity (ibid: 128). The key then is to understand how organizational and institutional pressures are met by the individual's own sense of self-identity (Ibarra, 1999; Kreiner et al., 2006) and how a sense of balance or security is achieved in particular circumstances over time (cf. Giddens, 1991).

Our attention to how individuals become managers reflects the importance of all of these processes if we are to understand how managers understand themselves (Czarniawska-Joerges, 1994; Watson, 2009), and how this understanding shapes, and is shaped by, their behaviour. Such identity work is often revealed in career narratives through which managers seek to make sense of their career progression (Ibarra and Barbulescu, 2010): from the socialization processes associated with individuals starting careers and/ or joining organizations (Ibarra, 1999; Ashforth, 2001); through to their on-going efforts to make sense and cope with their organizational setting (Weick et al., 2005). The generation of narratives around career development may, of course, gloss over what is actually a much more fragmented and fluid set of career transitions (e.g. Learmonth and Humphreys, 2012). Nonetheless, such accounts yield important insights into how managers relate to particular constructions of managerial identity. Moreover, the sense that is made of career progression in a context in which professional and managerial discourses may conflict or be conflated as a consequence of hybridity—in ways that either fracture or consolidate managers' sense of their identity throughout the course of their careers—becomes extremely important in understanding the constructions placed by managers on their emerging roles and sense of professional identity.

Finally, the link between hybridity and identity work is a close one. Those inhabiting hybrid roles, subject to contradictory demands from different communities or trying to reconcile different logics in their day-to-day work, almost inevitably engage in more intensive identity work to generate a sense of coherence and suppress inconsistencies in their self-image. Such subjects who find themselves caught between two worlds, or forced to inhabit two worlds simultaneously, are described by some as being in a *liminal* position (Tempest and Starkey, 2004; Beech, 2011). This liminality may occur temporarily, as part of a transition from one role to another, such as a promotion or a change of career direction (Tansley and Tietze, 2013). For hybrid managers, however, who rely upon being at the same time both manager and professional, for instance, or manager and scientist, or indeed manager and academic, this represents a more permanent tension which must be negotiated, necessitating more intensive identity work (Paton and Hodgson, 2016). While many point to the advantages of this liminality—the creative freedom it might afford, or the opportunities for innovation through combining different fields of knowledge (Garsten, 1999; Swan et al., 2016)—it remains the case that many struggle to reconcile the competing demands, both in their everyday conduct and in pursuit of a coherent sense of self. We therefore turn to the question of how hybrid healthcare managers engage in identity work to manage this tension.

Hybrid Managers in Healthcare Organizations

Changing managerial identity has certainly been an important recurring theme in the context of healthcare (Learmonth, 2005; Currie et al., 2010; O'Reilly and Reed, 2011). Given the importance of hybrid management roles to contemporary healthcare organizations (Buchanan, 2013; Noordegraaf, 2015), it is not surprising that considerable attention has focused upon the occupational position, management capabilities and professional orientations of healthcare managers who either continue to combine professional workloads with managerial responsibilities or who have moved from clinical backgrounds into predominantly managerial roles (Llewellyn, 2001; Currie and White, 2012; Burgess and Currie, 2013; Croft et al., 2015; McGivern et al., 2015).

As we have already seen, hybrid middle managers play a crucial role in healthcare organizations when compared to so-called *pure play* managers who do not have clinical backgrounds or experience (Buchanan, 2013). Not only are they numerically by far the most important type of manager in the wider NHS workforce,[1] as we have already seen they are also important in helping bridge the clinical-managerial divide within healthcare (Llewellyn, 2001). They also play a potentially important role in helping develop relationships and broker knowledge across multidisciplinary teams (Currie and White, 2012; Burgess and Currie, 2013) and are seemingly well placed to help complex healthcare organizations both exploit existing knowledge and explore new sources of knowledge (Burgess et al., 2015).

Much of the work on hybrid middle managers nevertheless does highlight the organizational and professional challenges they face. Despite their supposed advantages, they occupy a precarious position at the edges of established professional hierarchies, and this can pose personal challenges (Burgess and Currie, 2013). Doctors can be very reluctant to take on the mantle of manager, given the potential dilution of their professional status it implies and the practical difficulties they face in trying to combine managerial and clinical work (Kippist and Fitzgerald, 2009; Currie et al., 2010). At an organizational level, clinician-managers can also struggle to reconcile professional expectations and organizational objectives (Currie and Procter, 2005; Kippist and Fitzgerald, 2009; Croft et al., 2015). The resultant default career choice, for hybrid clinician-managers, can, for example, be between retaining a strong clinical professional identity or taking on a 'full leadership role' (Dellve and Wikström, 2009: 935; Burgess and Currie, 2013).

Recent research by McGivern et al. (2015) has highlighted important differences between such *incidental hybrids*, whose orientation to management is more secondary and whose primary interest is in clinical work and the protection of professional interests; and *willing hybrids*, whose orientations are much more managerial and who are more effectively able to blend their managerial and clinical roles. Even where hybrid managers are more willing, however, their baseline professional identity as clinicians can have a much stronger bearing upon their self-image and actions than any acquired managerial identity (Llewellyn, 2001; Dellve and Wikström, 2009; von Knorring et al., 2016). Not only do hybrid managers tend to have less management education and training, they also tend to default to a more clinical perspective on management issues (Iedema et al., 2004). Indeed, recent research suggests that, while hybrid managers draw upon both professional and managerial discourses, the former tends to dominate, with the result that managerial role constructions tend to default to a much stronger clinical identity (von Knorring et al., 2016). The net effect, according to von Knorring et al. (2016: 430), is the rendering of managerial identity as effectively invisible and the reinforcement of the stratification of power in healthcare that favours the medical profession.

At the same time, research also suggests that hybrid managers—particularly those in more powerful organizational positions—can be skilled at reconciling and holding competing bases of identity. Llewellyn (2001), for instance, highlights the power of senior clinicians to occupy the 'two-way space' through which clinical and managerial needs are mediated and reconciled and to carve out new identities as medical-managers—limited only by their lack of financial management expertise. In a similar vein, Iedema et al. (2004) take a discourse approach to show how doctor-managers are able to adopt highly complex dialogic strategies that weave together into a seamless flow of talk seemingly incommensurate discourses (clinical, managerial and a 'hedging' discourse that is focused on reconciling contradictory positions).

It is clear, however, that significant intra-professional status and power differences within the medical profession itself ensure that some hybrid managers may be able to reconcile these tensions more effectively than others (Currie and White, 2012; Burgess and Currie, 2013) and some may find the liminal position particularly challenging (Croft et al., 2015). Nurse-managers are a particularly interesting case in point as, while they may find it easier to resort to managerial discourse to strengthen their position (Brooks, 1999), at the same time, they have also been shown to be less willing to embrace certain aspects of management—such as commercial or entrepreneurial activity (Bolton, 2005). Moreover, while nurse-managers can rely upon their clinical background to engage in strategically important work (Burgess and Currie, 2013; Burgess et al., 2015), research also suggests that, due to their comparatively lower occupational status, they have to depend upon alternative, more informal and personal sources of influence (Currie and White, 2012).

Consequently, status differentials are an important set of contingency factors to consider. If differences in social position result in different 'dispositions' towards sense-making, and this results in different outcomes associated with that sense-making (Lockett et al., 2013), then power and legitimacy are essential pre-requisites to the deliberate and strategic mediation of clinician-managers' identity work. However, this leaves questions about the character of the identity work undertaken by a fuller range of hybrid managers, some of whom might lack the power and legitimacy of clinicians. In such cases identity work might be more 'reluctant' (Currie, 2006) in character, and result in more 'accidental' career trajectories into management (McGivern et al., 2015).

In the empirical work that follows, we draw out the sense-making engaged in by healthcare managers in accounting for their transitions into managerial roles and how this reflects the juxtaposition between their clinical and managerial identities. In approaching their managerial roles in particular ways and in rationalizing their moves into management, the accounts reveal the various ways in which the construction of managerial identity has been, and continues to be, an on-going process in which narratives of career development are infused with processes of sense-making. It also brings out how varied those constructions are when we draw out the distinct identity narratives that emerge and how these constructions are also influenced by diverse professional and organizational experiences.

Managers' Backgrounds and Experiences

Across all three organizations there were no clinical managers and surprisingly few general managers without a good deal of clinical experience. Table 5.1 below gives a detailed breakdown of the clinical backgrounds and qualifications of managers across the entire sample. Most of the 68 managers interviewed (42=62 percent) came from a clinical or clinical-related professional background (5 doctors, 23 nurses, 5 scientists, 7 allied health professionals (AHPs) and 2 social workers). That included all of the general managers at the Care trust (most of whom were former nurses who

Table 5.1 Clinical Backgrounds and Qualifications

Trust	Cohort	Numbers with clinical backgrounds	Clinical qualifications (or PhD)	Total in cohort
Acute	Clinical	2 Doctors 2 Nurses 1 Scientist	2 MD 2 RGN* 1 PhD	5
	Functional	1 Nurse	1 RGN	7
	General	1 Nurse 4 AHPs	1 SRN –	8
Care	Clinical	2 Doctors 3 Nurses	2 MD 2 RGN + 1 RMN 2 AHPs	7
	Functional	–	–	6
	General	10 Nurses	7 RMN + 3 RGN* 2 Social workers	12
Specialist	Clinical	1 Doctor 3 Nurses 1 AHP 1 Scientist	1 MD 3 RGN* – 1 PhD	6
	Functional	1 Scientist	1 PhD	8
	General	3 Nurses 2 Scientists	1 BSc + 2 RGN –	9
Total		42	31	68

had progressed into management) and over half of the general managers at the Acute and Specialist trusts (63 percent and 56 percent respectively). As already noted, only two of the functional managers had any sort of clinical background or experience. Of the 42 managers with some clinical background, most had at least one relevant medical or nursing professional qualification (the exceptions were the AHPs, social workers and some of the medical scientists). Nursing qualifications varied and included Registered General Nurse (RGN), State Registered Nurse (SRN) or Registered Mental Nurse (RMN). There were a smaller number with newer degrees in nursing in addition to other nursing qualifications (in groups marked * in table 5.1).

Amongst the general managers, apart from those who had departed little from a clinically oriented educational and professional pathway (e.g. nurses at the Care trust), there were a substantial number encountered who also had clinically related educational qualifications (at BSc, Diploma and/or MSc level). Table 5.2 below summarizes the various educational qualifications (excluding medical and nursing degrees) across the sample as a whole and highlights the preponderance of health-related qualifications across all

Table 5.2 Non-clinical Educational Qualifications

Trust	Cohort	Non-clinical health degrees	Mgt degrees	Other degrees	PGDip Health (Mgt)	MSc Health (Mgt)	Total
Acute	Clinical	1			(1)	1 (1*)	5
	Functional		1	4	(3)	1 (3)	7
	General	2	1	1	4	4 (1*)	8
Care	Clinical	3		2	3 (1)	4	7
	Functional		1	2	(3)	1 (1)	6
	General	1	1		4 (3)	4	12
Specialist	Clinical	2			1 (1)	2 (1)	6
	Functional	1	1	5	1 (2)	1 (2*)	8
	General	1	2	2	1 (2)	1 (2*)	9
Total		11	7	16	14 (16)	19 (11)	68

(*indicates MBA)

groups, the comparatively small number of managers (mainly functional) with backgrounds in management or other non-health subjects and the very small number without any sort of clinical or health formal educational experience whatsoever. There were even some expectations of healthcare experience and/or qualifications amongst pure play managers (especially at the Care trust; moderately so at Acute; less so at Specialist).

As expected, therefore, hybrid managers in our sample greatly outnumbered so-called pure play managers, by more or less the ratio of 4:1 that was identified by Buchanan et al. (2013: 11). The majority of hybrid managers were found among the clinical and general managers interviewed. There was also some variation between the organizations in terms of the prevalence of hybrid managers, with the Care trust relying on them to the greatest extent.

Managers with a nursing background constituted by far the largest group of hybrid managers (there were 21 in total, compared with 9 clinical managers and 6 occupational therapists and social workers). This reflected an established career track: many nurses had moved into management via a standard progression through the nursing grades, before moving into senior nursing positions, including ward sister and matron. For example:

> The Ward Manager's post is still quite clinical so you spend part of your time managing the unit and the staff within it and also part of your time actually clinically working there. The Matron's post was less so but still had a clinical part in it, so I still worked on some of the units with the

staff . . . And then the Service Managers post sort of evolved after that . . . So my clinical work has got less and an awful lot smaller and it's more management . . . I still work clinically on the unit occasionally but that's more to do with staffing issues.

(Hannah, General, Specialist).

Advancement within nursing had often involved a wide range of experiences in a variety of clinical domains (particularly in Acute) and/or service operations (particularly in Care). For example:

I've moved quite a bit, if you look at my history. Some of my colleagues have stayed in their post for 20 years and not moved. So I've had the real chance to be able to manage . . . adult services, older people services with the social care element of it, acute inpatient services, A&E services, drug and alcohol services, and now [this] service . . . I see myself working [here] for quite a while. So long as I'm successful.

(Hasin, General, Care)

At the Specialist trust, clinical specialization and engagement with research were more valued and so constituted an important additional route into management—often involving development opportunities for experienced nurses that were more project/task based. For example:

I was anaesthetic nurse in theatres here. Worked my way up the pecking order; ended up as a Senior Sister in theatres. But that was more clinical. Then I was given an opportunity . . . to establish a new role as a clinical specialist in critical care and resuscitation. This was before we had a critical care unit, so I was instrumental in the development of [that] . . . You can imagine, there was a lot of work.

(Nina, Clinical, Specialist)

While this gives a good general indication of the pattern of career progression across the three types of case, it does not say much, however, about managers' orientations to their career development into (and in some cases, out of) management. What follows are a number of clearly identified career identity narratives (and their sub-narratives)—that give a flavour of the variability of management career trajectories identified across the sample.

Managers' Perspectives on Becoming a Manager

Motivations for pursuing a career path into management were quite diverse. However, three broad narratives could be discerned in the accounts of managers' transitions into management.

Aspiring Managers, Keen to Make a Difference

For a small number of managers—particularly the pure play managers, but also some of the nurse managers—it was a clear ambition and guiding vision in their career:

> I came to [Specialist] newly qualified as a nurse. I did two years on the wards and worked in chemotherapy, radiotherapy and combined therapy services, surgery as well . . . I'd had a lot of work experience, so I didn't want to just work on a ward for x number of years and become a ward sister and become a ward manager. I wanted to look at a management pathway . . . I have always wanted to be in a leadership role.
>
> (Becky, General, Specialist)

Amongst the hybrid nurse-managers, about half of them had begun with aspirations of management, or had developed a keenness to move into management because of the opportunities it gave them to exert greater influence and make more of a difference to patient care:

> I ended up locuming within this organization and I was asked to apply for the team leader job of the team that I was working in, because they didn't have a team lead at the time . . . So, I was kind of like, well, must be onto a winner. I applied for it and that's where I am.
>
> (Gloria, General, Acute)

In all cases, especially Acute, a transition into management was seen, moreover, as a natural and desirable next step—as the quotes above and below both suggest:

> The therapy manager job came up . . . I applied and I was successful in getting that position. And I loved it, because being able to make a difference on a bigger scale was there. And to be honest, when I'd thought about how my career would go when I was in my early 20s, I always thought the pinnacle would be to manage a therapy department that needed sorting. That's where I thought I'd be when I was 65. And here I was at 40.
>
> (Melissa, General, Acute)

For aspirational nurse hybrid managers, the crucially important factor was the desire to make more of a difference that only a move into management could effectively realize:

> I felt this job, because it was a clinical service manager post, would be my first proper full time operational management role. But also because of the clinical focus it would mean I would also have the ability, really, and the power to actually drive some of the things that I felt were important, in terms of the quality of care. That's when I came into this role.
>
> (Beth, General, Care)

These managers were clearly what could be described as willing hybrids (McGivern et al., 2015), who shared a belief that moving into management was not only a natural progression but also gave them the chance to make a difference. Moreover, for them, there was a clear symbiotic relationship felt between their clinical background and their managerial responsibilities: transitioning into management roles gave them perceived opportunities to match their clinical orientations with managerial ambition.

At the same time, the quotes also suggest that there could be serious constraints on realizing their desire to make a difference without moving into a general management career path. Advancement purely within a nursing career path was limited anyway, and so moving into general service line management roles was often the only option:

> You've got to that glass ceiling [and] if I don't make a sideways move or I don't take a more leadership or managerial role, I can't make more difference. It's always been [that] I can't make any more difference to who I work with or the client group I work with, so I'm going to have to try a different tack. So it's been out of frustration really that I've kind of passed eight years and woven the path that I've woven.
>
> (Gloria, General, Acute)

Lack of opportunity to exert influence without moving into management was particularly emphasized by the handful of nurses in the sample who had occupied senior nursing positions, including modern matron and nurse consultant roles. However, the two following quotes on each of these roles also highlight the frustrations that even senior nurses could feel due to the lack of direct operational influence that came with these positions:

> As a Matron . . . because you haven't got operational management of people it's: this would be a really good idea if we did this, and this would be good. But actually getting it in, you don't have that responsibility . . . You get pulled into other things . . . [It] starts at the top of people's agenda, and then you sit in operational management meetings and before you know where you are, you're on Any Other Business at the bottom.
>
> (Beth, General, Care)

Similarly, but this time with regard to the nurse consultant role:

> [It's] not got the same credibility . . . It hasn't got that same level of importance maybe as, say, the matron role . . . I think part of that is because . . . the role is so vast that it's hard for you to make a difference because of all the different components.
>
> (Beryl, Clinical, Specialist)

Consequently, while there were strong aspirations within this group, this was accompanied for some by a sense of frustration at the absence of alternative career paths that offered nurse-hybrids sufficient influence. It also encouraged an element of rationalization in how they viewed their move into management and their shift towards more of a managerial identity. This reflected the historical lack of dual career ladders for nursing professionals and the options that management gave for nurses wishing to develop their professional career (Brooks, 1999). On occasion, it meant that the strong aspiration towards management was rather more a result of lack of alternative options and so, to some extent, a rationalization of needing to move into management to progress. For example:

> It's just very hard to know where to go in the NHS and particularly because most nurses go down a very clear pathway of: you start on a ward, you become a senior sister, you become a ward manager, you become a matron, you become a divisional nurse and then you become a nursing director. That's the pathway for a nurse. If you are so [minded] to go that way. And I suppose mine has gone slightly off that trajectory.
>
> (Becky, General, Specialist)

Nevertheless, while the extent of internalization of managerial values and approaches might have differed between them, there was a clear identification with management and their career trajectories were associated with a natural sedimentation of managerial identity on top of their clinical experience. As Annette put it:

> I took a service manager job [at a big teaching hospital] and that was a big difference, because, that was real general management as I would call it. I didn't have responsibility for the clinical areas, it was about the operational performance and you managed the medical teams with clinical directors and all the administration processes. So, it was a very different job, but a very good grounding.
>
> (Annette, General, Specialist)

This marked out that group as not only to some extent willing hybrids, but also those for whom it was comparatively easy to reconcile their clinical background and experience with their managerial identity through a focus on improving patient care.

Accidental Managers, Ambivalent about Management

It was clear, however, that many hybrid managers had come into management as much by accident as by design. More than half of the nurse-managers felt that this was the cases, as did virtually all of the clinical managers. So, for example:

I've never had a clear view of where I wanted to end up really. I've taken opportunities when I've wanted to take them if the opportunities arise and I felt interested in doing that . . . I tend to take the stance where, you know, if somebody else did it, do you feel you could do either the same or a better job? . . . Things have just evolved really as I've gone along.

(Hannah, General, Specialist)

Indeed, many of the hybrid managers interviewed similarly attributed their career progression as much to a series of opportunistic or accidental moves associated with organization change as to a chosen trajectory with a clear vision at the end. Some were very explicit that they had simply been 'in the right place at the right time':

You come out of college or uni don't you and you're supposed to have this plan of what you want to do with your career. And actually it's being in the right place at the right time or the wrong place at the wrong time, and it's whether your face fits or doesn't.

(Belinda, General, Acute)

In some instances, as will be seen, this was related to a particular organizational change, such as reorganization or the need to cover vacancies. In other cases, it was seen as an experience that had characterized managers' progressions more generally. For example:

I don't think I ever had a sense of where I was going . . . But, posts seemed to come up that were the next natural step, fairly quickly, really. So, within five years of working there, I'd gone up two grades and was managing an aspect of the service . . . A couple of years after that, I got the management of the whole service, the outpatients and the day service.

(Gabrielle, General, Care)

Such opportunistic moves were much less apparent for clinical managers and those hybrid managers from a medical or scientific background, whose career development tended to follow a much more a standard pathway through clinical grades (from medical degree onwards). However, for nurse hybrids as well as other non-medical general managers this was a fairly normal progression route.

Importantly, it was the shifting sands created by regular waves of healthcare organizational reform and reorganization that created the backdrop to understanding the career development options open and taken. Often, such changes actually or potentially disrupted existing and established career paths into management:

I was coming to the end of my secondment and . . . the arms-length body review was taking place across the country with the new government coming in . . . They were looking to downsize, there were people going to be put at risk and all the rest of it, and I thought well, the NHS is about to go through a really tough time. Jobs are going to get shorter. I still had six months left in my secondment but I started to look for jobs.

(Pavak, General, Specialist)

However, the effects were not simply negative: there was evidence across the trusts that change within the sector had opened up alternative career paths and opportunities that hybrid managers, already predisposed to 'muddling through', were able to exploit to develop their careers. In some situations, the opportunities that opened up were connected positively to service growth, development or redesign:

[The Director] of Diagnostics, Therapies and Facilities . . . had a big patch . . . but he also had facilities . . . So he created a new structure and he said, "I want you as my deputy, and I want you to manage the laboratory as well. So keep therapies, which you can do in 20 per cent of your time" . . . So that's what I did and I was the Deputy Divisional Manager.

(Melissa, General, Acute)

In others, they were connected to less positive aspects of organizational change:

There was a bit of re-shuffling around and people left so I was asked if I'd take over Outpatient Physio. The OT manager here went off sick, so I ended up taking over OT as well. I was already managing speech and language. Then we had a restructure; we all had to apply for our own jobs; six people and one post. I got the post, which was awful.

(Belinda, General, Acute)

Moreover, it was clear that, across the trusts, managers' career development was often associated with high levels of what could be described as externally oriented 'institutional work' (Lawrence and Suddaby, 2006) associated with new service provision. At the Acute trust, rationalization and improvement of existing service processes was often the guiding objective:

I was approached . . . to see if I wanted to take on a modernization role . . . to set up integrated care pathways and services out in the community. So I took on that role . . . and I set up a lot of services in the area and worked with the clinicians, like the secondary care consultant and the GPs and the community specialist nurses . . . It really was bridging across the services. So that was quite a big role, spanned a whole range of work. I managed quite a big team.

(Roxanne, General, Acute)

At the Care trust, the creation of new or consolidation of existing services was often the principle aim:

> A brand new service was being set up . . . and that was always attractive to me, because I knew I could do it. I knew I could set things up, and it would be successful . . . Basically, it was about taking good practice from all areas, and then putting that into place, drawing up things like assessment forms, and then actually going out and training all of the different agencies . . . So, that was a very diverse role.
>
> (Justine, General, Care)

However, whatever the sources of change that created these threats or opportunities, the accidental pathways into management could be differentiated between those (mainly nurses and AHPs) whose route into management was an unexpected but comparatively straightforward transition; and others (notably, clinicians but also some nurses), whose step into management was much more hesitant and pursued only after a considerable amount of conscious reflection and evaluation:

> It wasn't a planned career path . . . One of the senior consultants in my department said: "you know, we're struggling to find a clinical director and I think you'd be the best person for the job. You're going to have to do it." And I went home and said to the wife: "oh my God!" And, in all honesty, I did it because, I thought, well, somebody has got to do it and if I say, no, how can I expect somebody else to do it?
>
> (Brian, Clinical, Acute)

At one level, this suggests that clinical managers could simply be considered to be incidental hybrids (McGivern et al., 2015), encouraged or pressed into a managerial role (cf. Harrison and Miller, 1999). However, it was evident too that there was much more agonizing than this might suggest about what it meant for their changing professional identity which was clearly anticipated would become more managerial. There was also a good degree of rationalization of the move—as evident in the above account and in the account below from a nurse at Specialist:

> [I was] asked to consider trying [the job] for six months . . . So I thought about it because I felt very comfortable with the clinical leadership and managing what I'd done and I felt I'd built up a really good service, I was very proud of. My heart was very much in that and I'd never considered going into a purely management role, it had just never entered my head. So I agreed I would try it for a period of six months, which went to a bit longer. I realized that, hey I'm not bad at this, I quite like it as well.
>
> (Nina, Clinical, Specialist)

Interestingly, this dilemma was much more strongly expressed by hybrid managers at Specialist and Acute than at Care—where it was much more natural for nurses to move into general middle management positions. Nevertheless, having cloaked themselves in the managerial role—however reluctantly at first—such managers were not only able to rationalize their moves into management, they were also able to reconcile what they originally considered to be quite distinct logics and identities through practical engagement and, as Nina suggests above, some degree of experimentation.

Reluctant Managers, Conflicted about Management

Nevertheless, amongst clinicians and also some of the nurse-managers, there were a number who were much clearly reluctant to engage with management; or whose progression into management was accompanied by clear felt and expressed tensions between their clinical and managerial identities.

> Being a general manager is not a career I want to pursue. I've worn the T-shirt and I can look anyone in the face who's done medicine and sympathize with them. But to me pushing beds round or asking people to see patients to stop a breach really isn't my thing.
>
> (Oliver, Clinical, Acute)

Oliver's view of management had been shaped by earlier experiences in management. For other clinical managers, such as Brian at the Acute trust, there was also a good degree of reluctance, although the transition into management was also characterized by subtler and stealthier processes of seduction, co-optation and guilt (cf. Harrison and Wood, 1999):

> The first couple of years was very hard. It's a steep learning curve, it's very different from what we've done in our training and managing a body of people is not something that we do, as a doctor . . . There was a lot of lost night's sleep, to be honest, to start with. But, at the end of 18 months, I found myself coping okay. The sleepless nights were fewer and further between and I actually thought, well, having got to this point, it's daft to not do five years . . . At the end of five years, I found I was doing it really quite calmly . . . Then, inevitably, people say, well, we need you to do the next step, because no one else can do it. It's a familiar story, isn't it?!
>
> (Brian, Clinical, Acute)

A similar reluctance, centred upon conflicting clinical-managerial identity, could also be found in the accounts of some nurse hybrid managers who also shared a strong clinical identity:

> Went into nursing. Loved it. And kind of developed my skills and my professional qualifications and pathways, which I just wanted to get

more into managing, a senior clinical role really . . . I was being encouraged to go into director's roles . . . But I actually decided that I like the detail. I didn't want that really high level overarching role that a director would take on board. I liked getting involved with the detail of things and . . . improving patient care. So it really challenged me about where I wanted to go next in my career.

(Roxanne, General, Acute)

Although the move into management for many of these managers had still been a relatively smooth transition (e.g. from team leader or senior clinical roles), in some cases it was the unexpected and accidental nature of the move (including 'acting up' during reorganizations or having to combine managerial work with clinical case-loads) that created very stressful experiences. So, for example:

I've been given the portfolio that has sat in somebody else's portfolio . . . and that portfolio is massive anyway. But what comes with that is a corporate outpatient project with [savings] assigned to it . . . And this project has been passed from pillar to post, I understand, for about four years and I think they thought: "oh, [she] did that at [a nearby acute trust]." So I think, even though I had an element of choice, I was being told by people down there that my name was against it . . . I think people see it as a slight poison chalice . . . I'm very much feeling the pressure because . . . if it actually goes to . . . the exec team, they say: "so, when are the savings going to be realized?" . . . So it's a lot of pressure suddenly coming on.

(Bethany, Clinical, Acute)

For others, it was not just the intrinsic pressures associated with managerial work but the context in which managers were expected to act that created problems or generated reluctance and sometimes drove managers back into clinical work:

I did paediatric neurology for six years. Then just got frustrated with all sorts of things . . . I was at the old senior one level, so an element of day to day management responsibility. But at that level, you're very aware of the politics and I just got really frustrated with where the NHS was at that time. So I ducked out and locumed.

(Gloria, General, Acute)

For some managers, such as Justine, it was simply having to combine managerial work with a continued clinical caseload that created a serious work overload and led to a considerable amount of stress:

I became a service manager . . . and I was still carrying a caseload of a 100. I did that for about a year and I just found that I couldn't do it. I was quite ill, depression, handed my notice in, didn't have anywhere to go . . . and then they actually asked me to stay on in a consultative role when I returned from sick.

(Justine, General, Care)

Her response was to seek advancement through more sideways moves within management that retained a clear clinical focus:

I feel quite ambitious, not in a promotional kind of way, because I actually don't want the responsibility of an 8b, and I've been very clear with people about that . . . I'm very interested in kind of a sideways move, but actually into a more challenging area where I'm not so comfortable . . . So, yeah, for me definitely no upward movements but definitely other challenges . . . I love it here, I love the work.

(Justine, General, Care)

For other nurse-hybrids who were reluctant about management or who encountered stressful experiences, the solution to their career development dilemma was found in the displacement of career development efforts back into nursing or more diversified middle management activity.

The tension between clinical work and general management orientations was felt most acutely by hybrid managers in clinical positions and especially in the Specialist trust, where clinical specialization and expertise were very highly valued. It was in those cases that 'incidental hybrid' managers were more common and there was evidence too of a much more superficial orientation towards their managerial as opposed to clinical identities:

People who are clinicians and managers don't seem to get the balance right because they'll always throw back to the clinical part and they won't be able to think as a manager. There's very, very few clinical managers that I've come across that have been successful, like clinical directors, because they don't have training.

(Joanna, General, Specialist)

Having said that, it was clear too that even reluctant clinician-managers could, in many cases, move beyond superficial engagement when they saw the benefits of taking a more management-oriented role:

I really didn't fancy going back into pharmacy so I became the manager of Medicine and that was an incredibly operational role and I did that for two years and that was very much the classical bed pressures, getting people out of A&E, [etc]. But I did other things as well like introduce proper governance arrangements in medicine . . . and we turned medicine round. It was a good experience, and it certainly gives you an insight into organizations and the challenges.

(Oliver, Clinical, Acute)

For reluctant nurse hybrids too, there could a strong element of ratio-nalization that could lead to a much stronger *ex poste* engagement with management thinking than originally intended or anticipated. As Roxanne admitted, despite her earlier-noted reluctance to move into management:

> [I] really got involved in the modernization programme and worked with the critical care network . . . I was keen to develop those modern-ization skills of process mapping, Lean, that sort of thing. And because of my nursing, clinical background it felt like a really natural move, that it bridged that knowledge of clinical processes plus developing better management processes and ways of delivering critical care.
>
> (Roxanne, General, Acute)

As her account suggests, there was no reason why intense reflection might not lead to even deeper internalization and identification with management in due course.

Though rare, there were even, exceptionally, one or two instances of reluctant clinical managers being more than willing to embrace their mana-gerial identity:

> I quite like to describe myself as a medical manager. Because I quite like to not pretend I'm one of the clinicians who only does management resentfully . . . I like to say: "no, you know what? I'm one of the bad-dies. I'm on the other side."
>
> (Brian, Clinical, Acute)

This conscious positioning by Brian interestingly draws ironically upon negative connotations of management in order to bolster his manage-rial self-identity and presumably, enhance his credibility and legitimacy (cf. Alvesson, 2010).

Pure Play Managers: Ambitions and Opportunities

Finally, it is worthwhile noting briefly how pure play managers (Buchanan, 2013) fitted into this landscape of management development. General man-agers without any clinical experience or background were rare across the sample (numbering only 9 in total, 4 of whom were on the GMTS and as such recent graduates rotating through different positions before specializ-ing). Most of these managers without any clinical experience were found in the Specialist case, with a small number at Acute.

At all three trusts, such managers were naturally much more conscious of their generic management capabilities and identity and not surprisingly, did not experience the same internal tensions between clinical and managerial orientations. However, they were still expected to work closely with their clinical and hybrid manager counterparts and of course, with pure clini-cians. For those few who had come into management directly from outside healthcare, this meant a good deal of effort being expended in establishing their credibility and legitimacy:

> I'd never worked for the health service and I found it quite difficult to get in because I didn't have experience. I got to . . . three or four interviews for . . . head of podiatry but never actually got the job. And the feedback was: "We think you're a bit of a risk, you've got no experience."
>
> (Hugh, General, Acute)

The task was easier for the three general managers and those on the GMTS who were effectively working their way up 'through the ranks'. However, three further general points are worth emphasizing about this group of managers as a whole. First, 'accidental' progression into management roles was no less important in understanding their career development and trajectories. Take the following account by Greg for example:

> A lot of [opportunities came] where I was either working in an organization or with an organization and then was asked . . . or encouraged to apply for a post there. So it tended to be wherever my career took me. When I was working in primary care, I started doing this work with the Modernization Agency, which put me in touch with a network of trusts, who said . . . we've got a role coming up here. So it's always been sort of that route, rather than me sitting down and thinking, you know, I need to go and work over there next. It's just things have come along really.
>
> (Greg, General, Acute)

Second, Greg's experience of working up through the ranks in healthcare was a more common route into management than direct entry from private healthcare or the private sector more generally. In fact, nurse-hybrids (and some AHPs) were just as likely as pure play managers to have had private sector experience:

> It did help because we used to have to go out and sell ourselves to different places. So it helped me in terms of the cost side and selling a service. I think that did prepare me in how careful you've got to be and how you can lose it very easily . . . We had a lot of work with [a private healthcare company] as well, so we went in their offices. So, yeah, I knew how they worked so I was quite at an advantage that I did know. But not every nurse will have that. But that is helpful to understand that.
>
> (Diane, Clinical, Specialist)

Despite these benefits, nurses such as Diane (who were found particularly at the Specialist trust) tended to be much more critical about their experiences in the private healthcare sector. Also found at the Specialist trust were one or two pure play managers with experience beyond healthcare who were recruited to contribute to the trust's business development agenda. Those managers had more deeply internalized managerial identities (as indicated, for example, in Gavin's account earlier).

Third, what was noticeable about those on the GMTS scheme in particular was that, while they also tended to have more general industry experience and shared a strong sense of managerial identity, they did not necessarily express strong managerial ambitions. For example:

> I found myself along a [GMTS] journey then and along a career path that wasn't necessarily intended. It's just happened. And then you get to that point where I think well, actually, this is a career now. So if I'm going to do something else you've got to start again and drop down the ladder . . . I do see myself staying in healthcare. Whether or not I see myself staying in an acute setting I'm not quite sure. Again, I'm quite open to that at the moment.
>
> (Stewart, General, Acute)

Like their established pure play counterparts, those on the GMTS were relatively mobile within the healthcare sector. However, while they clearly valued and had benefitted from the opportunities the GMTS opened up to them to move directly into management positions, their progression was a lot more opportune and/or accidental than one might expect from aspiring managers—and just as easily rationalized as their clinical counterparts.

Summary

In highlighting the distributed nature of management in healthcare, and relating it to questions of hybridity, liminality and identity, this chapter has brought out and explored two main issues related to the experience of becoming a manager in healthcare: first, it has identified the wide range of orientations to management found amongst healthcare managers and examined how that relates to and reflects their clinical-managerial hybridity; second, it has examined what it means to act as a hybrid manager in the quite distinct settings found across the organizations explored in this research. There has also been some consideration too of how the experiences and orientations of pure play general managers compare with those of their hybrid middle manager counterparts.

Two main themes emerge from this chapter. First, it suggests that there may be a much more complex, subtle and dynamic set of underlying orientations to hybridity than current approaches often tend to present or to presume. Hybridity, reflecting managerial or clinical orientation, affects not only roles, activities and career paths but also, more fundamentally, self-identity. This chapter has delved into managers' identity narratives to explore the very different sorts of career development trajectory associated with aspirational, ambivalent or conflicted views about management, as well as more deliberate or accidental progression into management roles. It has also highlighted the very different levels of engagement with managerial identity they suggest—from those with more internalized managerial identity to those whose engagement is more superficial or incidental (cf. McGivern et al., 2015). Such differences are clearly likely to have direct implications for the formation of a professional community around healthcare management, as well as the likelihood of knowledge sharing and learning within that community and beyond.

Second, the organizational context in which managers have progressed has also been brought to the fore, and the discussion has highlighted the ways in which distinct organizational and institutional contexts played a role in shaping the opportunities and constraints afforded to (hybrid) managers. It suggests that quite different types of healthcare organization and their associated systems and cultures may promote or inhibit different types of manager, or induce very different behaviours among their managers (cf. Dopson et al., 2008). So, for example, in developing their identity and careers, the effects of reorganization that are dramatically affecting management development in one part of healthcare (e.g. at Acute) are only marginally offset by the greater entrepreneurial demands on managers charged with developing new service provision elsewhere (e.g. at Care). It therefore suggests that contemporary changes that are affecting healthcare organizations are likely to have important consequences for shaping the local landscape in which such processes of management development and identity formation play out.

By exploring managers' backgrounds and experiences in some depth, this chapter has stressed the importance of understanding managers' predispositions and how managers' receptivity to management and to different forms of knowledge associated with it may have been shaped by their career development experiences and by their (changing) organizational circumstances. Building upon this more complete picture of healthcare managers and the precise context in which they act, the next chapter turns to an exploration of the types of knowledge valued, accessed and used by managers, in order to gain further insights into the factors enabling or impeding the mobilization of management knowledge in the delivery of healthcare.

Note

1 Buchanan et al. (2013: 11) suggest that in the hospitals they studied, 'hybrid managers' with combined clinical-managerial duties outnumbered 'pure plays' with no clinical responsibilities by a ratio of four to one.

6   Managers Knowing

> You almost need to learn little bits of everything . . . You need to understand
> how a nurse rota works and . . . when a surgeon goes in to do a complex
> procedure, broadly what he's doing. So you can understand the time pres-
> sures, how many people are in there, what they're doing . . . You're never an
> expert in anything.
>
> (Thomas, Functional, Specialist)

Introduction

The above quote neatly highlights how managers in healthcare not only
face a distinct set of challenges but also need to develop a diverse set of
skills. This prompts questions about whether the highly fragmented work
of managers militates against the development of a distinct and coherent
knowledge base over which healthcare managers exert mastery and through
which they can assert their professional identity. In this chapter, we drill
down to examine what sources and types of knowledge managers access
and use in practice to cope with these many challenges, what possibilities
and limitations this suggests for applying more general management knowledge to a healthcare setting and what, in turn, this means for understanding
healthcare managers' professional basis and identity.

Given the pressures on management associated with continuing financial cuts to public service provision and increased pressures on managers to
deliver efficient, effective and safe healthcare (Hassard et al., 2009; Buchanan
et al., 2013; Hyde et al., 2016), it is perhaps not surprising to find that
attention has been increasingly directed towards understanding the knowledge base available to and used by managers in the NHS (e.g. Ferlie et al.,
2012, 2015). For some time, healthcare management has been perceived as
lagging behind developments in management practice. This negative pro-
filing of middle management work in the NHS has meant, among other
things, greater emphasis being placed on the need for healthcare managers
to mobilize 'leading-edge' management thinking more effectively (Pollitt,
2013; Fischer et al., 2015). In turn, this has led to much closer examination
of the underpinning knowledge base of managerial work in healthcare, as

well as the factors enabling and inhibiting the mobilization and exploitation of different forms of management knowledge.

However, we still know comparatively little about how managers in healthcare actually mobilize and utilize management knowledge and what this means for management learning processes and the development of a distinct managerial identity (Ferlie et al., 2012). Moreover, to what extent and how are current changes in healthcare overcoming or reinforcing any barriers to the translation and application of management knowledge? Do managers' predispositions to act in particular ways based upon their established knowledge bases and orientations to learning complement or contradict wider developments in healthcare provision? To address these questions, we examine the effects of different forms and sources of knowledge on management practice, including clinical and other specialist knowledge bases as well as codified management knowledge in the form of widely applied tools and techniques. We also assess the constraining influence of more local, situated forms of knowledge as well as the impact on managers of their personal experience. Before all this, however, it is useful first to examine briefly the nature of management knowledge itself.

The Ambiguity of Management Knowledge

As was discussed in the previous chapter, healthcare management—like any other form of management—has struggled to develop not only a coherent professional identity but also a distinct knowledge base (Currie, 1997; Currie and Procter, 2005). Yet, expectations on managers to coordinate and control work effectively inevitably mean that they need to be receptive to the wide array of management ideas, tools and techniques available to them from within and beyond their organizations. These not only help them meet performance expectations but also help them make better sense of their managerial responsibilities and their identity as managers (Watson, 1994). That wider knowledge base, however, is far from being complete, coherent, neutral and uncontested, and this is for a number of major reasons.

At one level, the nature of management is inherently multidisciplinary (involving, *inter alia*, operational, financial and human resource management activity). Moreover, the range of disciplinary perspectives this leads to inevitably opens up different ontological and epistemological assumptions about the nature of management and the validity of different forms of management knowledge (dependent, for instance, on whether management is seen in more mechanistic or humanistic terms; or whether more quantitative or qualitative methods are valued). An engineering-based or financial management perspective, for example, is unlikely to put the same emphasis on the behavioural aspects of management, as is a more psychological perspective. Nor are the same epistemic practices likely to be used across management sub-disciplines in the development of new types of management knowledge (cf. Knorr-Cetina, 1999).

At another, more profound level, management knowledge itself is highly political and contested (Clegg and Palmer, 1996). The history of management thought is itself a contested terrain, in which competing visions of the nature of management and the development of different forms of management knowledge have historically vied for pre-eminence (Barley and Kunda, 1992). Major paradigmatic shifts in management thinking from earlier more functional perspectives to later more critical approaches mark out an extremely broad territory in which the nature of management itself and its underpinning knowledge base are both viewed very differently depending, for example, upon the perspective taken on societal order/conflict and societal regulation/change (Burrell and Morgan, 1979). Certain theoretical approaches within this broad domain—such as institutional theory (Powell and DiMaggio, 1991; Greenwood et al., 2008)—might have some hegemonic influence on current thinking. However, alternative perspectives on management and organization continue to proliferate and to question basic assumptions about the nature and appropriate use of management knowledge (Fournier and Grey, 2000; Alvesson and Willmott, 2003). The resultant complexity is added to when one considers the very different theoretical perspectives on management that exist within any particular paradigm.

Also important in understanding the kaleidoscopic nature of management knowledge in theory and in practice is its tendency towards commodification and mediation by a range of social actors involved in its (co-)production and reproduction. These include not only academia, industry practitioners and the state, but also other influential actors, most notably management consultants and the media (Thrift, 2005). Management consultants have historically played an extremely important role not only in engaging with practitioners to co-produce, and generalize from, more localized forms of knowledge; but also in proselytizing and packaging particular management practices, thus contributing towards the wider circulation of management ideas and associated managerial discourse (Czarniawska and Joerges, 1996; Sahlin-Andersson and Engwall, 2002; Sturdy et al., 2009; Sturdy, 2011; Engwall and Kipping, 2013).

Indeed, the widespread diffusion and adoption of particular management practices owe as much to their commodification by leading practitioners, prominent academic gurus and consultants as they do to their grounding in theory and empirical research. Examples of this can be found in numerous management concepts and practices such as culture management (Peters and Waterman, 1982), total quality management (Powell, 1995), lean manufacturing (Womack et al., 1990), business process re-engineering (Hammer and Champy, 1993) and the learning organization (Senge, 1993)—to name but a few. Each has had a global impact in its time and each clearly has the qualities that resonate with practitioners and which has made them readily commodifiable and transferable (Røvik, 2002). There are, of course, huge potential problems in translating any such management ideas into practice in specific contexts and researchers have also pointed out that the circulation of management ideas itself is not a neutral process and often results in the transformation of that knowledge itself as it connects with practice (Czarniawska and Sevón, 1996; Gherardi, 2000; Gherardi and Nicolini, 2000; Røvik, 2002). Moreover, each of these particular 'packaged' forms of management knowledge has also, in turn, attracted its own serious critique (see, for example, Willmott, 1993; Grint, 1994; Williams et al., 1994; Zbaracki, 1998). Attention by critics is frequently directed towards the failure of these types of management programme to properly consider social aspects and to ignore their effects upon employment relations (see also Delbridge, 1998; Stewart et al., 2009).

Allied to this tendency towards commodification, management knowledge is significantly influenced by the vagaries of fashion and has been shown to follow fairly predictable waves of uptake, adoption and decline (Abrahamson, 1991, 1996). Such managerial fads and fashions are instigated and promoted by prominent management gurus, consultants, academics and others who are adept at symbolic manipulation (Huczynski, 1993). Successful fads and fashions tend to capture the zeitgeist of contemporary management discourse (Grint, 1994) and resonate well with the value and belief systems of managers having to cope with practical performance concerns and receptive to ideas that reflect hegemonic values of rationality and progress (Abrahamson, 1996). As active participants in the fashion setting process and not simply 'cultural dopes' that are easily subject to manipulation by persuasive consultants (cf. Garfinkel, 1984: 68), managers are further able to draw upon such ideas to help make sense of their management practice and enhance the legitimacy of their actions. In doing so, they not only potentially represent themselves as 'heroic' figures solving organizational problems (Jackson, 1996), but also contribute to the on-going construction of what it means to be a manager in practical and professional terms (Czarniawska-Joerges, 1990; Clark and Salaman, 1998). Consequently, managers have a good degree of influence over how such management ideas are accessed, translated into practice, developed, shared, re-produced and recycled. However, perhaps the most important implication of this to bear in mind here is how it contributes to the already fragmented, situated, mediated, provisional and contested nature of management knowledge (Blackler, 1995).

Management Knowledge in a Healthcare Context

Against this background of ambiguity and disagreement about the nature of management knowledge, the question of whether and how management knowledge (whatever its nature or source) diffuses or translates into healthcare management practice throws up a further complex set of issues. It has long been recognized that so-called leading-edge management thinking does not easily or necessarily translate into a healthcare context (Ferlie et al., 2005). Indeed, the well-researched 'translation gap' that exists in

understanding how clinical knowledge developed through research is translated into clinical practice (e.g. Eccles et al., 2009) is paralleled by another,
less widely explored translation gap that pertains to problems in the diffusion of management thinking into and through healthcare management
practice (Nicolini et al., 2008; Ferlie et al., 2012, 2015; Fischer et al., 2015).

Part of the reason for this problem of translation lies in the dilemma that,
while management within healthcare is sufficiently similar to management in
other contexts to make generic principles and practices ostensibly relevant,
it is sufficiently distinctive to make the application of generic management
knowledge problematic (Currie and Suhomlinova, 2006; Buchanan, 2013).
Whereas some types of codified management knowledge in the form of texts
and bundles of management practices do appear to influence management
thinking and action directly or indirectly (e.g. McNulty and Ferlie, 2002),
evidence of their impact on practice is often patchy, implicit and/or frequently challenged (Ferlie et al., 2015; Fischer et al., 2015; Hyde et al., 2016).
Moreover, specific management tools and techniques which are developed
and applied elsewhere (such as lean operations in manufacturing) do not
easily align with processes of healthcare delivery and thus often fail to translate directly into healthcare settings (Waring and Bishop, 2010; Radnor
et al., 2012; McCann et al., 2015).

Conversely, healthcare management is a well-developed institutional field
of activity that has its own modus operandi based upon widely accepted
management principles and practices, which are continually being shaped by
health policy initiatives and by the distinctive strategic imperatives and
operational demands of healthcare organizations (cf. Reay and Hinings,
2005). Such well-established institutional conditions not only potentially
raise barriers to the diffusion of knowledge from outside the sector; they
also tend to encourage an 'inward-looking' search for solutions to healthcare management and organizational problems (McNulty, 2002; Currie
and Suhomlinova, 2006). Furthermore, healthcare management is strongly
influenced by its own very specific and highly salient external demands
for public accountability and regulatory control. One consequence of this
for management processes and management knowledge is that healthcare
managers are subject to very stringent regulatory requirements, as might be
expected where patient care and safety and the use of public finances are of
paramount concern. Highly publicized cases of problems with healthcare
delivery amplify these demands and significantly heighten the level of public
visibility and regulatory focus on management action (e.g. Francis, 2013).

Another important consequence, however, is that institutional barriers
within healthcare inevitably inhibit the transferability and diffusion of management practices and disrupt flows of knowledge and learning (Newell
et al., 2003; Ferlie et al., 2005; Dopson et al., 2008; Ward et al., 2012;
Oborn et al., 2013). This is particularly so when one considers major differences within management—such as the differences between clinical and
non-clinical groups that were explored in the previous chapter. With regard

to the mobilization of management knowledge, the characteristic patterns of flows of knowledge and learning experienced by managers and clinicians through their education and professional development are vastly different, as are the epistemic practices through which managerial and clinical knowledge is developed and re-produced (cf. Knorr-Cetina, 1999). While clinicians and managers clearly need to interact as well as act collectively in healthcare situations, the frames of references they bring and the interests they represent are quite diverse and reflect their grounding in quite different experiences and communities of knowing (Llewellyn, 2001; cf. Boland and Tenkasi, 1995). Indeed, it has even been suggested that opportunities for dialogue and prospects for change are lessened by the dialectical nature of the relationship between clinicians and managers (MacIntosh et al., 2012).

The interaction between the forms of knowledge that they represent can certainly be considered two-way. On the one hand, there is a good deal of evidence to suggest that the systematization of management knowledge associated with greater managerialism in healthcare (Kirkpatrick et al., 2005) has led to an extension of managerial control over clinical work and some erosion of clinical-management practice as well as change in the knowledge base required (Davies and Harrison, 2003; Noordegraaf, 2015). However, it is also apparent that, while professional clinical practice is increasingly being shaped by managerialism, the development and application of management knowledge itself remains fundamentally constrained by the power of clinical directorates within a classic professional bureaucratic context (Buchanan and Fitzgerald, 2011; cf. Mintzberg, 1979). Indeed, this leaves senior clinicians with a continued ability to appropriate management control (Llewellyn, 2001: 596–597; Currie et al., 2009; Waring and Currie, 2009).

Moreover, given what we know about the ambiguity of management knowledge, it inevitably struggles to meet the dual requirements of scientific rigour and clinical relevance that form such an important part of the dominant medical/clinical discourse in healthcare (Oborn et al., 2013). Establishing legitimacy and avoiding too much deference to clinical discourse is made even more difficult perhaps when one considers developments in healthcare thinking. The comparatively recent shift towards 'evidence-based medicine' (Dopson and Fitzgerald, 2006), reproduces and even amplifies the values of scientific method that are, in contrast, so difficult to replicate in producing so-called 'evidence-based management' (Walshe and Rundall, 2001; Learmonth and Harding, 2006; Rousseau, 2006; Morrell and Learmonth, 2015). Furthermore, it is clear that lack of clinical grounding continues to limit the influence of managers in affecting clinical practice by furthering the spread of evidence-based medicine (Dopson and Fitzgerald, 2006; McGivern et al., 2009). Consequently, management knowledge within healthcare is both a powerful influence upon, as well as significantly constrained by, clinical practice and discourse. Any proper examination of management knowledge in healthcare therefore needs to recognize the recursive nature of the relationship between the two and the ways in which each impact upon the other.

From Knowledge to Knowing in Management Practice

At the level of management practice, it is also important to recognize the complex and subtle ways in which forms of management knowledge and practices of management inter-relate. So far, the implicit presumption has been that management knowledge, despite being situated, provisional, contested and mediated (Blackler, 1995), can somehow be considered to be a tangible asset or resource to be exploited by the organization (Grant, 1996). Indeed, until comparatively recently, approaches to management knowledge in healthcare tended to adopt this 'epistemology of possession', emphasizing the more concrete or 'objective' properties of knowledge (Newell et al., 2009: 14–18). Emphasis was placed upon the embodiment of knowledge in individuals and attention was focused upon constraints involved in the capture and 'transfer' of that knowledge into and across healthcare (Ward et al., 2012).

That approach drew significantly on earlier conceptions of flows of knowledge and learning between individuals and groups within organizations which rested upon Polanyi's (1968) important distinction between explicit and tacit knowledge. Such an approach does throw some important light upon some of the main challenges of socialization, externalization, combination and internalization involved in attempting to convert one form of knowledge into another for the purposes of knowledge sharing and knowledge creation (Nonaka, 1994; Nonaka and Takeuchi, 1995; Spender, 1996). So, for example, socialization processes are highly important for the sharing of highly tacit forms of knowledge (see also Hansen, 2002); and some of the key challenges facing organizations are in capturing and codifying individual know-how (externalization) and in ensuring that explicit forms of knowledge are effectively shared and understood (internalization) (Nonaka and Takeuchi, 1995).

At the same time, however, it is important to recognize that explicit and tacit forms of knowledge are mutually constitutive and thus inseparable (Tsoukas, 1996; Gourlay, 2006). So, for example, exploiting forms of knowledge that are more codified and explicit (such as specific management tools and techniques) is not just about somehow 'enculturing' new ways of working (Blackler, 1995); these forms of knowledge are actively shaped by individuals' interpretations and tacit understandings (based upon personal dispositions that are shaped by context and experience). Examining the impact of management texts, for example, involves going beyond identifying where they appear to be consciously referred to and even apparently used (Ferlie et al., 2015). Further understanding is needed of whether and how they are inscribed in practice as well as what generative part they play in contributing towards the development of management knowledge (cf. Cook and Brown, 1999). Gabbay and Le May (2004), for example, emphasize in the clinical context the importance of recognizing collectively constructed *mind-lines*, as opposed to more explicit forms of knowledge, such as evidence-based guidelines.

Recent thinking in healthcare management has thus followed wider developments in knowledge management and organizational learning theory by adopting a more practice-based approach and questioning the conception of knowledge as something that is a property of the individual and that can simply be transferred into practice (e.g. Nicolini et al., 2008; Greenhalgh, 2010b; Ward et al., 2012; Oborn et al., 2013). Instead, it has embraced a more socialized and situated conception of knowledge that recognizes the intimate connection between knowing and practice (Orlikowski, 2002; Nicolini, 2011) and which stresses the importance to knowledge mobilization of social networks and the occupational and professional communities of practice within which individuals are embedded and through which they share their understanding and learning (Lave and Wenger, 1991; Brown and Duguid, 2001).

Practice-based perspectives on knowledge are diverse and according to Nicolini (2011: 603–604), range from those that still retain some conception of knowledge as effectively a property of collectives of individuals via communities of practice (Wenger, 1998); to those that explore the recursive relationship between forms of knowledge and knowing in practice (Cook and Brown, 1999); to those that go further in stressing how interconnected and mutually constitutive knowing and practice are (see also Orlikowski, 2002; Tsoukas, 2005). However, they do share in common an orientation towards teasing out the ways in which knowing and practice interconnect and what this means for understanding processes of knowledge diffusion and management learning (Gherardi, 2001, 2006). Moreover, they are also sensitized to the impact not just of social relations but also of material conditions in influencing the development of particular forms of knowing and learning in practice (Orlikowski, 2002; Swan et al., 2007). Furthermore, as Nicolini (2011) also points out, practice-based approaches are also concerned with understanding how knowing and learning are shaped by the web of power relations in which they are embedded. Such analyses range from an interest in how the nature of the employment relationship influences the development of communities of practice (Contu and Willmott, 2003); to understanding the different configurations of power/knowledge that are constituted through particular management discourses (Foucault, 1980).

The propensity for managers to mobilize knowledge through networks and networking activity is explored in more depth in the following chapter. In the meantime, it is important to recognize too that learning boundaries between networks and communities of practice can also create a double-edged sword, by promoting learning within occupational specialisms, while inhibiting knowledge sharing and learning across different (but connected) domains of practice (Scarbrough et al., 2004; Lindkvist, 2005). Indeed, this is not only an inevitable feature perhaps of clinical-managerial interactions in healthcare, but also an inhibiting factor on team-working in healthcare more widely (Lloyd et al., 2011). Moreover, in recognizing the importance of divergent interests as well as different ways of thinking, attention is also drawn to the disruptive effects of new ways of knowing and learning on existing practice and how this may need something more than the translation of meaning from one domain of practice to another (as implied by the notion of a 'translation gap'). Instead, what may be required for learning to occur and knowledge to be shared is a collective joint commitment to a more profound transformation of practice (Carlile, 2002, 2004).

In the remainder of this chapter, we examine the orientations of managers in our study towards different forms and sources of management knowledge and how these were interrelated in and through their management practice. We explore how their approach to management was influenced by their particular professional background; how particular codified forms of knowledge may have been mobilized and utilized by managers; how organizational reporting requirements influenced the managerial knowledge base required; and how important personal experience and experiential learning was to their management practice. As well as highlighting common findings, significant differences encountered across each of the trusts and managerial cohorts are also drawn out. Inevitably, such an analysis reveals not only the very complex nature of healthcare managers' knowing in practice, but also some clearly identifiable trends that raise questions about the relationship between managers' predispositions to knowing/learning and the expectations associated with wider changes within the sector.

Managers' Orientations to Types of Management Knowledge

The Influence of Clinical and Other Specialist Knowledge Bases and Practices

The data presented in tables 5.1 and 5.2 in the previous chapter clearly indicated how pervasive clinical background and experience was across the sample of managers. It was clear too from the interviews that an understanding of the clinical aspects of managerial work was an important starting point when it came to the knowledge base of managers, as too was proceeding from a good understanding of the distinctive features of healthcare management:

> You need a good clinical understanding of the work, and I think that's important because the whole idea that a manager's a manager and you manage a carpet factory then you manage a day hospital—I don't think it's the same. I think you need to understand the business, and it's quite different, health.
>
> (Leo, Clinical, Care)

Indeed, the combination of professional clinical experience and clinical and health-related educational experiences that most managers had provided them with the baseline technical understanding that enabled them to communicate effectively with their teams and, in particular, to engage with medical staff:

> If you've got that clinical background it is a major advantage. There's managers within my business group—our theatre manager and some of the heads of nursing—[that] are more clinical based. I quite often find that they do have a massive advantage [as] they've got that clinical knowledge.
>
> (Stewart, General, Acute)

At the same time, it was clear too that educational qualifications by themselves were not necessarily sufficient and that some clinical experience was both desirable and necessary:

> There was a time when a Degree was really valuable, and a management qualification was really important. But, gradually, we've realized that having a management qualification or being an NHS management trainee does not necessarily equip you to be a manager. It's the clinical experience that equips you to be a manager . . . Managers that come without the clinical experience . . . don't really progress.
>
> (Hasin, General, Care)

Moreover, even with some clinical background and experience, managers often still struggled to establish credibility in the eyes of clinicians, and this could often only effectively be achieved through using other strategies that combined their clinical knowledge with interpersonal skills and/or personal experience.

These findings echo what was found in Chapter 4 about differences between the trusts in the ways in which they tended to handle clinical-managerial differences. In the Specialist trust, despite relatively harmonious relationships between powerful clinical and managerial groups, there was still a pronounced divide that needed bridging and that could cause problems for middle management. Doing so tended again to rely upon structural mechanisms combined with relational skills:

> They don't trust you; they see you as a manager; and, until they realize that you're actually working with them instead of against them, it makes your job very difficult.
>
> (Joanna, General, Specialist)

This could lead to individuals performing crucial boundary spanning and brokering roles that brought together management and clinical communities:

From the engagement point of view, the management consultants saw me as a way in, because I knew the consultants, I knew a lot of the medics, a lot of the senior team at the trust. I could get in and deliver their message without it being all management spiel.

(Becky, General, Specialist)

Similar structural mechanisms were also used to bridge the divide at the Acute trust. In contrast, and as we saw in the earlier chapter, clinical understanding was more personally embodied in the knowledge base of individual managers at the Care trust, where most general managers were experienced nurses. Structural mechanisms and relational skills were therefore important in helping bridge the divide between managers and clinicians. However, these relational capabilities were not as beneficial as the integrative capabilities found in the ability of hybrid managers to move from one perspective/role (managerial) to another (clinical) (cf. Owen-Smith et al., 2002). As such, and as we saw too in the previous chapter, a great deal of reliance was placed on those who could span the boundaries between managerial and clinical groups and who possessed the personally embodied knowledge and skills necessary to bridge the divide (Burgess and Currie, 2013).

In all three cases, however, management knowledge was strongly influenced by the processes and practices associated with the dominant clinical discourse. So, for example, concepts of diagnosis and prescription were used as a general way of framing managerial problems, and that fed into what was considered managerial 'know-how'. Consider, for example, the following explicit account and the presumption it contains about what is the most reliable and valid way of knowing:

I don't think I need my clinical background to do my job. What I think is that as an AHP the way that we have practiced absolutely influences the way I work and perform as a manager . . . As a physiotherapist . . . I would meet a patient, and I would assess them. And then have a conversation with them about what the treatment options are . . . and then treat. And then at the end of it, are you better or not? . . . And those are actually fundamental principles that I apply in my role now. So we assess a situation . . . What is the problem . . . what are our options? Okay, how are we going to take this forward? . . . We'll treat or we'll implement the change that we need to implement, and do it, but we need to review it. And is it better or not?

(Melissa, General, Acute)

Such an *encultured* understanding (cf. Blackler, 1995) that reflected the professional norms, values and practices of clinicians was a dominant influence upon management thinking. Moreover, it forced managers to conform in their management problem-solving and decision-making to an appropriate way of thinking (i.e. clinically) that was based upon a particular epistemology of knowledge (diagnostic, evidence-based) in order to create convincing and credible management arguments.

However, that was not the only influential professional knowledge base at play in shaping managerial discourse. Financial expertise was important too, and what was apparent from those interviewed was how natural and normalized the emphasis on finance had become, and how this shaped orientations to management work. As one manager made clear, it was influencing the balance of management skills and knowledge base required and was also shaping perceptions of the essential criteria to be used in problem-solving and decision-making:

> One of the best pieces of management advice I ever got was get the money right. If you don't get the money right, nothing else ever works . . . As soon as you get the money right you can concentrate on the clinical services.
>
> (Kerry, General, Care)

While this internalization of financial management discourse was particularly pronounced amongst general managers and their functional counterparts, it was also noticeable from interviews with clinical staff how readily they and their teams related to it as well. At the same time, there was clearly some effort of translation required in applying financial management principles and practices direct to the healthcare sector. As Matthew, a finance manager at the Specialist trust, put it, "The whole basis of finances are different." Similarly:

> Our head of finance was new into the NHS—he came from KPMG—so he had workings with the health service but didn't really understand community services; and it was quite a steep learning curve for him to understand it wasn't just about making cuts . . . You had to understand the implications that that would have on the services that were delivered and how clinicians operate.
>
> (Hugh, General, Acute)

Indeed, financial concerns shaped managerial discourses at the three trusts in very distinct ways. There was a much stronger emphasis on new business development and the greater opportunities it afforded at the Specialist trust (and parts of Care); whereas there was a much greater preoccupation with the challenges of improving operational efficiency and coping with cuts in government funding at the Acute trust.

What this all suggests was that engagement with clinical discourse was important in enabling managers to articulate management knowledge and influence discussions and decisions within their organization. Clinical expertise therefore continued to influence strongly the ways in which management knowledge was developed and effectively imparted. Managers clearly had to work with, through and around other dominant groups with well-established professional knowledge bases—notably clinicians, but also those who were carriers of other influential know-how (notably, finance).

At the same time, however, the direction of travel was rather one-way: unless there was some countervailing pressure associated with financial imperatives that could be mobilized by managers to help counter, shape or soften the clinical perspective, managers were much more reliant upon taking the perspective of clinicians than promoting their own perspective based upon a distinct managerial agenda (cf. Boland and Tenkasi, 1995). In other words, establishing clinical credibility and/or harnessing financial imperatives were the keys to establishing management knowledge, identity and influence. Even for hybrid managers, their managerial know-how tended to be subordinated at all times to the dominant clinical perspective.

Exploiting Codified Management Knowledge, Tools and Techniques

As table 5.2 also indicated, management educational qualifications were far less prevalent than clinical or health-related formal qualifications. However, around a quarter of managers still had some type of formal management educational qualification (usually PG Diploma or MSc/MBA). Clinical groups were less likely to have non-clinical or non-health qualifications and functional managers were those most likely to have degrees unrelated to health, as well as more management educational qualifications. Formal management educational qualifications were more common amongst general managers at the Acute and Care trusts. At the Specialist trust, they were comparatively rare (although one general manager there did, exceptionally, have an MBA).

Further educational development through more health-specific or clinically oriented MSc programmes was therefore the norm. The emphasis tended to be on the enhancement of healthcare knowledge and improvement of analytical skills relevant to a healthcare context as opposed to developing those generic management skills most often emphasized by managers as important to the job (identified in Chapter 4 as interpersonal and communication skills as well as technical knowledge of finance, HR and IT systems—all of which it was commonly presumed could be developed through training). For example:

> The MSc did just elevate me clinically to a higher level, which is everything a masters is supposed to do, so that was around critical thinking, being able to understand and utilize research and to develop evidence-based practice.
>
> (Leo, Clinical, Care)

Again, it was the diagnostic element of managerial problem-solving that was emphasized. Similarly:

> [In] the transition from nurse to manager, it's getting that confidence to be able to challenge evidence, data, financial, systems. You've got to be quite confident in those to be able to challenge those, and I guess going through a formal MSc in public health helped me to develop that skill set.
>
> (Roxanne, General, Acute)

Managers only very rarely made explicit reference to established and codified systems of management knowledge which were consciously drawn upon and applied to their work. Clinicians inevitably referred less anyway to management knowledge per se than to the importance of relevant clinical expertise. Functional managers naturally drew upon their own expert knowledge in the routine performance of their work (e.g. accounts, IT protocols, project management). There were some instances where more generic management tools and techniques such as process mapping or strategic modeling were explicitly referred to by managers (particularly functional managers) keen to use them to make sense of management problems. Referring, for example, to "some of the tools of trade . . . like the Boston Box," Emma noted:

> I love frameworks and tools and techniques . . . My old team used to laugh because they used to say, Emma wants to put everything in a box. But I suppose it's just the way my brain works; it helps me think things through if I can use some sort of tool to start to work an issue through, and categorize things. That's my way of making sense of it.
>
> (Emma, Functional, Care)

However, where explicit reference was made, the emphasis was generally not on direct application to day-to-day work but more to their use to facilitate more strategic managerial reflection:

> If you're doing a full developmental day with a team, then I would absolutely use some tools to help take them through. But in terms of day to day management of my team . . . problem solving, it's probably far more intuitive. I'm not constantly . . . doing a SWOT analysis of everything.
>
> (Emma, Functional, Care)

Even if Emma's personal approach was fundamentally underpinned by a rationalistic management epistemology, there were clearly limits to how she felt this could be applied in practice and a recognition that a more generative approach was necessary that combined formal tools and techniques with more intuitive, tacit learning (cf. Cook and Brown, 1999).

Similarly, there were a number of references made by some general managers to attempts to import and apply lean thinking principles to the sector, particularly at the Acute trust. There was a sense from the majority of people we spoke to that the heyday of these initiatives in healthcare had passed and it was clear too that their application had been patchy due to problems experienced in embedding the initiatives in practice (cf. Waring and Bishop, 2010; McCann et al., 2015). What was interesting, however, was that the use of 'lean thinking' could be promoted to provoke discussion about different ways of acting—provided it was not 'packaged' as such:

> We had an all-day event yesterday with the new community teams . . . about how we can amalgamate and transform these teams. And really what we did in that day was effectively Lean, in the sense that it was value stream mapping; we were going through, looking for elements of waste . . . but it was never packaged as that.
>
> (Glen, General, Acute)

Promotion of a similar reflective and 'diagnostic' logic (that also made use of a clinical metaphor) was also apparent in what Melissa had to say about service improvement:

> I'm trying to bring in the ideas [and] concepts of service improvement, because . . . people identify that there's a problem and they jump straight to solutions . . . It's the natural thing to do. What I'm trying to get them to do is saying: "well, hang on a minute, why have we got the problem?" They don't answer that, they put sticking plasters on things all the time. Another plaster, another plaster, and the problem is never resolved properly because you never understand why we've got a problem in the first place.
>
> (Melissa, General, Acute)

Despite these examples, what was more apparent across the cases was the relative infrequency of references to more external, *encoded* forms of management knowledge (cf. Blackler, 1995) that were actively harnessed, adopted and/or adapted to deal with management issues in each trust. The exception here was the knowledge base of functional managers whose managerial remit and career development required them to be aware of and apply particular specialist management tools and techniques (in finance, HR, etc.).

In large part, this absence of codified forms of knowledge reflected not simply difficulties in translation (due to differences in meaning) associated with their application, but also major impediments to application (as was the case with lean principles) due to the transformations in practice that were required if they were to successfully confront and overcome the barriers associated with different orientations and interests (Dopson et al., 2008; cf. Newell et al., 2003; Carlile, 2004). There was clearly some heuristic value for managers in using such systems of knowledge to analyze and interpret local strategic and operational needs: tools such as process mapping, strategic modeling and lean thinking were undoubtedly used as such. However, although they could clearly be used to help generate new ways of thinking about operational processes (cf. Cook and Brown, 1999), their legitimacy and acceptability was clearly in doubt, and there were limits on how well they were received and internalized as part of legitimate management practice. This was not just for those on the receiving end: as the quotes suggest, those managers who were keen to promote different ways of thinking were very self-conscious and even self-effacing in their attempts to do so. This suggests that such ideas had some way to go before they could be considered properly embedded in management practice and constitutive of managerial knowledge in any significant way.

The Effects of Thinking Institutionally and Acting Locally

The difficulty in translating codified forms of management knowledge into everyday managerial practice was augmented by strong isomorphic tendencies and a more inward-looking search for solutions (cf. Currie and Suhomlinova, 2006). In particular such tendencies were driven by the need to respond to institutional reporting requirements and the continuing search for best practice across the sector:

> The other phrase that is used a lot here is: "Don't reinvent the wheel", so if another NHS Trust has done something, well let's just do that. Let's copy what they've done.
>
> (Christian, Functional, Acute)

The above quote reproduces an assumption consistently found in policy documents that 'good practice' can be assembled and abstracted to be applied elsewhere. Importing established best practices across healthcare organizations, however, is far from straightforward, as account also needs to be taken of how they translate into different local circumstances and effectively deal with different interests and practices (Newell et al., 2003; Dopson et al., 2008). Nevertheless, there was a clear privileging of home-grown management (sector, trust) systems and practices. While these might owe some debt to a wider, more diffuse management knowledge base, they were predominantly driven by formal, sector-specific requirements.

Principal amongst these were the institutional requirements on healthcare trusts to meet expected standards of care and to do this according to accepted performance targets and standards (as defined by CQC, NICE, Monitor, etc.). This emphasis upon monitoring of levels of care and performance had clear consequences not only for the balance and focus of managerial effort, but also for the primacy attached to locally situated management knowledge that was embedded in bespoke or tailored systems and processes (as opposed to more abstract management ideas and practices). So, for example:

> We already have a really, really high standard of quality. We've implemented a . . . Choice and Partnership Approach to manage our demand and capacity and, within that, comes the need for very clear pathways, review, constant review, flexibility of services, listening to what users want . . . We're perceived, within the directorate, as being quite structured, quite robust and a lot of those principles fit with the IAPT [Improving Access to Psychological Therapies] principles . . . the separation of an assessment and a treatment process and making sure it's evidence-based, and meaningful, and collaborative.
>
> (Gabrielle, General, Care)

Moreover, it was clear that external institutional pressures required more recording and reporting of information about performance in relation to targets. This predisposed the trusts to apply and/or develop management systems and procedures that were geared towards standardization and formalization of process and which were, consequently, more bureaucratic:

> The organization needs you to be able to tick their boxes, so being able to understand their must-dos and their must-haves and their givens, the data stuff—if you can pay attention to that and translate your activity into that in a comprehensible way, that can carry you a long way.
>
> (Laura, General, Care)

It also meant that one of the continuing challenges facing all of the trusts was the tension that existed between 'corporate' attempts to standardize processes and practices and the more local needs that managers felt were important to meet in their own particular part of the organization:

> We still have to evidence that the quality of care that you are providing is at a level that the PCT don't want to de-commission this service. So, without saying: unless you do it we're not going to have money for your team any more, therefore you are going to be out of a job . . . [the] messages that we try to get across to them [are] actually this is about protecting the organization by providing this information. It's just the nature of the world . . . You all have to be able to evidence what you're doing
>
> (Carl, Functional, Care)

Where there was already an established and strong corporate identity (as at the Specialist trust) and/or more of a bureaucratic ethos (as at the Acute trust), there was more of a predisposition towards, and perhaps greater acceptance of, the collating, processing and assessing of performance data required to meet organizational reporting requirements. Formal management meetings observed at the Acute trust, for example, tended to be driven by the agenda of regular performance monitoring and reporting requirements. Greater tensions within management were apparent at the Care trust where a more highly differentiated organization (spatially and operationally) meant that there was much greater heterogeneity in management practice and in corresponding flows of information between the centre and periphery.

Consequently, a strong emphasis on the importance of 'home grown' knowledge was added to by contemporary institutional pressures and influences that demanded standard bureaucratic responses to reporting and evaluation needs (cf. Bevan and Hood, 2006). As such, forms of knowledge that were *embedded* in the structures, technologies, systems and procedures of management (cf. Blackler, 1995) had a major effect upon managerial agendas, orientations and practices. Financial pressures also had a part to play in accentuating these reporting requirements and so managerial expertise and identity was again circumscribed in a major way by knowledge and expertise emanating from this professional domain.

The Importance of Experience and Experiential Learning

There was a strong and consistent view held across the sample that it was experience and experiential learning that were of greatest value to managers' skills development and their underlying knowledge base. As Belinda at the Acute trust graphically put it:

> You can go on management courses till the cows come home, can't you, but you can either manage or you can't, and I think a lot of it does come from experience and your own personality.
>
> (Belinda, General, Acute)

As already noted in Chapter 5, managers' career development and job experiences varied considerably, and it was not always direct managerial experience that was of importance—clinical experience was important too. This was obviously concentrated amongst the clinical manager cohorts, but there was also a preponderance of those with clinical experience and qualifications amongst the general managers—particularly at the Care trust, where there were more hybrid managers and the common route to management was through nursing:

> I've grown up through the ranks . . . I've had that experience as a clinician, as a student nurse, as a senior member of staff, so I've gained

that experience and I think that's what's helped me grow into this position . . . Without that, I wouldn't have been able to achieve where I'm
at because I think you miss a real sound foundation to becoming a
manager.

(Kate, General, Care)

Moreover, echoing comments that were made earlier, clinical experience
was often considered as something that easily overshadowed any more
indirect or more generalized managerial experience that might be drawn
upon.

I feel having the clinical background has been a real advantage.
Because you can see it's not just about a process, a management style,
a service. You look at things in a very different perspective when
you've been hands on. You've been on that ward, you've delivered
treatment, you've delivered patient care. You've had that interaction
with the patient.

(Becky, General, Specialist)

Indeed, it could be frustrating for managers if their clinical experience and
expertise was forgotten or not explicitly recognized:

I keep reminding the team that I am a physio . . . Some of the junior staff
that have never worked with me in that role, you know, they forget that
they can come to me for that kind of advice and support and they see
me as 'the manager'.

(Gloria, General, Acute)

The opposite applied too, however, particularly in the more medically prestigious Specialist trust, where some nurse hybrid managers (e.g. Hannah)
felt they were still treated as if they were just 'acting up' as managers.

Experiential learning, however, was not necessarily associated with a
smooth journey that gave managers great opportunities for reflective learning. Indeed, as hinted at in Chapter 5, many of those interviewed had
experienced enormous changes, challenges and transitions in the path to
reaching their current position (with jobs being re-defined, re-combined or
made open to competitive application). 'Muddling through' (cf. Lindblom,
1959) also typified a good deal of the learning involved in the development
of skills. General and clinical managers, in particular, tended to emphasize
the 'trial and error' associated with learning how to do their jobs.

Most of it, in all honesty, is muddling your way through a problem and
finding a solution that works and thinking, well, actually, you know,
with hindsight, that worked

(Brian, Clinical, Acute)

Many also stressed—some quite positively—the importance of making use of the range of experiences available and stretching people's capabilities:

> I'm trying to [take] my Band 7s . . . out of their comfort zone a little bit, so I've rotated them all, as much as they're all kicking and screaming. And it was a bit of a nightmare to start with; they've all done each other's wards because there was some very insular people there, and that's helped . . . I'm doing things with [their] consent.
>
> (Nancy, Clinical, Acute)

However, what is evident too in these quotes (and many others across the sample) is that this muddling through not only reflected the often sporadic nature of day to day managerial work, but was also in large measure a consequence of the real constraints and demands on managers' time that resulted from resource limitations and pressures on managers to deliver under conditions of *normalized intensity* (McCann et al., 2008) that emanated from major and rapid change. Managerial learning was taking place, but it was as much about learning to cope without sufficient time and resources as it was about being able to learn new things.

The social learning that occurred through interaction with others was also an important aspect of developing managerial knowledge and skills. Formally, this occurred through established mentoring and coaching relationships with senior colleagues. Where managers had established relationships with chosen mentors, considerable value was placed upon the guidance, knowledge and support that this provided.

> Everyone in the senior finance team have got a coach who comes in once a month for each of us. And we spend an hour with him, and I was actually with him yesterday, and I found it really useful. It's really good.
>
> (Felix, Functional, Acute)

Although mentoring and coaching was highly valued by some of the managers we spoke to, there were limits too in the extent to which managers were able to access and make use of that type of support. This could be for a variety of reasons, including different individual predispositions to mentoring/coaching, the lack of availability of senior mentors, problems in finding the time to be able to focus on developing close relationships, and gaps in mentoring provision as staff left the organization. Formal coaching, in particular, was more limited an experience and did attract some scepticism. Moreover, the general guidance and support provided by mentors did not necessarily help managers directly in their day-to-day work. However, it did lessen the sense of isolation that could be experienced and gave them access to practical insights about coping with day-to-day challenges and developing careers.

In addition to formal opportunities to engage in mentoring or coaching, social learning occurred in a variety of more informal ways, including the implicit learning from each other, direct observation and even conscious imitation and role modeling:

> My manager is a real business manager. She's got a real business head on her, and it's interesting to learn from her, because she's a radiographer by background. She does think completely differently to me, but I think we actually complement each other quite well. I've learnt an awful lot from her.
>
> (Belinda, General, Acute)

Learning what it meant to be a manager was clearly strongly influenced by social aspects and by the socialization processes involved. Where that occurred in a setting where there was intense interaction within and between managerial groups, it provided good opportunities for managers to develop their skill sets through sharing tacit understandings. However, it did mean there needed to be sufficient managerial role models available:

> I've probably learnt more about how not to manage and lead . . . I've seen very few role models so far in the NHS who I would say, "God, I want to manage like that."
>
> (Becky, General, Specialist)

Where opportunities for such intense interaction were more limited, it tended to foster a greater reliance on more formal means of passing on knowledge and learning that did not translate so readily into practice (e.g. through management courses). Although such events might open up managers to a wider potential range of influences, it was the strong ties needed to share tacit understandings that were more highly valued.

Overall, the garnering of management knowledge through experience did enable managers to deal very practically with the problems and issues they faced and naturally led to the very direct application of acquired skills and tacit understandings (or extrapolation of past learning) to the solution of immediate operational and practical problems. However, there were also a number of downsides to this strong emphasis on the *embodied* and *embrained* knowledge and skills of individual managers (cf. Blackler, 1995).

First, it made it difficult for organizations that were trying to externalize knowledge and codify and disseminate it across the organization.

> I wouldn't envy somebody coming in and trying to do my role. I don't think they'd be able to do my role the way I do it . . . Unless they came from within and they had that kind of exposure and that knowledge, it would be very, very difficult to do.
>
> (Ian, Functional, Specialist)

A good example of this was in the Care trust where a comparatively small number of managers had built up a successful track record in writing tenders. Although this was considered an increasingly important activity for the trust to engage in (and therefore a skill that needed to be spread amongst its managers), a continued reliance on those individuals' expertise had led to some 'stickiness' (Szulanski, 1996) that was making it difficult to capture the tacit skills and spread them elsewhere. Other examples of such 'sticky knowledge' were encountered—particularly in the knowledge brought to bear by clinicians and certain functional specialists, but also in relation to the tacit management skills of general managers linked to particular services (especially at the Care trust where operational units were more differentiated).

Second, and related to this, the organization's collective memory and its impact on longer term organizational learning and capability development depended a lot upon people staying with the organization:

> [I've got] to the point now where the knowledge I've got of the organization is scary to be honest. Not just from knowing the people but knowing the services, knowing the interlinks and the dependencies and how reliant they are for infrastructure and if this fails what does that mean? It's not something you could necessarily teach somebody. You couldn't sit down and say: "Right, I want to give you all of this knowledge."
>
> (Ian, Functional, Specialist)

Quite apart from the challenge this implies in harnessing socialization processes for the sharing of tacit understandings (Nonaka and Takeuchi, 1995), this also raises important questions about the effects that reductions in managerial capacity are likely to be having upon the absorptive capacity of healthcare organizations (Cohen and Levinthal, 1990) as well as their general ability to retain crucial managerial knowledge and expertise (cf. Cascio, 2005). Although many managers had been in their posts for some time (see table 3.5 earlier), there was still the ever-present danger of redundancies associated with cuts and reorganizations.

Third, for some of those interviewed, an over-emphasis on immediate operational demands was a major constraint upon the development of more strategic and creative thinking and tended to reinforce more localized learning based on problem solution on a 'management by exception' basis. This 'sticking plaster' approach, as Melissa put it earlier, is redolent of the management-by-exception logic of *single loop learning* (cf. Argyris and Schon, 1978)—as opposed to 'double loop' or 'triple loop' learning that goes further by questioning underlying assumptions about existing ways of operating. It is also perhaps worth noting here too that such constraints on learning could result not just from pressing operational needs, but also organizational success—as was suggested in the point made earlier about possible complacency at the Specialist trust.

Managers clearly put a great deal of emphasis on personal experience as a primary source of knowledge and learning. While this was more meaning-ful to managers and heightened their receptivity to learning, training and development that made use of social and experiential processes, it did have a down side in making it more difficult for knowledge and learning to be externalized and generalized (cf. Nonaka and Takeuchi, 1995). Constraints upon the spread of more abstract forms of management knowledge also signified a clear preference for the strong ties needed to share tacit under-standings, rather than the weak ties that could have been used to access wider sources of knowledge (e.g. Hansen, 2002). There were exceptions to this, as evidenced by a few highly networked general managers within the sample who made significant use of wider sources of knowledge within their professional communities of practice (e.g. some psychologists at the Care trust). However, the general picture presented was one of the precedence of more personalized and social forms of knowledge accumulation and learning (cf. Zollo and Winter, 2002). The 'stickiness' of certain forms of knowledge (Szulanski, 1996) provided further evidence of the challenges of generalizing knowledge and learning even within trusts—particularly where the organizations themselves were highly differentiated (as was the case at the Acute trust and, especially, the Care trust).

Management Training and Development

Given this emphasis on the value of experience as a source of knowledge and learning, it is unsurprising to find very mixed views expressed about the value and logic of various forms of training and development, includ-ing the GMTS, continued professional development and wider initiatives within the sector (such as the *Gateway to Leadership*, *Aspiring Directors*, *Breaking Through* and *Athena* programmes). Dismissive statements about the value of training courses were not uncommon, as illustrated in the fol-lowing dismissive response:

> When we were on the training scheme we did lots of courses in leader-ship and management and weeks away doing it, and I never really learnt anything . . . It's not until you start doing it.
>
> (Felix, Functional, Acute)

However, opinions were quite mixed, and a number of main themes emerged in the views expressed by managers about their training. First, there was clearly a good deal of importance attached to training that developed or updated professional technical skills—particularly for clinical managers, but also for functional specialists (e.g. new accounting practices or HR regu-lations). For general managers, however, such technical training tended to cover very routine aspects of their work. While the quality of training was generally well regarded, its mundane nature did make it seem less valuable to general and functional managers, as well as highly unattractive to clinical managers.

> I've been delivering some health and safety and reporting training to the consultants . . . You get the odd one who will come, but certainly not surgical—sorry, lords and masters. They forget that they're managers as well . . . and that's something I remind them of with the health and safety law, what their responsibilities are.
>
> (Hayley, Functional, Specialist)

Second, virtually all of the interviewees placed a strong emphasis on the value of practical and applied training—particularly that making use of action learning sets and project/case assignments and where developing interpersonal skills was the intention—through various forms of interactive learning, including role play.

> The trust put on a senior manager training course . . . It was excellent, a week's training where we looked at the theory around leadership and management styles, different ways of working. I got a lot out of that week . . . I had a couple of people in the service [who] were really challenging to manage, really difficult . . . They brought actors in and you gave the scenario to the actor and then you came in and you had to do the role play around it . . . I learnt such a lot from that process about what I was doing and how that wasn't particularly helpful . . . I found that I was able to transfer that learning to other situations as well.
>
> (Jocelyn, General, Care)

Indeed, the opportunities that such courses offered for personal reflection could be really valued by general managers—especially those at the Care trust:

> We had a five-day course away from services, and it was the best course ever because it was very much around emotional intelligence . . . It was absolutely fantastic. Because I got to learn about my colleagues, I got to learn about how people can be at work, why people are the way they are at work. I got to learn about a range of leadership styles; how to apply them, when to apply them. And the best bit is, I got to learn about myself, which was really important.
>
> (Hasin, General, Care)

A particularly striking example was training that involved personality assessment using the Myers-Briggs indicator. Respondents who had undertaken this training across the Acute trust and (particularly) the Care trust were highly enthusiastic about its use as an aid to staff development and team working—a reflection perhaps of the Care trust's orientation to personal psychology, but also symptomatic of the emphasis that managers tended to place in interviews on the importance of personal skills:

> I've known what my Myers Briggs profile is for quite some time, but one of the things that we did do on the first part of [the course] . . . was a real in-depth look at Myers Briggs . . . And that was really insightful because although there's lots of theory attached to it. I could relate and think, do you know, I do do that. So I got a lot from that particular session, and again it was about more self-awareness.
>
> (Melissa, General, Acute)

Third, virtually all of those interviewed valued the opportunity that training gave them to have time for reflection away from the daily pressures of work and to network with their peers and share experiences, knowledge and learning. At the same time, many complained of the difficulty they had in taking time out from busy schedules to make the best use of training opportunities.

> If you really want to push on and you really want to expose yourself to as much training and development as you want, then there are opportunities [in the organization] to do that. I think one of the biggest hindrances to that is that once you're actually in a post, the day-to-day grind of doing your day-to-day job [makes it] difficult to find that time to be able to remove yourself from the position for maybe two, three days . . . You almost have to force yourself to try and do that if you want to continue learning and development.
>
> (Stewart, General, Acute)

Even if managers were able to take up training opportunities, there was always the danger that immediate operational demands would 'crowd out' the time needed for further reflection or for the direct implementation of learning. For example:

> I was fortunate to go on . . . a really good [named] leadership programme . . . and it was really empowering at the time . . . I'd literally only been away one day a week for ten weeks and come back and I've got another service to manage. It's like okay . . . now where do I fit it into my week?
>
> (Gloria, General, Acute)

Moreover, these significant difficulties in scheduling training were augmented by a sense that training was not always synchronized with the development needs of managers at particular points in their career:

> When you're doing a management course that tells you how to manage staff or gives you the theory about managing staff, it's really difficult

without having practiced in HR. It's kind of like catch 22 almost . . . You need the experience to apply the learning, but you . . . need the learning . . . to do the job.

(Theresa, Functional, Care)

A similar 'catch-22' situation was emphasized in the following account:

Theory was something I'd got in my head but I hadn't got the experience necessarily to be able to apply it; and other periods where I'd got experience that I really could have done with some more formal development to work out how best to use that.

(Ruth, Functional, Care)

Furthermore, the emphasis on very practical training did have a down side in shifting the balance away from longer term, strategic reflection based upon more abstract forms of knowledge (Reynolds, 1998) and towards what was immediately relevant.

For those who had managed to secure places on wider leadership developmental programmes, the experience was seen as unambiguously beneficial. Although synchronization with career trajectory could still be an issue, access to such programmes was generally considered as providing enormously valuable opportunities for networking and, for some, an inspiring entrée into leadership:

It [included] four days of assessments, which was quite tiring actually. Just four consecutive days of being observed and watched in group exercises, individual things, every psychometric test you could possibly imagine in the world . . . They worked with you on a personal development plan to meet the development areas, and then we got coaching to follow that up and we also established a network from the group . . . We were staying away together as well. But that was brilliant, and I think had quite an impact on my career after that.

(Ruth, Functional, Care)

Perhaps not surprisingly, though, for those who did not have the same access, such programmes could be seen as too selective, over-emphasizing self-presentation and style and divorced from the 'real work' of management. Consequently, although seen as positive and valuable experiences, such programmes did attract some scepticism.

A similar degree of scepticism was evident in views expressed about the GMTS. Although highly regarded for the grounding it gave graduates, it was not considered as valuable in giving graduates the 'hands-on' experience they ultimately needed to manage. Views on the GMTS were not just restricted to those 8 managers (5 in Acute and 3 in Specialist) who had come through that route. For example:

I've worked with a number of graduates now, probably four or five in my time. I've got one who was very, very good, and he's sat next door in there now as one of my senior managers . . . He seemed to be able to do what a lot of the graduate trainees couldn't; and that was communicate with other human beings. A lot of them seem not to be able to do that.

(Greg, General, Acute)

On the other hand, it was seen as extremely useful in helping prospective managers gain a wider range of experiences of their organization and of the sector:

One of the big things they tell you pretty much on day one is that one of the main focuses on the Graduate Scheme is networking . . . We attended loads of events where there'd be directors of finance there, chief execs, and . . . you're encouraged to network . . . It's like a skill that you can't really learn, it's just a case of doing it.

(Thomas, Functional, Specialist)

This socialization into networking was particularly the case for those in functional specialist areas (finance, HR, estates, IT) who relied more heavily upon the network of professional contacts they were able to develop who shared a common orientation to the healthcare sector.

Together these factors suggest that training opportunities provided some potential for the development of appropriate management skills and expertise. However, there were real tensions in the ways in which training was designed and how it was delivered and received. Quite apart from the more practical issues associated with the value of particular sessions or types of training and the difficulties in scheduling them into busy managerial schedules, there were clearly challenges in developing training programmes that suited middle management needs and which provide them with the timely opportunities they needed to help them gain both practical insights and opportunities for reflective learning.

I think I've learned more on the job than anywhere else . . . There are times you are managing the situation and you think, now what did I learn on that management course? . . . Maybe that just says something about the quality of the courses I've been on? But I don't know . . . It would be great to have something that you could go away to and would help you quickly.

(Robert, Clinical, Care)

Returning to the importance of experience, there were clearly limits as well on how well formal training and development could furnish managers with the expertise and skills they felt they needed and could relate to their day-to-day practice. There was, however, a perceived value in training that was focused on emotional and social development.

Summary

Despite a good deal of variation in the clinical and managerial backgrounds and experience of managers within the study, as well as some significant differences between the trusts that have been identified and examined, what was perhaps most striking when we consider the mobilization of management knowledge was the overall consistency in orientation towards various forms of management knowledge and management learning processes. Five key themes have emerged from this chapter that relate to the mobilization of management knowledge by healthcare managers.

First, it has shown the continued influence of clinical expertise and clinical thinking upon management knowledge, counteracted only really through the power of financial management discourse. While some clinical knowledge and experience was necessary (if not always sufficient) to establish the credibility and credentials of managers, it also shaped their ways of framing and thinking about managerial problems in more subtle, indirect ways. At the same time, financial management imperatives were probably the only real countervailing influence that managers could try to harness to enhance their independent influence. While this might, in turn, shape management thinking and practice, it also inevitably favoured the influence of that particular specialist management group, as well as reinforced corporate discourse centred upon the need for efficiency improvements (cf. Armstrong, 1987). Second, the continued challenges faced in translating and embedding more abstract management knowledge into healthcare settings were also quite apparent (cf. Waring and Bishop, 2010; McCann et al., 2015; Hyde et al., 2016). At the same time, there was still clearly some scope for using that knowledge in more subtle and catalytic (even cathartic) ways to prompt more strategic and different management thinking. Third, the very strong influence on management practice of 'home grown' knowledge was also a key influence. That was driven by formal reporting requirements and embedded in standardized systems and practices. These were sometimes imported directly from other healthcare institutions and reinforced by the comparative longevity of healthcare managers in the NHS and their individual trusts (see table 3.5 in Chapter 3). Fourth, the crucial importance to managers of individual experience and the very strong continuing emphasis upon personally embodied management knowledge was also apparent—particularly that embodied in the knowledge base and skill sets of hybrid managers. Finally, it was apparent that the formal training and development programmes that managers had access to often fell short of delivering the kind of knowledge prized by managers, in a format which suited their careers and daily job responsibilities.

Taken together, what these findings point to is a significant tension between, on the one hand, calls for the use of more leading-edge (codified) managerial knowledge by healthcare managers (e.g. Bate and Robert, 2002; Kings Fund, 2011); and on the other hand, the principal ways in which healthcare managers actually engage in knowing and learning. That is, managers tend instead to defer to more clinical ways of thinking with one eye firmly set on financial imperatives, while at the same time, having to resort to standardized, bureaucratic reporting system requirements, while privileging individual know-how and on-the-job learning. Despite the limitations of formal training and development programmes, what was still valued by many, however, was the opportunity to socialize, to network and to be socialized as healthcare managers. To examine these processes in more detail, we turn next to a consideration of the networks that managers accessed and made use of in their conscious attempts at networking.

7   Managers Networking

> If you just look around a trust like this, you've got people with experience in practically everything and anything you can think of, but we don't use it. We don't, because of our failure to network with one another and use other people's skills and knowledge and understanding, we just don't use it. You've got all these people with all this knowledge and we don't use it, and we don't manage to tap into it . . . We're so busy trying to keep afloat that we just don't look forward.
>
> (Greg, General, Acute)

Introduction

The quote above indicates the perceived potential latent within the NHS, in terms of breadth and depth of knowledge and experience, both clinical and managerial, and the frustration felt when this potential goes unfulfilled. This final main aspect of the study addresses the issue of networks and networking, a theme which complements and connects with the preceding discussions of management/leadership, management identity and management knowledge. Network relationships are the predominant way knowledge and understandings are shared across professional and organizational boundaries in a large and diverse 'meta-organization' (Ahrne and Brunsson, 2005) such as the NHS. Networks, in a more formal sense, have also been seen as the organizational solution to providing an integrated service across organizational and professional boundaries, through the establishment of managed networks connecting fields of practice or patient pathways (Edwards, 2002). As a consequence, there has been substantial healthcare management research interest in recent years on network organizations, social network analysis, and also in related concepts, including communities of practice and social capital (Braithwaite, 2010, 2015; Griffiths et al., 2012; Ferlie et al., 2013).

This chapter builds on the previous discussions of managerial roles, identity and knowledge and will consider the role, prospects and limitations of networks and networking in healthcare. In doing so, the research is not concerned with mapping the dimensions of particular formal networks,

but instead approaches the theme through examining managerial perceptions and experiences of networking, as a practice, covering both the formal
and informal relations in which they are embedded. As such, a deliberately
broad scope of enquiry has been chosen: the focus is not on specific professional, intra-organizational or even inter-organizational networks and
networking; instead, an attempt is made to encompass all forms of network relations, including non-work networks and relationships which are
not primarily functional or goal-driven in a conventional sense. This broad
range of networks observed in the study will then be described and catego-
rized, before addressing the deeper question of how and why healthcare
managers network. The study suggests four broad reasons for networking:
for knowledge, for support, for career development and for influence—
although, as will be seen, these motives may overlap and both synergies and
conflicts exist between them. At the same time, there are several features of
the modern NHS which effectively impede or undermine networking. We
discuss these in detail before concluding by reviewing the importance of
networking in the sector and the distinctive way the various management
groups attempt to form and benefit from networks—not only to enhance
their effectiveness and resilience as managers, but also to forge the kind of
collective communities that might secure greater occupational/professional
security and legitimacy.

Understanding Networks in Healthcare

The late 20th century saw a wave of interest in the notion of the network across social, managerial and organizational research, best exempli-
fied by Manuel Castells' claim in *The Rise of the Network Society* that
"networks constitute the new social morphology of our societies" (1996:
500). Much of this work rests on the recognition of the importance of
knowledge and knowledge flows across society, business and culture,
and the concomitant need for flexibility and speed of action. Networks
are thus seen as highly dynamic and fluid systems of inter-related nodes,
capable of rapid expansion or adaptation. The model of the network has
been used to represent and analyze a vast array of social phenomena: as
methodological tools to understand the functioning of communities and
society (Putnam, 2001); as designs for new and more effective organizations (Miles and Snow, 1986); as models to account for the vital flows of
knowledge within and between contexts, organizations and communities
(Brown and Duguid, 2000); and as the solution to the failings of markets
and bureaucracy (Powell, 1990).

It is the last of these virtues which explains the particular attraction of
the network concept to healthcare, and in particular the NHS. As noted in
Chapter 2, the evolution of the NHS has been described as moving between
distinct eras, marked by efforts to replace the classic bureaucracy of the NHS
with a new emphasis on competition and market relations, enshrined in the

creation of the internal market separated into 'purchasers' and 'providers' in 1991. While the reforms of the Labour government between 1997–2010 sought to moderate the internal market, this involved a reinvention of managerialism through governance in the form of national targets and local performance management (Exworthy et al., 1999; Kirkpatrick, 1999). Given this history, it is unsurprising that interest should focus on networks in an attempt to break the sterile oscillation between markets and bureaucracy. Hence many describe a move from hierarchical 'command and control' to a reliance on (quasi-)market relations, followed by a more recent move in the last fifteen years towards a networked collaborative model (Powell and DiMaggio, 1991; Kickert et al., 1997; Exworthy et al., 1999; Sullivan and Skelcher, 2002)—not only in healthcare, but across the UK public sector (Clarence and Painter, 1998; Newman, 2001). Globally, similar shifts have been observed in the reform of the public sector (e.g. in the US: Goldsmith and Eggers, 2004; in Europe: Kickert et al., 1997). Networks have been proposed as a means to traverse boundaries and reconnect a fragmented and complex healthcare system (6 et al., 2006), and to produce solutions to the kind of 'wicked problems' encountered in modern healthcare (Ferlie et al., 2013). The current financial pressures upon public services, including healthcare (McKee et al., 2002; Fulop et al., 2012), have lent further weight to such calls.

In practice, the implications of this shift in healthcare include enthusiasm for new working arrangements such as distributed leadership (Buchanan et al., 2007) and formal or informal knowledge brokerage (Burgess and Currie, 2013). In parallel, there is renewed interest in the relevance of communities of practice (Wenger, 1998; Bate and Robert, 2002). In particular, communities of practice are networks where members learn collectively and are at the same time socialized into a common way of thinking and acting through frequent and face-to-face social interactions. Increasingly popular in 'post-bureaucratic' private sector organizations, it is argued that communities of practice enhance knowledge sharing and knowledge creation among members across divisional, organizational and even sectoral boundaries. They have had some significant impact in healthcare research and practice, principally in the deliberate formation of formal, managed networks of practitioners, sometimes referred to as *networks of practice* (Agterberg et al., 2010). A key example would be the establishment of managed clinical networks consisting of "linked groups of health professionals and organizations from primary, secondary and tertiary care working in a coordinated manner, unconstrained by existing professional and organizational boundaries to ensure equitable provision of high quality effective services" (Edwards, 2002: 63).

Rather than identifying networks in advance, and exploring their nature and use, the approach adopted in this study was to ask individual managers themselves about their network relationships, emphasizing a broad rather than a narrow scope of enquiry. In this way, the aim was to avoid the widespread preoccupation in health management literature, noted by Ferlie et al. (2010), with formal or 'managed' networks. As a consequence, the analysis is not only concerned with formal, structured, closed and centralized networks; it also seeks to consider informal, loose, open and flat or distributed networks—such as friendship and affinity groups, or highly dispersed communities bound by 'weak ties' (Granovetter, 1973). Similarly, the research does not adopt a sociometric approach to networks, attempting to quantify network relationships by measuring the frequency and duration of contact (as is common in social network analysis, for instance). The approach adopted here focuses less on counting and measuring the incidence of networks, and more upon understanding the "situated and contextual quality of relationships" (Anderson-Gough et al., 2006: 236)—in terms of the nature and significance of networks and the specific practices of networking undertaken by our interviewees.

Locating Networks in Practice

As a consequence of the methodological approach adopted, a wide range and variety of networks were identified and explored through the interviews and the ethnographic encounters. Table 7.1 summarizes the main categories of network discussed and analyzed throughout the study.

This typology is not intended to be exclusive, exhaustive or abstract—rather, it is deliberately drawn from the descriptions of interviewees themselves. So, for some, their operational networks—those people who they relate to routinely in the performance of their roles—may also be a professional network (of accountants, for instance) or an elite network (of fellow directors or divisional heads). This point will be returned to below when we address network multiplexity. This list does, however, start to draw out some broad distinctions—between intra-organizational and extra-organizational networks, open and closed networks, and work and personal networks, for example.

In parallel, these networks may themselves be differentiated along a number of different dimensions, such as the degree of co-ordination, strictures on membership, the way in which the network was formed and its location within or across organizational boundaries (see table 7.2). The kind of dimensions set out here reflect those adopted in other typologies of healthcare networks which typically depict a continuum between 'loose' and 'tight' networks (cf. Marsh and Rhodes, 1992; Ferlie et al., 2010), differentiated in a 2 × 2 matrix by level of integration and by level of regulation (6 et al., 2005). The dimensions do not, and could not, neatly correspond to the typology of networks in table 7.2. For instance, alumni networks could range from the relatively formal (prescribed action learning sets) to the informal (loose affiliations of friends who socialized together); some elite networks were described as highly instrumental, built on engineered introductions and self-promotion, while others seemed relatively organic,

Table 7.1 Typology of Networks

Nature of Network	Description
Academic/ Scientific	Links to universities, research or scientific bodies
Alumni	Connections made through participation in a specific training or educational programme which persists beyond end of programme
Peer/Cohort	Relationships formed with others who joined this (or another) organization at the same time
Commercial/3rd Sector	Links to private sector organizations or charities
Elite	Connections to senior decision-makers, within the trust/ organization or at a regional/national level
Functional Specialist	Relationships or collectivities bound by a shared work specialism
Government	Relationships with individuals within regional or national government
Managerial	Relationships between groups of managers, including both occupational networks and more operational groups
Mentor	One-to-one relationships with a formal or informal mentor, typically but not necessarily outside the organization
NHS	Connections to individuals in other NHS organizations, including SHAs/PCTs, GPs/CCGs, etc.
Operational/ Clinical	Relationships typically formed through the day-to-day execution of responsibilities
Personal	Friendships, non-work relationships, family connections, etc.
Professional	Links with general or health-specific formal professional bodies, in accounting, HR, facilities, health and safety, etc.
Public Sector	Non-governmental public connections, with for instance schools, legal bodies (e.g. coroners), prisons, armed forces, BBC
Political	Networks specifically cultivated to develop influence— typically diverse in composition, hence not captured by other categories

Table 7.2 Dimensions of Networks

Structure	Formal	Informal
Co-ordination	Tight	Loose
Membership	Closed	Open
Formation	Instrumental	Organic
Position	Internal to organization	External to organization

resulting from a shared interest or an accidental social connection. A small minority of categories of network were largely homogeneous in terms of their dimensions: personal networks were generally organic, informal, loose and external in scope; while most professional networks were closed and relatively formal. Nonetheless, the dimensions provided a means to differentiate particular networks, and also to identify similarities between networks which on the surface were very different in composition and nature.

This analysis of networks by type and using these dimensions revealed key aspects of the different organizations examined, and also served to highlight the differences between the management groups. For instance, managers in the Care trust made most frequent reference to external (extra-organizational) networks, reflecting the multiple connections in their work between different primary, secondary and community health bodies. By contrast, in the Acute trust, markedly fewer references were made to networks of any kind, internal or external. This reflected the overall size of the organization and perhaps, in part, its more functional and bureaucratic organizational structure (when compared with the fluidity of service delivery in the Care trust).

With regard to the pattern of networks discussed by the three management groups, it was unsurprising to see that functional managers relied most heavily upon their professional or functional specialist networks, and enjoyed connections to some powerful elite networks either through these professional associations or by their representation of a professional area at board level. To a lesser degree, clinical managers also retained important network contacts through their clinical or scientific professional associations. In some cases, they were clearly active and highly committed (in the case of medical directors, for example). In other cases, their involvement was more latent (as in membership of a nursing body retained as a career to fall back on, or as a way to retain legitimacy when managing clinicians). While the background of some general managers enabled them to participate in clinical or professional networks, more typically they would rely upon networks established through day-to-day operations, which were necessarily less formal. They also tended to be less enduring, due to the disruptions brought about by organizational change. A substantial number of the general managers spoke with feeling of the perceptible absence of supportive networks in their role, compared to their clinical and functional counterparts, a point returned to below.

While the networks identified and discussed helped to corroborate and enrich understanding of the management groups and the organizations in which they worked, this analysis necessarily delivers a rather static and structural understanding of how managers are positioned within network relations. To go beyond this and understand how and why managers engaged—or did not engage—with particular networks, it was necessary to explore more qualitatively how they discussed not simply their networks, but rather the activity of networking.

From Networks to Networking

While much has been written about the nature of networks since the seminal work of Granovetter (1973), the focus in the vast majority of this work is predominantly on the structure and composition of the network itself. The act of networking itself, by contrast, has been rather neglected, in favour of sophisticated mapping of network ties, structural holes and the like. As Scarbrough et al. (2014: 110) note:

> Research to date has tended to view networks primarily in structural terms, as channels, conduits or 'pipelines' through which knowledge is transferred. The more limited research available, focusing on networking processes, crucially establishes that networks are not static, but are dynamic and evolving as circumstances unfold. Yet relatively little attention has been paid to understanding and explaining the social and political processes underpinning the formation and effectiveness of network relationships.

As a consequence, "we know surprisingly little about the strategies individuals employ when networking, and in particular the underlying agency mechanisms involved" (Bensaou et al., 2014: 29). To address this gap, we seek here not only to consider the nature and dimensions of networks, but also to consider the relations, motivations and actions that shape, sustain and constrain an individual's participation in these networks.

Exploring such social practices in networks brings the study into contact with concepts used to explain activity and even 'success' in network building, such as the notion of social capital (Coleman, 1988). Social capital is frequently drawn upon to focus on the characteristics of the individual within the network rather than the network itself; at times it is used to ascribe a value to the individual in terms of their 'social connectedness'. Nahapiet and Ghoshal (1998: 243), for instance, define it as "the sum of the actual and potential resources embedded within, available through, and derived from the network of relationships possessed by an individual or social unit." While this turns the spotlight on the individual rather than the network, and links with studies which highlight the characteristics of 'good' networkers (Ferlie and Pettigrew, 1996; de Janasz and Forret, 2008) for others, such as Burt, social capital is nonetheless an effect of network positioning: "social capital explains how people do better because they are somehow better connected with other people. . . . One's position in the structure of these exchanges can be an asset in its own right." (Burt, 2005: 4). This concept certainly informs our analysis—the extent to which individuals rely upon networks to help them to achieve any of a number of goals informs our understanding of how management knowledge flows, as well as the formation of managerial identity. The danger, however, of prioritizing social capital is that the notion of capital prioritizes the economic aspects of social relationships, and frames these primarily in terms of "economic exchange, possession and organizational effectiveness" (Anderson-Gough et al., 2006: 236) while neglecting the less-instrumental reasons why individuals forge relationships: for emotional closeness, affirmation of self and identity, the reassurance of belonging in a community, etc. For this reason, social capital is not the primary way in which we have approached networks and networking in this study. Although we are attentive to the impact of networks in terms of individual and organizational effectiveness, it is not assumed a priori that this is the sole purpose or predominant consequence of networks. In practice, this required a broad and open approach to the topic in interviews; rather than speaking directly of 'your networks' and 'your networking', the issue was approached obliquely, with question such as 'who do you turn to with a work-related problem?'

Below, the discussion then focuses specifically on networking as an activity—the conduct of individuals to establish and maintain enduring relationships and the process by which networks are created, supported and sustained. The interviews revealed four motives for networking across our healthcare managers, although discussion of each varied substantially between trust and between management group. The key motives were:

1   Networking for knowledge
2   Networking for support
3   Networking for career advancement
4   Networking for influence

Through analysis of interview transcripts, it was possible to quantify the frequency with which references were made in the interviews to reasons for networking. It was clear from this analysis that, overwhelmingly, the main purpose of networking among our interviewees was to acquire knowledge. Over half of the references to networking motives in the interviews related the activity specifically to knowledge acquisition, either actively or passively. Around a quarter of the references were made to the value of their network connections in providing personal, emotional support. The remainder were roughly equally split between those referring to the value of networking in terms of career management (14 percent of references), and those referring to the active use of networking in order to influence policy, decisions or behaviour in or beyond the organization (9 percent).

Discussion of each of these motives varied significantly between organizations and also between management groups. So, for instance, discussions of networking for support were dominated by contributions from managers at the Care trust, while this motive was relatively rarely mentioned in the Specialist or Acute trusts. Similarly, managers in the Care trust were substantially more likely to discuss networking for knowledge than their peers in the other two organizations. When comparing the different types of manager across the trusts, the differences were less pronounced, although networking for knowledge was much more frequently discussed by managers with a clinical background than by the other groups of managers. One striking difference also emerged between male and female managers: male managers were twice as likely as female managers to discuss networking for career or influence, while female managers were more likely to mention networks as a source of personal support.

Before discussing these motives in detail, it is important to introduce a methodological caveat on the incidence of references to each motive, as noted above. That is, the frequency with which each motive was discussed by a particular group, or within a particular trust, does not necessarily equate to the frequency with which individuals engaged in this behaviour, or even the importance of this behaviour to them. Critically, interviewees may have only discussed motives which were felt to be 'legitimate' to discuss in their particular organization or environment. This may particularly affect discussions of networking for support, or networking for career. Rather than this representing a limitation, however, this constitutes one of the strengths of the qualitative research methodology: the frequency with which each motive was discussed provides insight not only into the practices and orientation of each interviewee but also, inevitably, reflects to some degree the norms of their cultural, organizational and professional environment and their socialization in abiding by such norms. This theme will be expanded on below as we deal with each particular dimension of networking.

Networking for Knowledge

The primary purpose of networking, for almost all managers interviewed, was to acquire or share knowledge. As noted in the previous chapter, conceptions of 'knowledge' among the managers interviewed was varied, informed by their particular clinical/non-clinical background, the cultural norms within their organizations and their experiences of training and development. What was common, however, was a recognition of the difficulty of translating knowledge from one context to another, and given the weight afforded to experience over codified knowledge, a faith in learning directly from others in the same organization or sector of healthcare.

Hence, it is perhaps unsurprising to see a reliance on networking for knowledge. Widely discussed across all three trusts and all management groups, this was mentioned with particular regularity by managers with some clinical background. There were, however, significant differences in how this was understood or practiced, a key distinction existing between passive and active networking for knowledge. Passive networking for knowledge largely related to partaking in events, or membership of formal or informal groups, networks or associations. This was in order to be broadly informed about new or potential changes in policy, or to scan a community for new ideas which might be transferable, or indeed to learn lessons from failed initiatives elsewhere. We refer to this more passive activity as *peripheral awareness*, primarily to differentiate it from the more active networking for knowledge discussed below.

> The secret is always having the ability to look over the garden fence and see what's happening in somebody else's garden. Because that's the only way you learn. And you might learn something you don't want to learn. You know what I mean, you might see something you don't want to see. But also, from all this variety, as I've said before, why reinvent the wheel? Why do it?
>
> (Adrian, Functional, Specialist)

Active networking for knowledge we refer to as *problem-solving*. Here, interviewees discuss the value of networks and networking in terms of providing a resource for the pursuit of intentional enquiries or searches for information in order to fix a particular challenge or problem faced in everyday practice. This targeted problem-solving networking was typically related more closely to networks based around a particular specialism, operational or clinical networks. In many cases, such networks were specifically formed to facilitate such activities:

> The Clinical Leaders' network tends to start off with a general presentation and then you'll get into your area networks . . . [Town A, B and C] might sit as a sort of subgroup within the network and then you'd bounce off your problems from your colleagues and sort of see whether you could learn anything from others' experiences.
>
> (Hugh, General, Acute)

Similarly, various specialist functional networks, dedicated to particular occupational or professional groups, such as finance and human resource management, were able to take advantage of the size of the NHS to maximize learning opportunities.

> We only meet once a year, and we go round the table, at the end of the meeting, and it might be what we're doing here. And then you might say, "Well, I've got a problem with so-and-so", and this guy over here will say, "Well, hang on, I did that last year". And it's all very informal, but it doesn't half bring it out.
>
> (Adrian, Functional, Specialist)

Less formal, structured problem-solving networks included the action learning sets established on many development programmes. Those formed during the GMTS were highlighted by a number of interviewees, building on the strong group relationships formed during extended training and induction programmes:

> I still stay in touch pretty much weekly with probably 15 others [from the GMTS] . . . If there's a problem, we'll put it out there, you know, email it out . . . I'd say that is one of my key networks.
>
> (Thomas, Functional, Specialist)

This knowledge sharing, then, is supported strongly by the establishment of trust, underpinned frequently by long-term personal relationships and affiliations outside of the work environment. One interviewee captured this well, describing a relationship established on a training programme where a conversation about childcare challenges provided the basis for a personal relationship with tangible benefits for work-related knowledge sharing:

> My 'challenging situation' [discussed at a leadership course] was my five-year old at home at bedtime, but it felt a safe environment to have those discussions. And actually, the lady that ran the course, I emailed her three nights after and said, "You know, I tried X, Y and Z and, you know, woohoo, it's working!" . . . And I've now got an email relationship with this lady that, if I did have a problem in work, I'd find it really easy to just pick up the phone and say "Jacqueline, you know, I've tried this, what do you think?" Rather than an outside agency or a consultancy that once they've gone, they've gone.
>
> (Gloria, General, Acute)

Although, in principle, networking for knowledge was the most instrumental and practical mode of networking, it frequently had a complementary relationship with other, less pragmatic modes of networking, an issue returned to below.

Networking for Support

Networking for support represented the second most cited motive for forming and maintaining networks—the reliance on such relationships for emotional reassurance, personal validation, consolation or the expression of feelings outside of the immediate work context. The incidence of this theme was noteworthy, as it was mentioned by almost half of those interviewed. It was most commonly mentioned in the Care trust and much less so in the Acute trust. This substantial variation may result again from the perceived greater legitimacy of such therapeutic discourses in the Care setting and/or the relative formality of the culture at the Acute trust, where such discussions could be seen as inappropriate. As such, it may not have fully reflected the actual incidence of this form of networking. Discussions of networking for support were also complicated at times by the reluctance of some interviewees to define such relationships as a 'network'—these were friend-ships, often long-standing personal relationships which may be quite sepa-rate from their job role. For some, perceiving these as a network attributed an instrumentality to them which seemed inappropriate.

What was striking was the importance attached to such networks. Man-agers frequently discussed how difficult it would be to survive in a pres-surized and often emotionally challenging role without a strong support network, which might include current or former colleagues, friends, family members or more formal and explicit arrangements with mentors, peers, members of action learning sets, etc.

> We meet weekly. We talk about what's going on or we have a moan about something, but often it's helpful just to have a moan about some-thing with someone that you're comfortable to do that, rather than it becoming winding you up . . . She'll say: "what are you getting worried and stressed about that for?" . . . I have gone: "have you heard what they've done?" But she just kind of goes: "it will all get sorted" . . . We bring each other down at times.
>
> (Carl, Functional, Care)

Descriptions of this form of networking ranged from the clearly emotional—as a safe place for 'venting' emotions or 'having a moan' outside of the work context and as a relationship which enabled someone to remain 'grounded'; to the more functional—as a kind of 'informal coaching', or a place to get 'objective comment' on one's decisions and actions. This distinc-tion was not a clear-cut one, however, and this reinforces the importance of relational attributes such as trust and interpersonal understanding for effec-tive knowledge sharing or meaningful advice. Equally, some descriptions emphasized the performative benefits of emotional support, as enhancing managers' personal resilience and therefore their ability to do the job well—or to stay in the job at all.

Frequently, networking for support was mentioned as a secondary issue in interviews—as something beneficial for the individual but less important than the acquisition of knowledge to improve practice. Many represented networking for support as a positive, perhaps unintentional, by-product of more formal networking (for knowledge, for example). In many situations, such relationships formed as a result of joint participation in a training or development programme, but often extended beyond the lifetime of the pro-gramme itself. For example:

> Going back to the Athena course, that has been invaluable because it's not only making the connection and networking to start with and meet-ing up and speaking to each other. At any point at any time I can think "oh god I'm not really sure about this." Gemma in Bedford, she might have an idea about that . . . We can just email each other, ring each other

and that's really beneficial. I think it's really important. Some days it could be just "oh god I'm having a crap day." It could be just an offload, but it's at the right level. I couldn't do that to my matrons, although I have great relationships with my matrons it wouldn't be appropriate. And equally you don't want to go to your Divisional Director. It's about professional pride, not because I don't get on with them.

(Nina, Clinical, Specialist)

As the above quote suggests, often the importance of external networks—separate from the organization or immediate working surroundings—was stressed, given the need for confidentiality and the need to maintain a professional bearing with work colleagues. Indeed, it seems that the absence of such relationships could reinforce the more dehumanizing aspects of working in a large organization:

I think that no matter how well you think you've set your network up . . . there are occasions when you can feel quite isolated in a trust as big as this. And you can't imagine who you could go to and just actually say that without it escalating into something that's really taken out of all proportions.

(Elena, General, Care)

Broadly speaking this more defensive aspect of networking for support is frequently ignored or under-represented in research in this area. The last quote above hints at a highly regulated organizational and institutional environment—or at least an environment where there is a pervasive sense that one might be under surveillance (cf. Foucault, 1977). In this form of networking then we find an important potential means in which managers could recover a temporary sense of privacy or anonymity.

Networking for Career

The role of networking in supporting the career advancement of managers was discussed by less than a third of those interviewed. For this form of networking, the need to be informed about new opportunities and openings coexisted with the perceived importance of being known by key decision-makers. Given the diversity of positions, organizations and career structures, it was noticeable that this motive was cited consistently across all three trusts and across all management groups. A number of interviewees also pointed to the emphasis placed upon encouraging this mode of networking by key management and leadership development programmes in the NHS;

One of the big things they tell you pretty much on day one is that one of the main focuses on the Graduate Scheme is networking . . . We attended loads of events where there'd be sort of like the directors of finance there, chief execs, and you know, it was always kind of like you're encouraged to network.

(Thomas, Functional, Specialist)

Networking for career development was practiced either collectively or individually. Collectively, career networking typically relied on membership of particular communities or participation at key events such as research conferences or senior training programmes where a manager could raise her or his profile and establish a personal reputation, while at the same time making personal connections to individuals.

I came and talked about my involvement in lean methodology within the Trust and how we'd made some powerful changes that led to some high quality impacts within the services. So I presented here, and then following that was kind of networked into the organization, and then they created a job and approached me to apply.

(Glen, Clinical, Care)

Individually, career networking often seemed to build upon some kind of formal or informal mentorship arrangement. Several interviewees were quite open about the importance of approaching career networking tactically, to ensure mentoring connections were made with influential individuals and with a long-term career strategy in mind.

I was very keen to come back to this organization after the training scheme. And as a ploy, as a tactic in me trying to do that. My mentor whilst I was on the training scheme was X, who's now the acting Chief Exec here. And I kept my contacts from when I was working here previously, and then obviously heard that there was a new Associate Director that was coming into this business group and I arranged to meet with him fairly early on as well. So certainly having that network and the training scheme, drumming it into you to make sure that you network with as many people as possible. I think that's true in one sense, but I think it's also about networking with the right people at the right time, and it's just picking your opportunities and just being a little bit cute about who you speak to and who you make your networks with.

(Stewart, General, Acute)

As with the notion of networking for support, there is often a sensitivity to suggestions that this might be behaviour which is in some sense inauthentic, instrumental or even manipulative. Several interviewees expressed deep reservations over the perceived need to network for career advancement; or some discomfort in engaging with what they understand as self-promotional or inauthentic behaviour.

> There's a lot of people on this course that ask a question for question's sake and they do the mingling on the tables at dinner. Every time they got up to ask a question, they'd get up just to say their name and say where they came from. . . . I still find it strange now.
>
> (Danielle, Functional, Specialist)

Reflecting this sensitivity, several interviewees who described themselves as engaging in career networking either denied that their career progression was dependent on their social capital, or argued that any career networking was marginal in its impact and that their own networking was unintentional or not strategic.

> I was interested in the work-life balance thing . . . and he recommended X [as a mentor], who's the Director here [laugh]. Yeah, so I had quite a long relationship with him. It was very much like me and him . . . I didn't get this job because of that, I'm pretty confident of that [laugh]. He's told me that, and if you've met him, he's not the sort of bloke who'd lie about that.
>
> (Thomas, Functional, Specialist)

On the other hand, particularly for those who had joined the NHS in mid or late career, the absence career networking could be perceived as an impediment to their career progression:

> My colleagues that have been in the organization with the NHS for 20 years plus, because they've moved around jobs . . . people they trained with [are] also now directors of nursing somewhere else. So because they've grown up in the NHS [they've accrued that kind of network anyway]. And I haven't!
>
> (Hugh, General, Acute)

Importantly, career networking has value not just for the individual but also for the group or organization. Some interviewees described how their strong networks enabled them to identify and attract higher quality recruits.

> You need a network, you can't function without a network . . . I've got a lot more from doing things and building up those networks. It's like the graduate trainees. I've had a lot who've ended up here, in years past, without even me actually applying, because they know that the training they'll get is the right training and they know that I'll look after them . . . If you look at it another way, and this sounds quite cold, I've got a free member of staff for three years, virtually,

who is going to add value to the organization who, ultimately, could be a permanent member of staff. And that's just from spending a little time networking.

(Jessica, Functional, Acute)

Overall, this particular practice was highly valued, despite deep ambivalence about the practice in some quarters, and a widespread recognition among those who engaged in career networking that it required sophisticated interpersonal skills to enact successfully.

Networking for Influence

The specific use of networking in order to secure some influence over a decision or behaviour in another organizational location was the least common outcome or intention of networking in the study, mentioned by only 11 interviewees. However, those interviewees who discussed networking for influence frequently spoke at some length and detail about this approach to networking, particularly within the Care trust where service delivery was more fragmented and where there was more reliance on networks of connections than in the other trusts.

Networking for influence was typically undertaken deliberately, consciously and strategically, and those who described themselves as networking for influence typically emphasized this as vitally important, for themselves and often for their field/area of activity/division. Ross, a general manager in the Care trust, epitomized this approach:

Networks: they're fundamental to me. They're absolutely the actual core of how I approach my work . . . It's not just some kind of pleasurable experience, I engage with a network approach to management, because I think it gives you the best chances of delivering things.

(Ross, General, Care)

In terms of networking practices, a broad distinction could be made between networking based upon a reciprocal exchange of favours; and a broader attempt to act to push or represent a particular agenda through links with senior management, key role-holders or influential external parties. Ross at the Care trust summarized both of these as parallel activities, describing part of his approach as building reciprocal favours, or "just scratching each other's backs", and another as strategically representing a set of interests ("having a cup of tea with the chief exec, it's purely about me making sure he doesn't forget about the agenda here"). In each case, this involved deliberately maintaining a list of useful and influential contacts across a wide network—one interviewee mentioned having "a little secret map in my mind of who I think is sound around this place" or "the fullest black book of contacts of any of my peers".

Many of those who engaged in networking for influence were passionate about its importance, and contrasted their activity here with other colleagues who were politically naïve and therefore less effective as a manager. So, for instance, Christian described his role in enhancing the political skills of staff in his area:

> X sent a guy to me a while ago who was new, and she said to him, "You just don't get politics. You don't know how to operate." She sent him to spend some time with me to talk through how to play the game here— it's the same where you work and the same where everybody works.
>
> (Christian, General, Acute)

Effective networking for influence, then, relies partially upon a particular understanding of organizations and relationships, a specific set of interpersonal skills to effectively build up influence and crucially, time spent in a particular field, as all of those involved described the process of building up contacts as one which was lengthy and time consuming.

Multiplex Networking

Collectively, then, these distinct motives for networking affect the way in which different managers engage with the act of networking, with implications for their own understanding of what it means to be an effective manager, subordinate, colleague, business contact or friend. In engaging in different kinds of activity, managers connect with different kinds of communities, which in turn reinforces their self-identity in different ways.

It is important to note, however, that although these motives were identifiably distinctive, in the actual practice of networking—introducing oneself to a colleague, forwarding an email, attending a conference—individuals might be driven by a combination of motives. Indeed, the same activity might have resulted in a combination of outcomes which do not fit neatly into any one of the categories described above. In network research, this aspect of relationships may be defined as *multiplexity*, a term used to describe "a link between two actors in a network that consists of more than one kind of relationship" (Heebels et al., 2013: 704). As such, multiplexity has important implications for the embodiment of one's positionality and the formation and maintenance of ties, rather than the accumulated product of those ties (see discussion above). A recognition of multiplexity also helps to explain the earlier noted difficulty of developing a singular and consistent typology of networks, as any network may be at one and the same time a combination of different types of networks—an elite network which is also a personal network, for instance; or a network of one type may evolve over time into another. In drawing on this approach, we hope to address the critique of Heebels et al. (2013: 702) and others, who point to the neglect in organization studies of "the emotional aspects or the multiplex motives for the formation and maintenance of personal ties." As discussed above, while much research on networks relates to the accumulated product of networking, our interest here is in the collective and embodied experience of networking, and the implications this has for individuals' different characterizations of network. This, in turn, draws attention to issues of ethics and instrumentality in networking, given that it is an activity which "contain(s) powerful moral understandings and personal commitments" (Bensaou et al., 2014: 53).

Similarly, the practice of networking may be multiplex in its motivation and meaning, and this also relates to notions of authenticity or instrumentalism. So, for instance, interviewees described personal relationships outside of their organization which they found valuable for personal support in times of stress, but also mentioned that these personal networks also provided knowledge (in the form of professional or occupational advice) as well as reassurance or comfort. Similarly, many mentor relationships were primarily seen as focused on acquiring knowledge, in terms of learning from the experience of a senior colleague. But these relationships also frequently led to offers of employment or information about vacant posts and recommendations of interest to the person being mentored. So, in various ways, the four motives for networking—for knowledge, for support, for influence and for career advancement—interrelated in that they frequently complemented and supported each other.

To examine this multiplexity in more detail, we considered specific examples of situations where networking served more than one purpose, to identify areas where motivations overlapped. Particular complementarities appeared key in the accounts of managers. First, several identified a strong overlap between networking for support and for knowledge. For example:

> I have a colleague from X, kind of a mutual mentor that I've carried on all these years, because I left there in 2006. So we meet up every couple of months. But that's not about solving specific problems. That's about just getting through it. I mean the whole period of the organizational restructure in here I value very much having someone, like you say, a confidante, that I could just say how it really was and how awful it was . . . She put in various different ideas and suggestions which was food for thought, but that's my own kind of deliberately set up mechanism for doing that.
>
> (Ruth, Functional, Care)

What is striking here is the underpinning trust relationship which is formed as the two colleagues become mutual confidantes and informal counsellors; but how this personal knowledge enables more informed and insightful advice to be offered, based on a deep mutual understanding of each other's personalities and respective situations.

Similarly, interviewees discussed the potential complementarity between networking for support and influence, again based on the establishment of a personal relationship of trust, explaining how doing a favour for a previous service user provided an opening to ask for a testimonial for their service:

> That's the kind of example of just scratching each other's backs and things that develop out of relationships. He wouldn't have had that conversation with me unless he knew me. I wouldn't have had that conversation with him. Even though my directorate was, you know, scrabbling around, desperate for testimonials, I wouldn't have been able to get that unless I'd had that relationship with this guy.
>
> (Ross, General, Care)

A similar complementarity, between support and career networking, implicitly underpins many mentoring relationships, where it is difficult to draw a hard and fast line between a personal relationship of coaching and counselling and a more strategic and political relationship with a senior colleague initiated to raise profile and generate career opportunities.

A more pragmatic complementarity would connect networking for knowledge and for influence. In the account below, the organic continuity between these two activities is explained, underpinned by an implied and established mutual interest:

> So this guidance came out, this lady at [another trust] was party to this information before I was, she called me up, said "have you seen this?" "No, I haven't seen it"—sent it across, we had a bit of discussion about it "what should we do about this?" "Well, shall we put a united response back to the SHA on this?" "Yes a good idea." We'll do that kind of thing.
>
> (Carl, Functional, Care)

Similarly, a complementarity is often observed between networking for knowledge and for career progression, with the former being the overt motivation and the latter being an unspoken yet deliberate by-product of the relationship:

> Sometimes you learn just as much through experience, talking to those people, as you do the sort of formal training. It's that networking thing as well, isn't it? Once you're out there doing these things it's who you know. Because you never know when you might meet them in an interview room.
>
> (Hugh, General, Acute)

Finally, although not frequently discussed, there were occasions where a complementarity was illustrated between networking for influence and for career. One example here was the case of Justine in the Care trust who discussed using her strong connection with board members to make a case for taking on a contract in a new area for the trust, after which Justine herself was chosen to head up the new service—a significant enhancement of her management responsibilities in the trust. This example highlights one of the implications of multiplexity—that there might be multiple motivations to network, and therefore multiple outcomes, which may or may not have been foreseen by the networker at the outset. Here we get a sense of the more or less intentional or accidental trajectories that might be set in motion by particular kinds of networking, a theme that echoes the discussion of career development in Chapter 5.

Overall, then, the motivations or indeed the eventual outcomes of networking are not necessarily pure or simple: managers engage in networking for a variety of reasons, not necessarily instrumentally or deliberately; network relationships change and often mature over time; and individuals often find the benefits of networking are wider or simply different to what they initially expected. Critically, though, there are various synergies between networking activities which reinforce the importance of this broader conception of networking. One reading of network multiplexity would be to emphasize the collective benefits of networking, both for the individual and for the organization. However, it could just as easily be the case that conflicting purposes, or mismatches between the individual aspiration and the organizational and institutional conditions of possibility could create obstacles to effective networking. It is to an examination of these conditions that we now turn.

Challenges to Networking

Across these accounts of networking, a number of issues were raised consistently as obstacles to effective networking, and by implication, as obstacles to effective individual and organizational performance, career development or the maintenance of resilience in the face of pressures. In particular, time pressure and competitive tensions presented immediate challenges for many of our managers. For some, though, the more fundamental challenge was of a more personal nature, relating to issues of integrity and authenticity.

The most consistently cited challenge to networking of all kinds is time pressure and intensive work demands. The issue of work intensification and stress was raised as a theme by over two-thirds of those interviewed, often discussed at some length. The impact of the substantial (and often increasing) pressure of work on the ability to network was considerable and felt especially acutely when managers attempted to engage in less formal networking—such as establishing a relationship with a mentor, or maintaining learning sets after the completion of a training programme.

> We had learning sets with people from similar roles, backgrounds, et cetera, which I found really, really useful. The minute that programme

finished and we tried to carry those on, it lasted about a month. And everybody got subsumed again into their daily grind. . . . I make a commitment that I'm going to start doing that again. And then the next time I look up, it's been 6 months and I've just been sat in the office and never left the hospital. And it's terrible, really terrible how that happens. We just all get totally consumed by our individual organization's problems.

(Greg, General, Acute)

Other, more formal networks, such as professional associations and practice-related networks, also had their effectiveness undermined by the difficulty in maintaining active engagement levels:

There is the Allied Health Professional network but it's not always that well attended. Everybody is under such huge pressure now, there is just no time to do anything.

(Belinda, General, Acute)

I find that [the clinical networks] are out there but fitting it into the day job, you know? It's about managing how you fit everything in. The first thing that goes, rightly or wrongly, is yourself . . . If your diary's full and you're desperate for an appointment, well, oh, yeah, cancel the network meetings.

(Hugh, General, Acute)

There are a lot of events that [the professional body] hold as well, but I have to say to be honest I've only been to a few because I can't seem to get out at the minute.

(Danielle, Functional, Specialist)

With little immediate prospect of a significant decrease in work intensity, the challenge, even for those convinced by the importance of networking, was to maintain a balance so as to protect this long-term activity in the face of more immediate work demands. For example:

Networking with a focus is absolutely essential, that kind of going and learning and bringing the learning back, going and looking, absolutely essential. We don't do enough of that. There is a balance to be struck about how you create the capacity to do that and the spin-offs that can be learnt from that versus the number crunching, the day-to-day grind meeting, the must-dos, keeping the front door open and not taking your eye off that ball.

(Laura, General, Care)

The potential for knowledge exchange through networks is most clearly impeded by the presence of competitive tensions between trusts (Reynolds et al., 2012). This obstacle was affirmed by a number of interviewees across the trusts, but particularly among general and functional managers and most frequently in the Acute and Care trusts.

> When we meet, we are directorate managers, same level, but also, we are working for a foundation trust. A foundation trust has to survive on its own, as a business. And that's the dark side to the NHS, I guess, but that's what FTs have to do. And so there is a sharing of information. But *titrated* sharing of information, should I say, is a better way of putting that. Because some of it is service sensitive, business sensitive. So some information you would share, some you wouldn't. [There are certain] constraints on the free flow of information, definitely.
>
> (Hasin, General, Care)

The barriers described here related not only to information of a commercially sensitive nature, as might be expected; but also to knowledge which was not clearly confidential, such as lessons learnt from experience in a particular area, guidance on good practices or even information on future developments which were not widely announced. Ironically, then, while the search for good practice could encourage imitation and other isomorphic tendencies (as highlighted in the previous chapter), it could also encourage a level of *protectionism*.

At one extreme, this protectionism might be seen to constitute a complete barrier to network formation between particular groups or organizations,

> Basically, I don't network with them because they are the competition! So I can't ring them up and say, "Oh, I'm doing this business case . . ." I don't feel able to.
>
> (Graham, Functional, Care)

A common means to balance this tension, between the necessity of networking and the danger of knowledge sharing in a competitive context, relates to the "titrated" sharing of information referred to above by Hasin. In practice, this involved a careful selectivity in terms of what could be discussed at the expense of a fuller and more effective knowledge-sharing process. For example:

> So here, when you're in a foundation trust and you're surrounded by other foundation trusts, there's not a huge willingness to work together as organizations, because you're in direct competition. So you probably find less that people would get together and discuss the issues and the problems they're having, their risks, when you're in direct competition. I'm seeing [colleagues at another trust] tomorrow afternoon, we're going to have a conversation about a couple of things we might be able to work together on. And then we're going to avoid a conversation

about all the other issues that we've got because, you know, that could result in difficulty. So that doesn't help, I don't think. You would hope we'd all be mature enough to have those conversations but I think it just doesn't work.

(Greg, General, Acute)

Elsewhere, these formal competitive tensions appeared to be more strati-fied, presenting more rigid barriers to formal requests to knowledge shar-ing, but allowing a freer exchange of information through managerial tiers where personal networks had been established.

I would say we were permanently in direct competition with a fairly large trust [nearby] When we look where we are on some sort of report it will be like "Oh my God where are they?" . . . And yet we'll go to a conference at the end of the month and we will all go out and have way too much to drink together. So I know that I can ring their Head of X up and say, "can you just send me a copy of your policy?" and they'll send it me. Interestingly a little bit lower than that level that isn't there . . . The ward sister asked a similar ward sister over there for their document—not a hope!

(Bridget, Functional, Acute)

The implication of these reports of competitive tensions, is that the institu-tional context experienced by these managers was more market- than network-based (see Exworthy et al., 1999), a point we return to below.

A final, and more individual, obstacle to networking lay in the personal challenges faced by some managers when engaging in networking. For some, this related to their own perceived lack of the sophisticated interper-sonal skills necessary to network effectively. A strong injunction to network was a message clearly received by a significant minority of managers, par-ticularly those who had attended formal management/leadership training programmes.

What came through [on the course] was they were saying network, net-work, network. That's it. That is what it's about.

(Pavak, General, Specialist)

However, a number of interviewees spoke at length about their per-sonal distaste at this activity, either because they were uncomfortable with the instrumentality implicit in networking (particularly for career or influence), the sycophancy implied or the inauthentic behaviour it encouraged. Many expressed their unwillingness or inability to engage in 'brown-nosing' or 'sucking up to' senior or influential colleagues within or outside the organization, even when encouraged to do so—as Danielle explained in response to the active networking that went on at her training course:

> I found it uncomfortable—I wouldn't do that. And even though I've been here three years, that's not what I would do.
>
> (Danielle, Functional, Specialist)

Several interviewees who expressed this discomfort went on to say that they had nevertheless later come to recognize the value and importance of networking, and that they had eventually overcome their qualms in this regard:

> When you first start [on the GMTS] they go on about networking . . . I remember thinking I can't be bothered. And it just seemed to me like—forgive my terminology because I can't think of any way else to describe it—but brown-nosing. It just felt like that to me. But as you mature which I did when I started, you realize how important it is.
>
> (Felix, Functional, Acute)

While networking is often a form of socialization, then, it is clear that managers were equally socialized into networking, over time accepting its apparent importance or inevitability, and attempting to suppress their disinclination or to compensate through the development of networking skills. Many of those interviewed were committed and self-conscious networkers, able and willing to speak at length about their networking strategies and practices, and often able to identify the benefits of their networking for their own effectiveness and for their organization. As noted, many of them had been effectively socialized as a *networked manager*, through training programmes, advice and encouragement from leaders and mentors, and through their established membership of professional and clinical associations and groups.

The challenge for the networked manager is typically how to engage in this activity in a way which appears *organic* rather than instrumental, avoiding the appearance of manipulative or self-serving behaviour. The line in particular between instrumental and organic networking is difficult to draw, in part because instrumental networking is frequently only effective if it presented as 'organic' networking. Networking frequently fails when the instrumental intent in forming a relationship is explicit, as one interviewee made clear:

> One colleague . . . seemed as though she was just using [people]. And that's not the way to get a relationship or whatever. So you meet someone, you're not asking for a job the next week or whatever. It's more about keeping contact, what things are going wrong.
>
> (Pavak, General, Specialist)

The obvious inference is that most effective networked managers present themselves as skilled social performers who can network deliberately and strategically with a focus on a goal while ensuring that this appears both authentic and natural. However, recognizing the multiplexity of meanings and motives behind networking brings into sharp focus the tension between instrumentality and authenticity when networking. Multiplexity presents a deep challenge to those managers who would wish to maintain "a clear conceptual distinction between instrumental networking driven by individual agency versus spontaneous networking reflecting the constraints and opportunities of the social structure" (Casciaro et al., 2014: 726). The moral dimension to networking, neglected in much of the more functional research in this area, was palpable to several of our respondents. Even enthusiastic and committed networkers appeared sensitive to the taint of instrumentalism, if only for the reason that this might undermine the effectiveness of their networking activities (Anderson-Gough et al., 2006).

For all those who could describe in detail their rich and varied networks and their acquired skill in building such networks, there was also the particular problem faced by *isolates*—individuals and groups who lack the requisite connections to acquire knowledge, influence actions, forge careers and build supportive relationships. The particular subgroup of managers who most commonly described themselves as lacking in networks were general managers. Roles such as the service manager suffered particularly from a combination of intensity of work pressure, infrequency of contact with managers in similar positions, the absence of a standard training route into the role which might help form cohort relationships, and a lack of dedicated formal networks to share knowledge and best practice. The damaging impact of this, in terms of the challenge of acquiring knowledge, building career, representing their interests and building support networks, was particularly noticeable among this group.

There is frequently a perception that the isolation of particular groups of managers, in terms of their lack of networks, is not a particular concern of the trusts themselves. Specifically, this isolation is often seen to be a personal rather than an organizational issue, and the employing organization is seen to be predominantly focused on the output rather than the activity of management.

> I don't think the trust is massively interested in any of that; what the trust is interested in is that you deliver. They're not interested in you as an individual, not interested in how you get, not only support, but how you get technical help.
>
> (Beth, General, Care)

However, the comparative absence of network opportunities as well as a question mark over the ability of wider, more institutionalized managerial networks to provide a basis for knowledge sharing and learning (Addicott et al., 2007; Ferlie et al., 2010) do raise important questions about what opportunities organizations might be missing to benefit from this aspect of management development.

Summary

This chapter has explored networks and networking among healthcare managers. While networks are undoubtedly in vogue in this sector—as a perceived remedy for some of the challenges of a fragmented and complex NHS—there is a need to be wary of claims made about their supposed applicability and efficacy. Two particular cautionary notes are important to flag here. The first is that history rarely lends itself to such neat divisions of messy policy and practice into epochs, with bureaucracy preceding markets, preceding networks. As Exworthy et al. (1999: 17) note: "the NHS has never been fully marketized but neither was it ever a (traditional) bureaucracy. Furthermore, it is unlikely that is ever was or will be a (true) network." Such ideal types oversimplify the history of the NHS, where networks of providers and of course, clinical/professional networks are long established and routinely relied upon (Ferlie et al., 2010: 17). Second, and related to this, efforts to encourage the formation and reliance on networks are routinely stymied by the persistent recourse to hierarchy and/or by the competition that results from quasi-markets within healthcare (Addicott et al., 2007). Both of these constraints were evident in the particular challenges to networking that were faced by the managers in our study.

To draw out the complexity and challenges implicit in networks and networking, this chapter first identified the networks which managers engaged with, emphasizing their range and diversity and using this to illuminate some important differences between the organizations and managerial groups studied. Rather than focus on a static depiction of nodes and network structures, however, emphasis was instead placed on understanding the motivations that shape, sustain and constrain an individual's participation in these networks. The study suggests four broad reasons for networking: for knowledge, for support, for career development and for influence. These motivations overlapped in ways that reflect the multiplex nature of networks and networking activity. Identifying key complementarities and synergies between particular approaches to networking does illustrate the potential power and benefits of networking within these organizational and occupational contexts. At the same time, however, the analysis clearly brings out a range of factors which tended to impede or undermine networking within the sector. These range from time pressures and the competitive tensions between parts of the NHS to more personal and moral concerns. Such challenges also draw attention to those individuals and groups who are left as isolates due to the failure to engage effectively in networks.

The assumptions present in many of the more optimistic conceptions of the value of communities or networks of practice in healthcare suggest that improved knowledge sharing and community building will be an almost inevitable by-product of bringing together people with a shared agenda. Our data suggests several reasons why this might not be the case—in the tensions between 'organic' and 'instrumental' networking, for example; or in the potential conflicts emanating from the multiplex motives for networking— whether intentional or accidental; or in the organizational and institutional impediments to open and co-operative relationship building. In contrast to suggestions that healthcare organizations are increasingly networked organizations (Exworthy et al., 1999), our findings suggest instead that, in spite of the recognition of the importance of networking by both individuals and organizations, it remains for many a sporadic and opportunistic activity and one which rarely leads to a coherent or stable collective practice among managers.

8 Managing Healthcare
Tensions and Prospects

The previous four chapters have explored what it means to be and to become a manager in modern healthcare organizations by breaking this down into four major, related themes and examining each of these in the context of wider, contemporary changes occurring within healthcare and more local circumstances and changes occurring within particular healthcare organizations. The four themes relate to how the managers in our study viewed their management and leadership responsibilities; how they emerged and developed as managers during the course of their careers; how they accessed and mobilized different forms of knowledge; and how they related to different networks of practice in which they were embedded. In this concluding chapter, we draw together the main threads of our analysis to bring out what it means to manage modern healthcare organizations and to establish how our findings contribute to the wider knowledge base in this area, as well as to draw out implications for future research, policy and practice.

Before doing that, it is important to reiterate that the context within which the research took place—the English NHS—was one that had seen successive, major waves of organizational change associated with policy change and reform and that this was continuing to have a major impact on healthcare provision more generally, as well as on the work of managers in particular (e.g. Hyde et al., 2016). As well as addressing the broad sweep of change from administration, through general management and business management, towards leadership and entrepreneurship, we highlighted three major events to have impacted the NHS in England during our study: the efficiency challenges resulting in part from the financial crisis of 2007–8; the major reform and reorganization instituted through the *Health and Social Care Act (2012)*; and the impact on governance, management and culture of the Francis Report (2013). Consequently, an important backdrop to the research was the intensified pressures on the healthcare system as a whole. While these are, of course, not unique to the NHS (Reeves et al., 2014), we would argue that these financial and structural pressures have impacted disproportionately on the management cadre within the NHS in England. Alongside on-going reductions in managerial capacity within the English healthcare system, they have had important implications for managers' day-to-day work, their career prospects and their expectations of their future role (King's Fund, 2011; Buchanan et al., 2013).

At a more micro level, the research was also purposely designed to reflect some of the diversity found within the healthcare sector, specifically in terms of types of organization and types of manager, in order to help enable analytical generalizations to be made to similar types of healthcare setting (cf. Yin, 1984). To capture organizational diversity, three case study organizations were selected for in-depth study that differed significantly in terms of geographical coverage, the diversity of services provided and the number of organizations purchasing services from them. However, they also differed markedly in their financial security, strategic goals, organizational structures and management practices. A core element of our empirical approach, therefore, was to identify key organizational factors and aspects of change at each organization which our interviewees saw as impacting most powerfully on management practices, knowledge mobilization and networking activity (cf. Dopson et al., 2008). Collectively, these differences provide a detailed and complex picture of the context within which our managers were immersed, and represent an important element in developing our empirically based thematic analysis.

Managerial diversity was equally important to capture. We know that management in healthcare organizations is variegated, fragmented and distributed (Buchanan et al., 2007; Buchanan, 2013); and that relations between managers and clinicians are critically important for understanding management practices and managerial identity (Llewellyn, 2001; Davies and Harrison, 2003; Currie and Procter, 2005). As a group, management in healthcare has not only been the target as well as the vehicle of recent policy change (Hyde et al., 2016); it has also experienced a dramatic and negative shift in how it is represented discursively—with consequent effects upon managers' professional/occupational identity and status (Learmonth, 2005; O'Reilly and Reed, 2011). An important objective was therefore to ensure that the research captured as much as it could of the distributed nature of the management and leadership function in modern healthcare organizations (e.g. Buchanan, 2013), rather than focusing narrowly on particular management roles. Identifying the breadth of individuals engaged with managing was challenging in a context where healthcare managers themselves were reluctant to attach themselves to this increasingly stigmatized identity. To ensure this happened in a structured yet meaningful way, a framework was developed that differentiated between three types of manager—clinical, general and functional—based upon their relative levels of clinical and managerial experience. Although inevitably broad-brush, it could then be used to select and situate particular research participants. The richness of their interview accounts was then used to locate individual managers more precisely, as well as to explore their experiences in depth. As such, the framework constituted an important element of the analysis and has been used in the foregoing chapters to tease out some of the key similarities and differences found between and within managerial groups within their respective healthcare organizations. What follows next is a summary of those findings presented thematically that takes into account these important differences in context and management cohort.

Being a Manager

The diverse circumstances and challenges the groups of managers we interviewed faced were reminiscent of the sorts of differences in management context and practice that have always made it difficult for managers anywhere to rely upon a clear and coherent professional identity centred upon common 'best' practices and a distinct body of knowledge (Reed and Anthony, 1992; Watson and Harris, 1999; Thomas and Linstead, 2002). It is perhaps unsurprising, in light of this, that clinical and functional managers tended to derive their managerial practices, knowledge base, networks and professional identity as much from their own professional communities of practice as they did from a clear and shared sense of their role as healthcare managers. General managers themselves varied in their levels of clinical experience and in their identification with clinical or managerial roles and this too added to the fracturing of any clearly shared sense of common managerial work and professional identity.

As already noted, there were also significant differences between the trusts in the financial and other pressures they faced, the structural forms they took, the patterns of inter-professional working that occurred within management and the levels of organizational change or stability they experienced. Broadly speaking, general managers at the Acute trust faced the principal challenge of trying to achieve, maintain and improve upon the delivery of a safe and effective service, in a context where managerial work had become intensified due to financial pressures and where there was some instability within the organization, as well as some lack of integration between clinical and managerial groups. For general managers at the Care trust—many of whom shared a clinical background—the primary concerns revolved around the tensions that stemmed from growth and diversification and which had resulted in attempts being made by senior management to standardize and control its quite disparate and highly distributed activities—especially in the light of growing financial pressures. For managers at the Specialist trust, despite the challenges in having to overcome a more pronounced clinical-managerial status divide, there were fewer financial pressures being faced and a greater degree of stability in service operations that owed a lot to the trust's distinctive purpose and established reputation.

Nevertheless, despite these important differences in the content and context of managerial work, there was a surprising level of agreement among the cohorts and across the trusts concerning the important managerial issues and processes involved. Despite some subtle but important nuances, strikingly similar accounts were given of both the nature of general managers' responsibilities and challenges (in coping with the intensity of work and in dealing with the interface with clinicians); as well as the most important management skills that were associated with responding to these challenges (especially the emphasis on interpersonal skills and a deference to financial, HR and other, more composite and explicit forms of knowledge). These did not easily align with more established, standard prescriptions of the nature of managerial work (e.g. Mintzberg, 1973) as they tended to emerge from managers' own sense-making of their roles and responsibilities and cut across the many different ways in which managerial work has been defined and classified (cf. Hales, 1986; Watson, 1994). However, they did suggest a convergence towards perceptions of a common skill set across different groups and contexts within the sector. Consequently, while there was a good deal of difference in the context and content of managerial work, there was also a good deal of commonality in the managerial needs and skill sets seen as important.

Managing the clinical-managerial divide, on the other hand, did appear to require distinct strategies that were, in turn, more reflective of the cultures of the organizations involved. In the Acute and Specialist trusts, there was perceived to be much more of a barrier between the two communities which needed to be overcome and the mechanisms used in both cases were essentially structural—making changes to the hierarchy in order to build bridges between clinicians and managers. In the Specialist case, managers also emphasized the importance of enhancing their position through establishing clinical credibility and using their relational skills. In the Care trust, this credibility and a more direct form of communication was more personally embodied through the (clinical) experience and skill sets of managers. While such distinctions could be considered quite broad differences and not necessarily generalizable to other, similar healthcare organizations (due to the complex set of factors likely to be in play), they do nevertheless start to bring out some of the important ways in which local context plays a key part in shaping managerial processes within the sector. As such, they start to signal the value of contextualizing management practice by situating it within the local organizational conditions that affect management action and options (cf. Dopson et al., 2008).

What was even more striking, however, was the commonality in how managers talked about leadership and how clearly they differentiated it from management—in ways that tended to reify the former and denigrate the latter (O'Reilly and Reed, 2011; Hyde et al., 2012; Martin and Learmonth, 2012). The leadership aspects of the role were clearly idealized and valued over the more mundane, technical aspects of the job that were associated with managerial work (especially operational requirements, financial management and HR aspects). However, in practice, managers clearly faced challenges in being able to convert these aspirations of leadership into practical managerial action (through creating a vision, inspiring followers and thinking strategically, for example). Often, leader behaviours were manifested in the interpersonal skills deployed by managers to inspire their teams as best they could; though they were limited by the more pressing managerial demands they faced on a daily basis (Tomlinson et al., 2013). As such, leadership was often beyond the grasp of busy, preoccupied managers, and instead, their activities tended to default back to those associated with management (Carroll and Levy, 2008; Ford, 2010). That is, managers in practice inevitably fell back on a problem-focused and action-oriented conception of leadership that was more closely aligned with their day-to-day managerial responsibilities and which prioritized their practical management skills (Denis et al., 2010; Wallace and Tomlinson, 2010).

At the same time, however, what was also apparent was an interesting counterpoint to the elusiveness of leadership, as far as general managers were concerned. In interviews with clinical managers, there was a clear indication instead that leadership discourse sat rather more easily with the professional orientations and aspirations of clinicians. In other words, while clinicians may still be very ambivalent about taking on managerial responsibilities, couching management in terms of leadership was much more appealing as it was seen as being much closer to what they might aspire to as managers (Spurgeon et al., 2011; Hyde et al., 2012). Consequently, clinicians may be far more likely to engage with discourses of change within the sector that emphasize the importance of leadership (particularly insofar as it also contains within it an implicit critique of management) and by the same token, be far more likely to benefit from such an alternative managerial discourses.

Taken together, such findings not only add to a growing critical interrogation of the purported shift to a discourse of 'leaderism' in healthcare (O'Reilly and Reed, 2011; Martin and Learmonth, 2012; Tomlinson, 2013; McDonald, 2014; Bresnen et al., 2015). They also suggest that the effects of this shift may be subtle, complex and contradictory. On the one hand, it could suggest a greater sense of managerial integration and unity based on recourse to a shared discourse of leadership—albeit one that effectively co-opts clinicians into organizational concerns. On the other hand, the engagement of clinicians via leaderism could be seen as reinforcing their influence in their dealings with management, insofar as it gives them the opportunity to mobilize a powerful additional discursive resource (Bresnen et al., 2015). We do not believe this to be an either/or equation. In a progressively more managerial NHS, it is no longer the case that organizational decision-making is driven by clinicians. Therefore, in order to retain influence, clinicians have to align themselves with more managerial ways of doing and thinking. This results in a situation whereby gaining or retaining one particular source of influence may or may not require sacrificing another source of influence. So, for example, the group of clinicians at the Specialist trust were both the most cohesive and powerful group across our three cases, but also the most financially literate. Given the historical, institutional importance of clinicians within NHS organizations, we should not be surprised by their ability to resist, negotiate, or co-opt managerial discourses, even as the longer-term view suggests that their collective power has been compromised.

Becoming a Manager

While our study used the three-fold grouping of clinical, general and functional managers as a useful selection framework and heuristic device, our interviewees naturally consisted of a diverse group of managers with a wide range of educational qualifications and professional and personal experiences. Capturing and analyzing the detailed career narratives those managers presented not only enabled us to identify generalized patterns across the data, but also enabled us to get a clearer sense of some of the more common career trajectories associated with their progression into management positions. Importantly, this also helped to tease out some of the important differences in experience and orientation between clinical and general managers, as well as amongst different types of hybrid manager (e.g. McGivern et al., 2015). Clinical-managerial hybridity was explored within our sample of managers not simply because it is undoubtedly an important feature of healthcare management (Llewellyn, 2001; Buchanan, 2013). It was also examined in some depth as it has important potential implications for the influence of the medical profession (Noordegraaf, 2015); for understanding processes of knowledge mobilization in healthcare (Currie and White, 2012; Burgess and Currie, 2013; Burgess et al., 2015); and for what it means more generally for the professional identity of healthcare managers (Croft et al., 2015; McGivern et al., 2015; von Knorring et al., 2016).

Clinical managers and nurse-hybrid general managers (who formed a sizeable group) naturally placed a lot of emphasis on the clinical aspect of their professional identity, which was forged through their educational and professional qualification and associated continued professional development. It was rare to find clinical managers who aspired to a managerial career or who comfortably occupied a management position. However, it was not uncommon for nurse-hybrid managers to have management *aspirations*, particularly as this was seen as the main way for them to be able to exert more control and influence (cf. Brooks, 1999). However, other orientations to management within this group were also apparent with a number of interesting nuances. There was quite a sharp distinction, for example, between more *accidental* managers—those whose clinical career path had led them unexpectedly (i.e. not by design or inclination) into management positions (these were found across all three trusts, but particularly at Care); and more *reluctant* managers—those for whom management responsibilities had at first been resisted and then rationalized as an inevitable (but undesirable) next step in the development of their career (these were found particularly, but not exclusively, amongst medics).

For both of these groups, the clinical frame of reference was still a very strong one. Although there were some clinicians whose orientations were more towards management processes (e.g. the psychologists at the Care trust), and some who saw themselves in a hybrid, bridging or translational role (e.g. clinical directors at the Specialist or Acute trust), management activity still tended to be seen as an adjunct to a largely clinical professional role (cf. McGivern et al., 2015). Receptivity towards management responsibilities and ideas was, for these managers, much more of an exception than the rule. Having said that, there were a few notable exceptions of clinical managers who were not only more receptive to management thinking, but also more enthusiastic than one might expect in mobilizing management knowledge in pursuit of their management aspirations (for example, Nina at the Specialist trust, who had become a manager via the *Athena* programme; Brian at the Acute trust, who whole-heartedly embraced his managerial identity; and Nancy at the Acute trust who, unusually, had an MBA qualification).

Furthermore, for both accidental and reluctant managers, although clinical experience was still important in shaping views about managing, there was a greater degree of acceptance (if not necessarily internalization) of management practices and management thinking. Managers of this type (particularly those with nursing backgrounds) would typically draw upon and value the more experiential learning they had experienced as clinicians and 'proto-managers' in charge of wards and were also well attuned to the challenges faced in bridging the clinical-managerial divide (cf. Currie, 2006). As such, the analysis appeared to offer some support for the idea that management expertise—albeit quite localized and informally developed—could offer some support for those from certain clinical backgrounds attempting to further a professionalization project based upon a mixture of clinical and managerial knowledge and experience (Grey, 1997; Brooks, 1999). This personal embodiment of the clinical-managerial divide for such hybrid managers might have led to better opportunities for the translation of knowledge and meaning across medical and managerial communities of practice (Currie and White, 2012). However, it did cause some discomfort for the managers concerned, who struggled with balancing their clinical and managerial identities when attempting to bridge the gap between 'board and ward' (Currie and Procter, 2005; Burgess et al., 2015).

General managers had reached their positions through a varied set of routes. The most common denominator was some level of clinical experience, combined with some level of qualification related to healthcare or healthcare management. Experience in the NHS (especially clinical experience) was what characterized how managers in this group had developed their skills—particularly amongst the sizeable group of hybrid managers who had entered management from a nursing background (and who were particularly prevalent at the Care trust). However, many also had some formal management post-graduate qualifications and training (especially at the Acute and Care trusts) as well as plenty of direct managerial experience. Management experience was, however, still quite varied, although what was fairly consistent was the comparative absence of wider (i.e. beyond the sector) management experience and pure general management qualifications. Less than half of the general managers had some experience of working in the private sector, and in several cases, that experience was rather limited. Only in a very few cases did experience outside the sector or the NHS appear consciously to shape thinking about the nature of management and management challenges in healthcare. Most often what was emphasized by even 'pure play' managers was the distinctiveness of managing in a healthcare environment and the need to adapt to that.

Functional managers as a group varied most widely, of course, in their professional orientation and status—depending upon their particular occupational specialism. For these managers, career development depended upon the professional development pathway associated with their discipline. For some, this was quite established and formalized and involved expected levels of intense formal education and training leading to recognized professional qualifications (e.g. finance managers and also some specialists in HR and estates). For others, whose discipline was less professionally institutionalized, the nature and intensity of formal education and training was clearly less formal and intense, and career pathways were sometimes more diffuse or ill-defined (e.g. specialists in marketing and IT). While functional managers also had to engage with clinical knowledge and the complexities of management practice in healthcare, only a small fraction of them had any clinical experience.

Last but not least, amongst general managers in particular (and especially for hybrid managers), what were also particularly apparent were the quite distinct career paths of managers in each type of trust. The differences were not stark, but there was a clear sense in which the standard pathway for development of general managers at the Acute trust involved a combination of nurse hybrids taking on increasingly enlarged and enriched roles across different clinical domains within the trust; or general managers developing their career through direct entry into management and promotion through the ranks. Major threats to these career progression routes stemmed from financial pressures and associated job cuts, although these at times did open up some opportunities for managers to progress their career (e.g. through 'acting up'). Similar threats and opportunities occurred at the other trusts. However, career development for general managers at the Care trust was also connected with more institution-building opportunities for developing integrated services across the trust's many operational units and more entrepreneurial outreach activity associated with integrating health and social care services. At the Specialist trust, additional routes for career development were also associated with the trust's commitment to research. In all cases, managers had to navigate a challenging and changing context in order to establish not only their careers but also their professional credibility.

Managers Knowing

Managers across the groups and across the trusts were fairly consistent too in how they depicted the types of knowledge that they drew upon in their work and how they mobilized those different forms of knowledge and engaged with different types of learning process. There were some important differences that emerged in how different managers across the different trusts mobilized knowledge, and these will be brought to the fore in what follows. However, what was striking about the accounts, and consistent with the findings above on clinical/managerial identity, was the consistent tendency for managers to rely strongly upon knowledge gained from experience—particularly clinical experience and the experiential learning that went with that; as well as the obvious limitations that occurred in the translation and embedding of more codified systems of management knowledge into their healthcare management practice. This was not only due to the perceived more abstract nature of that knowledge base, but also to the strong continuing influence that more clinical ways of knowing had upon management thinking, as well as the influence of more 'home grown' management knowledge—often developed in bespoke fashion but in quite standardized formats to deal with the many external reporting requirements facing the organization. It also reflected orientations to knowing and learning about management that were not only highly pragmatic, but also somewhat individualistic and highly experiential in nature.

Clinical experience and clinical ways of thinking provided the bedrock on which managers built their managerial knowledge base, especially amongst clinical managers, but also amongst the large number of general managers with clinical (mainly nursing) backgrounds who occupied hybrid management roles. Clinicians who were willing to engage with management were likely to approach management in more intuitively diagnostic ways—influenced rather more perhaps by the guiding principles and epistemic practices of their professional background than by the logics of action associated with management (as reflected in the attraction of Evidence-Based Management (EBMgt) for those grounded in Evidence-Based Medicine, for example). General managers in hybrid roles tended to share these dispositions. However, the need to engage with groups of powerful clinicians also predisposed them to frame managerial problems in ways that were likely to make most sense to clinicians. As we saw previously, structural mechanisms and relational skills were important in helping bridge the clinical-managerial divide. However, these relational capabilities were arguably less beneficial than the integrative capabilities that enabled some managers to switch relatively easily from one role to the other (cf. Owen-Smith et al., 2004) and to combine clinical and managerial perspectives in order to enhance their credibility with clinicians and to construct more acceptable and persuasive arguments.

At the same time, it was apparent too that the *encultured* knowledge and understanding (Blackler, 1995) that derived from clinical qualifications and experiences was not the only frame of reference shaping managerial thinking. As already noted, managers placed a good deal of emphasis upon the importance of understanding finances (and other specialist aspects of their work, such as HR). For those trusts facing more acute financial pressures, financial issues were a major concern and financial imperatives were important in shaping management thinking and action. Indeed, it would be a surprise if that were not the case, given recent budget cuts and the greater managerialism that has infused public sector management over recent years (Kirkpatrick et al., 2005; Hyde et al., 2016). With respect to management knowledge and influence, this may or may not have equated with a greater degree of control exercised by accountants in those particular senior management teams (cf. Armstrong, 1987). However, there was certainly evidence in all three of the trusts that it was having a major influence on shaping local trust management discourse, by the emphasis that was being placed, variously, on efficiency and cost cutting, business development and growth/diversification strategies. At the level of middle management practice, financial expertise provided general managers with a powerful discursive resource with which to counter clinical influence and/or to shape clinical practice managerially. On the other hand, clinicians were just as likely to be able to mobilize this discursive resource, insofar as it had become part of their normalized practice.

When it comes to more codified and explicit forms of management knowledge, it was apparent that neither clinical managers nor hybrid general managers relied greatly, or at least explicitly, upon more externally derived, abstract and commodified forms of knowledge—such as the management tools and techniques referred to earlier in Chapter 6. There were certainly examples given of formal attempts to apply methods such as lean production principles to service operations. However, these were by and large considered of limited effect or unsuccessful—principally because of the many problems faced in translation into the local context, including significant problems of generating sufficient buy-in or overcoming scepticism or resistance (cf. Waring and Bishop, 2010; McCann et al., 2015). Where such methods were more successful was in their more implicit and subtle use in ways that helped guide collective or individual management reflection. The same applied to the many examples given where individual managers drew upon particular frameworks (e.g. SWOT analysis, process mapping) to guide their management practice and local discussions within their teams. These exceptions aside, for the most part, neither clinical nor general managers were particularly receptive to, nor proselytizers for, more abstract and commodified forms of management knowledge. These forms of knowledge neither matched the clinical requirements of managers with a strong clinical/scientific frame of reference; nor did they meet the requirements of hybrid general managers who were more steeped in clinical experience and the experiential learning that came from that. Although direct references to pre-packaged and imported forms of managerial knowledge, such as lean or total quality management, were rare, this was in contrast to the extent to which more generic managerial ways of doing and knowing infused the discourse of participants.

Functional managers were, of course, much more predisposed and receptive towards formalized and generic management knowledge—albeit knowledge that tended to be more focused on their particular functional role (such as financial management or HR techniques and practices). In turn, their knowledge base often fed directly into and helped constitute the knowledge and expertise deemed important by general managers. Other forms of knowledge were either more generally underpinning of general management activity (e.g. the contributions of IT and marketing specialists); or constituted a more distinct and separate knowledge and practice domain (as was the case, for example, with estates management). What was therefore particularly interesting about this group was the extent to which certain aspects of their knowledge base constituted some of the most important aspects of managerial work and discourse (and were recognized as such by general managers).

What was, however, a more important feature of management practice perhaps and a strong influence on how management knowledge was framed and mobilized was the need to respond to external reporting requirements driven by regulatory and government bodies. Those requirements created a very strong emphasis on the generation of performance information and a reporting regime that privileged more bureaucratic forms of control—in turn, engendering something of a 'tick-box' mentality. There were important differences between the trusts in the type, range and intensity of regulatory requirements they faced and in the degrees of systematization and formalization in their management information systems and reporting procedures that were designed to meet these needs. These stylistic differences apart, however, the over-arching effect was not only the creation of a more bureaucratic system centred upon reporting performance against pre-set targets; but also pressures to standardize management systems and procedures to deliver the information flows and decisions required. As such, managers (especially general managers) were heavily reliant upon home-grown systems of reporting that perhaps drew implicitly upon wider management know-how, but which were driven largely by institutional demands. While the design of those management information systems was often localized and bespoke, a desire to look elsewhere in the sector for 'best practice' solutions to meet these requirements also encouraged isomorphic tendencies and, arguably, a further distancing from alternative sources of management knowledge outside of the healthcare sector.

The resultant emphasis on more home-grown management solutions was accentuated further by the strongly held perception that experience was the most important way of developing the expertise required to perform managerial work. Most of the managers in our study put a very strong emphasis indeed on the value of experience—both managerial and clinical experience—as the basis for their effective performance as managers. While clinical experience was, of course, seen as of less importance for 'pure play' general managers and functional managers, an ability to relate to clinical aspects was nevertheless also seen as important in enhancing their credibility and legitimacy. For general managers it was seen as even more essential perhaps in helping them connect with clinicians, and this was often expressed through their clinical-managerial hybridity. For clinical managers, of course, clinical experience was built in to their professional training and development, although this did not mean that they did not face any challenges in managing multiprofessional or multidisciplinary clinical groups.

This strong emphasis on experience had a number of important effects. In particular, it tended to promote a more personally *embodied* or *embrained* view of management knowledge (Blackler, 1995), in which emphasis was placed upon individual know-how and the ability of managers to muddle through and learn experientially, rather than through the systematic development of skills through formal training and development. Nevertheless, there was also a strong emphasis on socially situated learning, and managers valued the opportunities that applied training gave them for critical collective reflection on key issues. They also valued the social learning that came with mentoring and coaching opportunities, and it was apparent across the trusts (and particularly at Care) that strong ties for knowledge sharing and learning were very highly valued (cf. Hansen, 2002).

At the same time, however, this emphasis on learning through experience, augmented by practically focused and highly socialized training experiences did have a number of downsides. Again, particularly in the Care trust, the over-reliance on experience and strong ties created some internal 'stickiness' (Szulanski, 1996) that impeded knowledge sharing and learning and which also introduced some limiting factors on the organization's ability to capture and codify certain types of knowledge and experience (cf. Nonaka and Takeuchi, 1995). It also tended to reinforce a reproduction of managerial knowledge and practice that was driven rather more by immediate situational challenges and needs; that was less based on generalized learning from experiences elsewhere in the organization; and which was even more divorced perhaps from wider, more explicit forms of knowledge. As such, it arguably reinforced further the more inward-looking tendencies that have been identified as an issue in the development of healthcare management practice (e.g. McNulty et al., 2002).

Managers Networking

A concern with the immediate and a predilection for the familiar were also to some extent characteristic of managers' networking activities and their approaches to mobilizing wider sources of knowledge and support. There were a number of significant differences found between the managerial cohorts and across the trusts in managers' positions in networks and how they accessed wider networks to which they were connected. However, the general picture that emerges from the research is one in which managers— especially general managers—were somewhat constrained in the opportunities available to them to connect across wider communities of practicing managers. Instead, local concerns and needs tended to drive much more internally focused networked interaction based upon immediate operational demands and pressures.

All of the managers we interviewed potentially had access to a wide range of networks that varied considerably in type—from the more formal, work-related or professional-focused networks to more informal, personal friendship networks. It was not the intention to undertake the almost impossible and rather mundane descriptive task of mapping out these wider networks, identifying their structural attributes and relational properties. Instead, attention was focused upon managers' perceptions of the networks of activity in which they were embedded. This led to a focus on the reasons they participated in networks and how networked interaction contributed to their on-going work and knowledge requirements, their continuing professional development and their personal emotional support. The most striking distinction can immediately be made between those groups which enjoyed the most extensive networked relationships—primarily clinical and functional managers—and the relative lack of external networks in the case of most general managers.

Both clinical and functional managers tended to be more highly networked and made much more use of professional networks that allowed them to interact with colleagues more regularly elsewhere. Most clinical managers were of course well connected with clinical practitioners in their particular professional domain as well as professional colleagues in their local trust and region (and in some cases nationally and internationally). Most functional managers belonged to formal professional associations, although their activity varied greatly, ranging from regular and proactive participation in formal events and other activities to merely remaining on mailing lists. At one level, this level of connectivity of both clinical and functional managers reflected the wider range of professional connections they depended on to develop their knowledge base, learning and careers. At another level, it also reflected the desire or need of these managers—especially functional managers—to avoid becoming too embedded in their immediate organization and its requirements. This does not mean that the occupational mobility of functional managers necessarily made them look beyond healthcare for future career development opportunities (although there were one or two managers that did talk about other possibilities beyond healthcare). However, it did mean that functional managers were, on balance, more able and willing to keep their career options open.

General managers, on the other hand, tended to be much more constrained in their access to wider professional/occupational networks and much more focused upon addressing operational concerns that predisposed them to network more within their own organization. The comparative absence of wider accessible networks for general managers also reinforced the likelihood that existing ways of knowing about managing would tend to be self-reinforcing. In other words, managers were not only focused on responding to local managerial challenges, but also more isolated than the other two groups from sources of knowledge and learning that were potentially accessed through networks of peers—not only outside the organization (where competitive conditions could constrain open dialogue) but also within the organization (where operational conditions varied widely and organizational structures could create silos).

At the same time, there were important differences between the three organizations. At the Specialist trust, the national and international reputation of its work ensured that clinical managers were well connected and respected nationally and internationally. General managers there benefitted too from its more cosmopolitan image (cf. Gouldner, 1958). In the more fragmented and fluid conditions of the Care trust, managers were engaged in multiple joint initiatives with a range of other agencies (in, social services, forensic services etc.). General managers there did experience a wider variety of network connections—at least with local and regional actors and agencies. There were also some well-connected clinicians (mostly psychologists) who had strong national connections. At the Acute trust, however, general managers reported that they connected with fewer and less diverse networks. Managers here presented the organization as relatively more insulated than the others, a feature that was exacerbated by its size, its limited geographical spread and its traditional functional organization structure. Moreover, whereas there was a much greater degree of staff longevity at the Specialist trust (due to its prestige) and the Care trust (due to the strength of local ties), this was not so much in evidence at the Acute trust.

When it comes to the purposes of, and motivations for, networking, it was apparent that the majority of managers considered networks to be important primarily in providing managers with the knowledge and to a lesser degree the emotional support that they felt they needed. That was especially the case for general managers faced with operational pressures that needed them to solve problems and take decisions constantly. Whether the knowledge and support sought was in the form of more explicit knowledge or tacit understanding, and from work colleagues within or beyond the organization, knowledge sharing and support often went together for these managers. Moreover, networks and networking were also considered important for more self-aggrandizing reasons—namely in contributing to individual career development and/or allowing managers to exert greater influence. Those general managers on the GMTS were most conscious of the value of networking for career development, as this was made explicit at an early stage of their socialization. However, for all managers, the benefits of networking for knowledge sharing, support, personal development and influence were considered important and the motivations for networking to achieve these benefits were also intertwined. So, for individual managers able to make use of networked interaction, networking tended to be *multiplex* in nature (Heebels et al., 2013).

At the same time, however, it was as interesting to see what networks did not enable as much as what they did. Internally, a focus on operational challenges and day-to-day needs meant that connections were much more operationally focused in nature and centred around standard communication and reporting mechanisms. As already noted, these could take very different forms: direct observation of comparable monthly management meetings in the Acute and Care trusts, for example, showed a very clear cultural differentiation between the more formal way of working observed at the Acute trust compared to a more informal way of working at the Care trust. However, the agendas and outcomes were very similar, and they shared a common focus on formalized processes of knowledge sharing and communication driven by performance reporting requirements (as opposed to more informal opportunities for knowledge sharing and learning). Contacts were of course available to managers across each trust. However, it was noticeable how consistently these were activated more in the interests of formal reporting/communicating or specific managerial problem-solving, rather than as more generalized avenues for knowledge sharing and support.

As already noted too, there were differences across the trusts and between the managerial groups in their access to external professional or other networks and in their propensity to engage in networking activity. What emerged as a clear overall finding, however, was the relative isolation of many non-specialist and general managers from more widely based sources of knowledge and support through clearly identifiable and well-established networks of practice. Clinical and functional groups benefitted more in this regard. For general managers, their operational demands tended to promote more of a propensity to look inside the organization for help with knowledge and support. Efforts to look outside the organization were not only due to the lack of opportunities, but also due to constraints that emerged as a result of commercial pressures that inevitably inhibited knowledge exchange and learning between peers in competing healthcare organizations. Moreover, many managers felt relatively uncomfortable with active networking that could be interpreted as more competitive and self-aggrandizing. Several raised the concern that overt and instrumental networking, or networking that *appeared* to be instrumental, was not only uncomfortable but also self-defeating, with the consequence that many emphasized the need for authenticity in terms of how relations were built and maintained.

It was also striking that, despite lip-service being paid to the notion of networking in major training programmes and some trusts, there was on the whole comparatively little explicit organizational support for such activity. All in all, strong local ties associated with internal team-working and tacit sharing of knowledge were (understandably) emphasized rather more than the weaker, extended ties that might allow access to wider sources of knowledge (cf. Granovetter, 1973; Hansen, 2002).

Managing Modern Healthcare: Knowledge, Networks, Practice

So, taking these findings together and returning to the question posed at the start of this book: what does it mean to manage modern healthcare? More specifically, what do the findings from our research say about the nature of management practice in healthcare and the forms of knowledge and types of network that managers have access to and are able to mobilize? How are these features of management in healthcare shaped by the context within which managers act? And how are they affected by the dramatic changes they are experiencing in their healthcare organizations and managerial roles as a consequence of healthcare change and reform? What generally does the research say about the viability of healthcare management as a community of practice and the prospects for encouraging development of a more coherent sense of what healthcare management is and whether or not it can be said to possess a clear and distinct professional identity?

What emerges above all else from the findings is a clear sense of fragmentation amongst the managerial cadre in healthcare that is not only an established feature of healthcare management, but which is also being significantly added to by the fractures induced within healthcare through successive waves of institutional change and reform. Conditions within which managers are expected to deliver effective healthcare and improve upon healthcare performance have, for some time, been in a considerable state of flux. While there may certainly still be opportunities available for management development, changes that have been recently introduced pose substantial threats to the capacity and capabilities of managers to deal with the challenges facing contemporary healthcare. Recent cuts in managerial capacity might suggest that these consequences are in part intended. However, there are also many unintended consequences as well that arise from the resultant pressures on managers to deliver without necessarily having the time and resources to make best use of the knowledge sharing, learning and networking opportunities available to them. Moreover, managers appear constantly to have to respond to fixations with specific recipes for improving management practice—such as the importance of leadership and the value of importing 'best practice' into healthcare. In doing so, effort may be displaced into the application of managerial prescriptions that bear only very tenuous connections to the real, practical challenges that managers face in their work on a day-to-day basis and to the ways in which managers learn how to manage. Managing effectively in that changing and volatile context is no mean achievement and can be considered something of an accomplishment—despite the very bad publicity associated with what are framed as serious healthcare management failures (e.g. Francis, 2013).

Healthcare Management as a Community of Practice?

Earlier, the notion of community of practice was explored as a possible starting point for framing some of this broader discussion (Lave and Wenger, 1991; Wenger, 1998; Brown and Duguid, 2001). Communities of practice may or may not be associated with particular formal professional groupings, but membership of a community of practice typically involves an immersion in the practices of that community and developing one's identity as a practitioner—learning from within about the particular field of practice, rather than learning about that practice as an outsider. Membership of a community of practice revolves around shared narratives of experience, shared paradigmatic modes of analysis and shared modes of representation (Boland and Tenkasi, 1995). Communities of practice also encourage their members to search and adapt knowledge from beyond the particular organizational setting in which they are immersed. In principle, therefore, being a member of a wider community of practice should enable extra-organizational learning and arguably assist the incorporation of wider sources of knowledge and different ways of knowing into management practice within the organization. At the same time, the benefits of learning associated with communities of practice are often gained at the expense of difficulties encountered when more than one community of practice with quite different epistemic practices need to interact. Consequently, while communities of practice are typically defined as closely related groups of practitioners who develop and share common understandings through frequent and close interaction, it is also important to remain sensitive to the variety of groups, communities and networks to which managers belong and to the potential interplays between them.

Deconstructing management in healthcare as a community of practice is a relatively easy task, given the diversity and fragmentation in practices and forms of knowing and learning that have become apparent as we have drilled down into these aspects of management in the previous four chapters. Indeed, it would be extremely difficult (and somewhat heroic) to conclude that what we have here (or could have) is a unitary and unified managerial community of practice within healthcare. Managerial groups clearly had very diverse and distinct bodies of knowledge and they connected with very distinct networks of practitioners, in different ways and for different reasons. This is particularly true of clinicians and those with distinct functional backgrounds (i.e. finance, HR managers); but it is also the case when we consider the very diverse knowledge bases encapsulated within both clinical and general managerial groups (e.g. different types of clinician, including psychologists and AHPs; and general managers whose professional networks were often related to quite distinct types of service).

Of course, if a research method is used that sets out to differentiate between management groups, then it is perhaps not surprising that it should reveal such diversity and fragmentation. Moreover, it was quite clear that there were still a number of important points of connection and similarities in experience amongst management groups, despite their apparent diversity. These included aspects of management practice (the skill sets required and the reification of leadership, despite its sublimation from practice); sources of knowledge (driven by formal reporting requirements and attributed more to experience than training); and types of networking activity (that were principally used for knowledge and support). Nevertheless, while it is important to draw out these similarities as the earlier chapters have done, it is important to recognize too the key differences and what these imply for the development of a coherent body of knowledge and professional practice within healthcare management.

Indeed, if we first consider the relationship between clinicians, managers and other groups within management, we emerge with further confirmation that management in healthcare is itself a highly contested notion (e.g. Learmonth, 2005). Within the NHS in particular, the management/leadership distinction is probably more sharply defined, and has greater palpable weight and political significance, than in many other sectors, for the reasons outlined in Chapter 2. Moreover, historical tensions between management and clinical professions have resulted in continuing suspicion of (and resistance to) management both as a function and as a cadre. The consequence is a complex and delicate ontological landscape, where many NHS employees who manage will, for a variety of reasons, be ambivalent or conflicted over the title 'manager' and may not even recognize their practice as 'managing'. Furthermore, the continuing denigration of management in healthcare (Hyde et al., 2016) runs in parallel with the reification of leadership as a much more desirable alternative to management. This is not just by general managers themselves, but also by clinicians otherwise deterred by management and yet more than willing to benefit from the powerful symbolism associated with 'clinical leadership' (Spurgeon et al., 2011; Hyde et al., 2012; Bresnen et al., 2015).

Consequently, management in healthcare is not just a heterogeneous activity (Buchanan et al., 2007), but also a heterogeneous identity—distributed amongst a wide range of occupational groups who draw upon highly diverse sources of knowledge, learning and experience and who interact through very diverse and distinct networks of interaction. In this complex milieu, there are clear, cross-cutting hierarchies of status and influence that continue to shape the contested professional terrain that links managers with other professional/occupational groups (cf. Abbott, 1988). Put simply, middle managers face not only the recalcitrance of clinical professionals in determining the extent to which managerial processes and practices are accepted and embedded; they also have to rely upon the discursive resources that emphasize financial goals and regulatory imperatives if they are to have any real effect. This leaves very little space for the development of a distinct body of knowledge that does not simply defer to clinical know-how and financial/regulatory controls. The net effect is that it is general managers who face the greatest challenge in sharpening their sense of professional/ occupational identity around a coherent and distinct knowledge base and set of practices.

One way of looking at this further is to consider healthcare management as consisting neither of one clearly defined community of practice; nor of several inter-connected, but professionally distinct groups that together constitute a more splintered knowledge *collectivity* (Lindkvist, 2005); but as nested communities whose membership is fluid and whose boundaries are blurred. Managers therefore have to resort to framing management action in ways that best harness the discursive resources available to them (often in ways that speak to financial logic or reporting requirements); while, at the same time, framing them in such a way as to make them acceptable to other powerful groups, notably clinicians. Despite the strong connections that undoubtedly link different managerial groups through their engagement in common practices of management, it is clinical experience, managerial hybridity and relational skills that play key roles in providing the credibility needed for general managers to engage effectively and exert influence (cf. Iedema et al., 2004). Moreover, the imbalance of power and dependence between clinical and managerial groups at these blurred boundaries— whether or not they are bridged by hybrid managers displaying integrative capabilities (cf. Owen-Smith et al., 2004)—always tends to ensure that the former perspective is privileged and as such, tends to reinforce, rather than undermine, the status quo (cf. von Knorring et al., 2016).

Tensions and Dilemmas in Managers Knowing, Learning and Networking

When it comes to flows of knowledge and learning, such schisms within the managerial community inevitably pose major problems too for legitimizing certain forms of knowledge and practice that managers might have access to and be able to mobilize—especially more codified and abstract forms of management knowledge. In other words, while there are clearly practical challenges in transferring or translating abstract management knowledge to a healthcare context, a bigger issue is the lack of legitimacy of such knowledge. Where more effort was made to be circumspect and flexible in the use of such tools and techniques in what could be depicted as a *generative dance* that sought to marry codified knowledge with tacit forms of knowing (cf. Cook and Brown, 1999), then there was perhaps scope for overcoming the dual hurdles of suitability and acceptability. Otherwise, there were clear problems in translating such codified forms of knowledge into practice, without them becoming distorted or simply rejected.

More localized forms of knowledge associated with formulating responses to standard reporting requirements (such as responses to CQC and the like), on the other hand, were far more readily accepted and embedded in practice. Despite the diverse contexts faced by general managers, what knowledge was shared typically related more to the knowledge associated with meeting wider organizational demands (e.g. for standardization) and/ or national institutional needs (e.g. reporting requirements). The problem here was that the forms of management knowledge they privileged again tended to be those associated with the standardization and routinization of practice. These were precisely the types of knowledge that, although they could be relatively easily codified, shared and embedded in practice, were antithetical to the sort of strategic thinking that managers felt was in danger of being 'crowded out' by routine; and to forms of learning that relied more on creative and innovative thinking.

Moreover, the strong emphasis that was placed upon personal experience in learning how to manage also tended to reinforce a more intuitive approach to management and the idea that the most important sources of knowledge and processes of learning were those that were personally embodied and developed experientially. The encouragement of strong ties for the sharing of resultant tacit understandings about how to manage may have been a preferred mode of learning and had some considerable benefits for managers' attempts to internalize new ways of working through socialization into their role. However, they also inevitably made it difficult to externalize or extrapolate knowledge and learning within and between organizations. Furthermore, they also tended to substitute for wider connections to alternative, more explicit and potentially valuable alternative forms of knowledge.

What these complex conditions appear to suggest is something of a dilemma. On the one hand, the highly fragmented nature of management poses considerable challenges to flows of knowledge and learning due to the many interests that need to be reconciled or accommodated if management practices are to be somehow transformed. On the other hand, management in healthcare is enough of a self-referential and self-reinforcing community of practice that it promotes views of knowledge and learning that default to acceptable, 'common sense' solutions that focus on the immediate, the practical and the essential. In other words, it could be argued that management in healthcare experiences the worst of both worlds: limited in its ability to develop and deploy a distinctive body of knowledge that draws on wider systems of knowing that have legitimacy within the sector; yet trapped in its own system of knowing that is shaped by professional constraints and practical demands and which thus defaults to the common denominator of local, intuitive, situated knowledge and learning. The overall net effect is the reinforcement of (and in some respects regression to) established ways of managing, knowing and networking that, in complex, changing and unfavourable conditions, at least offer managers some certainty, constancy, security and support. In other words, if healthcare management practice, knowledge and networking are evolving, then they are doing so in ways that emphasize even further the value of the pragmatic, the personal, the local and the situated, as opposed to the value of the idealistic, the systematic, the global and the abstract.

Despite the value of the substantial literature on communities of practice that highlights the interpenetration of socialization and knowledge sharing processes, we also recognize the limitations in too exclusive a focus on this type of arrangement (Amin and Roberts, 2008). The research here focused on a broader and more extensive concept of *networks*, a concept which allows for a greater diversity in terms of degrees of co-ordination and cohesion, strictures on membership, the ways in which they are formed and their location within or across organizational boundaries. Several of the wider networks that managers had access to certainly were perceived by managers as playing some part in knowledge mobilization and socialization. In spite of taking this broadened approach to exploring network connections, however, the main message to emerge in this respect was the challenges faced by general managers in particular in being able to access fully and be actively engaged with wider networks of professionals (not only across trusts but within their own trust too). Not only did this mean that general managers had much less opportunity to gain potentially valuable knowledge and support, but also that it tended to reinforce their strong reliance on local and experiential knowledge. These limitations add to the inward-looking tendencies that have already been identified and highlight further how the reproduction of managerial knowledge and practice was driven primarily by immediate organizational needs and management challenges. The result was a general neglect of more ambitious attempts to access and apply more abstract management knowledge or to generalize learning from experiences elsewhere.

Prospects for a Professional Managerial Cadre in Healthcare?

So, what does this all mean for the nature of management in healthcare and prospects for its professionalization, if that can be considered a viable and justifiable project? Well, there are a number of key points that emerge from this research and which have implications for healthcare managers' evolving professional identity.

First, if we return to the wider context of change, there is a major paradox here, in that, while many of the major changes in healthcare policy have been characterized as promoting managerialism, they have actually resulted in considerably worsened conditions for managers. For instance, the introduction of foundation trusts could be interpreted as a managerialist move, intended to create corporate entities out of hospital trusts, with the expectation that the increased efficiency that would result from more rational and financially driven strategy and planning would be reinvested into organizational development. These aspirations, on the face of it, appear to favour the work of managers: finance, over which managers are stewards, becomes a more legitimate means of exchange within the organization; the uptake of strategic management principles offers the means for managers to establish closure around an area of expertise; and the rationalization of organizations into divisions creates opportunities for management given the increased need for co-ordination. However, as our findings suggest, and particularly in relation to general middle managers, such changes, rather than creating a more professionalized cadre, have effectively contributed to their *de-professionalization*. Drawing on each of our empirical themes in turn, we can see this as being driven by:

- The continuing denigration of managerial tasks as the more mundane 'nuts and bolts' of healthcare activity; and the take-up by clinicians (albeit reluctantly) of discourses of leadership that help them retain and reinforce their influence over management.
- The over-arching perception that 'anyone can manage' and that 'managers just manage' offers little in terms of expertise around which managers might attempt to establish closure. Management knowledge is seen as either too abstract and divorced from context to be useful; or conversely, too diffuse and 'everyday' to represent proper 'expertise'.
- Where management knowledge is useful, it is as an adjunct to financial and other regulatory reporting systems. This not only regulates the exchange of management knowledge within and between organizations, but also casts managers as agents of government policy and regulatory control. Organizational failures can then easily be cast as failures of management, reinforcing the view of management as a homogenous group of bureaucrats unconcerned with public service and divorced from the clinical 'front-line'.
- Managers themselves are faced with increasingly precarious means of developing and maintaining a stable career and professional identity, in the context of hybridization and economic rationalization and in the comparative absence of a coherent, legitimate and accepted domain of specialist knowledge or strong professional networks.

Second, and related to the points made above about knowledge, the findings suggest that any likely professionalization of management in healthcare is ultimately constrained by its connection to a body of knowledge that is less influenced by more abstract and formalized bodies of management knowledge and more driven by immediate system requirements and bureaucratic processes (cf. Hodgson, 2002; Miller, 2014). The strong emphasis on situated learning and applied know-how in the light of local conditions do not easily lend themselves to a traditional mode of professionalization (Abbott, 1988). Consequently, the prospect of a robust and recognized profession of healthcare management offering managers a power-base comparable to clinical professionalism seems a rather distant and implausible goal, even if it were to be seen as desirable. On the other hand, it could be argued that the institutional weakness of healthcare management as an occupational group does at least mean that it poses less of a threat to the influence base of other professionals, including nurses, doctors and allied health professionals. A more promising route perhaps may therefore be to present management as a meaningful and productive complement to other professions, clinical or otherwise, through the powerful hybrid capabilities it brings (Noordegraaf and Van Der Meulen, 2008; Noordegraaf, 2011a). However, this is seemingly less likely if management continues to be sharply differentiated from leadership, stigmatized in public discourse and implicitly associated with an historic administrative role (Learmonth, 2005).

Instead, any professionalization project in healthcare management is more likely to be predicated on the build-up of local knowledge and expertise which relates to more enriched and entrepreneurial managerial roles. The problem with this of course is that it represents a much lesser and far less portable form of professional status and influence for managers. For individuals facing already challenging conditions, it also simply adds yet another regime of control and performance management. Moreover, the losers in such a scenario are, once again, those general managers who in practice remain detached from networks and other sources of legitimacy.

Third, the concept of hybridity itself has been shown to be more disparate and complex than is often realized. We perhaps know rather more about the impact of clinical-managerial hybridity from the perspective of the medical profession and the threats and challenges that it poses to the professional status and knowledge base of clinicians (Noordegraaf, 2015). However, what this research has attempted to do is to explore a variety of types of managerial hybridity and therefore to incorporate some consideration of the inter- and intra-professional differences that impact upon managers' sense-making of their professional career development. So, for example, comparing the accounts of clinician-hybrids and nurse-hybrids has allowed us to explore key similarities and difference as well as highlight some of the main contextual influences. As such, our research has revealed a much more complex set of career paths that lie behind the socialization of managers into their managerial roles and considerable variation in identification with management and internalization of its core values and practices. It has therefore identified a much more complex set of identity formations and associated identity work than is often considered (cf. Watson, 1994, 2008) and that is consistent with the uni-directionality implied by the concept of professionalization project.

Finally, interwoven through this analysis and discussion has been a consideration of organizational factors (particularly structural differentiation, clinical-management interaction, centralization-formalization tendencies and pressures due to exogenous and endogenous change) alongside institutional/policy driven effects (greater demands on managers and greater regulation and control). Together, these organizational and institutional factors shape the ways in which managers see their professional development and role, and informs how relates to their experience base, knowledge and networks. In doing so, we have explored some of the major similarities and differences between the trusts and their varied impact upon different managerial groups. That analysis will not be repeated here. However, it is important to emphasize how it demonstrates overall that there are important situational differences that can affect management practices and processes of knowing and networking. That is, different forms of healthcare organizations exhibit different characteristics that shape management practice and knowledge requirements in different ways. Often this tends to be forgotten when we talk about management as a whole across healthcare or, indeed, healthcare as a whole. In particular, the findings suggest that there are important organizational differences in clinical-managerial relations and appropriate internal integration strategies; in the importance of managerial hybridity as a personal embodiment of clinical-managerial professional identity; in orientations towards different forms and sources of knowledge and learning; and in opportunities for, and orientations towards wider networking activity. While some of these effects were more noticeable, others were more nuanced; and while some were more piecemeal in their effects, others combined to have a more holistic impact upon management. Whatever the exact effects, the important point to emphasize here is that variations we identified in practice, identity, knowing and networking were not only related to differences in managerial type, they were also frequent related to differences in organizational archetype (cf. Greenwood et al., 2002).

Consequently, it is important to note that in our analysis many of those factors have been shown to have an effect—often unexpected, sometimes subtle and insidious—upon managers' ability to be receptive to knowledge and to engage in knowledge sharing and learning within their organizations and across the sector and to develop appropriate networks and communities of practice. In particular, the research brings into question not only the idea that developing knowledge sharing and learning across communities of practice is difficult when these communities are so fragmented, disparate and diverse and the networks they rely upon so sporadic (and often truncated); but also that organizational processes can, if not considered carefully, have the unintended effects of reinforcing some of the problems faced by managers in accessing and mobilizing wider sources of managerial knowledge and learning. For the sector as a whole, there are clear implications here in the challenges faced in developing a managerial cadre that is both valued for the management skills and responsibilities they draw upon and enact, while at the same time being given sufficient opportunity to marry these skills with the needs of healthcare organizations in the interests of professional, personal and organizational development.

Directions for Future Research

Our research has demonstrated the value of situating analysis of management knowledge mobilization and utilization in the context of the particular organizational conditions and challenges facing diverse managerial groups.

However, that very complexity and diversity also prompts further questions about how the mobilization of management knowledge may be affected by conditions in other types of healthcare setting (for example, primary care). Although our selection of three archetypal forms of healthcare setting allows us analytically to generalize the findings to similar types of healthcare setting (cf. Yin, 1984; Eisenhardt and Graebner, 2007), different constellations of conditions may of course create different outcomes in other types of setting (for example, in inhibiting or enabling more the sharing of learning through particular communities of practice). Clearly, this suggests the value of further research that taps into the effects of conditions in other types of healthcare setting.

There is also the need for further research that might extend the breadth of coverage to a wider or more complete set of participants. This research has relied on small-scale purposive sampling, as opposed to large-scale random sampling, and as such, the findings are inevitably restricted to the range of experiences and conditions faced by the group of managers selected. The qualitative nature of the study has nevertheless allowed us to choose our participants carefully and then to examine their experiences in considerable depth, augmenting this with direct observation of their management practices. While broadening out the research to include larger samples of participants inevitably sacrifices some depth of analysis for breadth of coverage, there is clearly some value in extending the research out to examine variations in management practice both between and within trusts. Indeed, the framework of management types we developed in our study offers a practical framework for selecting and surveying managers on that basis.

Last but not least, the data we have obtained have provided rich insights into the ways in which different managers access, share and use managerial knowledge and how this relates to diverse organizational circumstances and professional backgrounds. However, each of these networks of interaction in which specific groups of managers are involved are worthy of study in their own right. Attempting to do so has been well beyond the scope of the current study. However, there is clearly more scope for exploring in greater depth any or all of the networks of interaction that involve the managers we studied. Research of this type might employ similar quantitative research methods but might also consider alternative techniques, such as more in-depth ethnographies, managerial shadowing or social network analysis. This research has signposted where further research may reveal important details about the structure and dynamics of such networks of interaction and how they influence managerial practice, identity formation, knowing and networking.

Recommendations for Practice

While this book has been principally concerned with analysis of management in healthcare, rather than the prescription of management solutions, there are clearly a number of important potential implications of the work for healthcare management policy and practice that stem from the research findings and which it is hoped will have some useful practical impact. These implications pertain mainly to management training and development, but also encompass steps that trusts and other agencies might take to improve the structural context within which managers are embedded.

First, the research points to a widespread tendency to denigrate management in favour of heroic conceptions of leadership. There are benefits to be gained from a clearer recognition of the contribution of effective management, and the necessity of explicitly presenting management and leadership as more equal partners in managing complex and changing organizations. Leadership training and development programmes (e.g. via the NHS Leadership Academy) may need to ensure that the development of leadership takes account of the complex relationship between leadership skills and management practice 'on the ground'. Local trust training and development programmes can also help maximize the transferability of context-specific leadership training to management practice by ensuring that analysis of leadership challenges and solutions is firmly situated in routine management problem-solving and decision-making scenarios.

Second, the research indicates that the challenge of codifying and translating management knowledge leads to an over-reliance on experience and localized, situated knowledge and/or a tendency to privilege other, more established forms of knowledge such as clinical or financial. The evidence underlines the value of exploiting wider networks and other social modes of engagement to try to overcome these epistemic boundaries and assist the mobilization of knowledge. It also suggests that it is important that management training and development combines an appropriate balance of different sources of knowledge.

Third, the challenge of managing the relationship between clinical and managerial communities is pervasive across healthcare organizations. Our trusts each adopted distinct structural, relational, or personally embodied means to manage this relationship, each reflecting their organizational contexts. The research suggests that there is no universal solution, and that trusts need to tailor their approaches accordingly to manage this divide. National leadership programmes should also be considered as an opportunity for cultivating networked interaction between distinct types of managerial groups (especially clinical and general). This approach would encourage development of shared perspectives between the communities of practice on the use and application of specific types of managerial knowledge. There may also be opportunities for trusts to develop mechanisms for such networked interaction focused on management issues and solutions at a more local level, provided that they occur away from immediate operational pressures.

Fourth, our research suggests that receptivity to management knowledge, and the innovative or creative use of this knowledge, is enhanced by training and development that allows space and time for reflection and knowledge translation. This applies across all managerial groups but especially to general managers. Trusts need to find ways of giving middle managers time out from busy schedules to take up any opportunities afforded by more advanced training and development programmes that are based on such reflective learning processes.

Fifth, the research indicates that networking for knowledge acquisition/sharing, support, career development and influence are closely inter-related. Therefore recognition of the embeddedness of knowledge processes in social networks points to the importance of supporting the formation of strong network ties to enhance knowledge sharing and learning. Perhaps greater recognition needs to be given (in national and more local training programmes) to the importance and benefits of both formal and informal networks of interaction as sources of knowledge and support for managers and how specific mechanisms for middle managers may help significantly (e.g. mentoring).

Finally, given the evidence pertaining to isolation and inward-looking tendencies among general management groups in healthcare, trusts might consider the advantages of providing greater opportunities for internal and external networking to assist knowledge sharing and learning. External (regional, area) networks of managers could be actively cultivated (either by individual trusts or through inter-trust collaboration), and trusts that are highly differentiated (geographically, organizationally, professionally) may benefit particularly from taking their own internal networking initiatives that have the dual advantage of helping managers share best practice as well as improving organizational integration.

Bibliography

Abbott, A. (1988). *The system of professions: Essay on the division of expert labour.* Chicago: University of Chicago Press.

Abrahamson, E. (1991). Managerial fads and fashions: The diffusion and rejection of innovations. *Academy of Management Review, 16*(3), 586–612.

Abrahamson, E. (1996). Management fashion. *Academy of Management Review, 21*(1), 254–285.

Addicott, R., McGivern, G., & Ferlie, E. (2007). The distortion of a managerial technique? The case of clinical networks in UK health care. *British Journal of Management, 18*(1), 93–105.

Agterberg, M., Hooff, B. V. D., Huysman, M., & Soekijad, M. (2010). Keeping the wheels turning: The dynamics of managing networks of practice. *Journal of Management Studies, 47*(1), 85–108.

Ahrne, G., & Brunsson, N. (2005). Organizations and meta-organizations. *Scandinavian Journal of Management, 21*(4), 429–449.

Alexander, R. (2012). Which is the world's biggest employer? *BBC*, www.bbc.co.uk/news/magazine-17429786.

Alimo-Metcalfe, B., & Lawler, J. (2001). Leadership development in UK companies at the beginning of the twenty-first century: Lessons for the NHS? *Journal of Management in Medicine, 15*(5), 387–404.

Alvesson, M. (2010). Self doubters, strugglers, storytellers, surfers and others: Images of self-identities in organization studies. *Human Relations, 63,* 193–217.

Alvesson, M., Ashcraft, K., & Thomas, R. (2008). Identity matters: Reflections on the construction of identity scholarship in organization studies. *Organization, 15*(1), 5–28.

Alvesson, M., & Karreman, D. (2001). Odd couple: Making sense of the curious concept of knowledge management. *Journal of Management Studies, 38*(7), 995–1018.

Alvesson, M., & Willmott, H. (2002). Identity regulation as organizational control: Producing the appropriate individual. *Journal of Management Studies, 39*(5), 619–644.

Alvesson, M., & Willmott, H. (2003). *Studying management critically.* London: Sage Publications.

Amin, A., & Roberts, J. (2008). Knowing in action: Beyond communities of practice. *Research Policy, 37*(2), 353–369.

Anderson-Gough, F., Grey, C., & Robson, K. (2006). Professionals, networking and the networked professional. *Research in the Sociology of Organizations, 24,* 231–256.

Anthony, P. (1986). *The foundation of management.* London: Tavistock.

Anthony, P., & Reed, M. (1990). Managerial roles and relationships: The impact of the Griffiths report. *International Journal of Health Care Quality Assurance, 3*(3), 21–30.

Appleby, J., Helderman, J., & Gregory, S. (2015). The global financial crisis, health and health care. *Health Economics, Policy and Law, 10*(1), 1–6.

Argyris, C., & Schon, D. (1978). *Organizational learning.* Reading, MA: Addison-Wesley.

Armstrong, P. (1987). The rise of accounting controls in British capitalist enterprises. *Accounting Organizations and Society, 12*(5), 415–436.

Ashforth, B. E. (2001). *Role transitions in organizational life: An identity-based perspective.* Mahwah, NJ: Lawrence Erlbaum Associates.

Barley, S., & Kunda, G. (2001). Bringing work back in. *Organization Science, 12*(1), 76–95.

Bate, P. (2000). Changing the culture of a hospital: From hierarchy to networked community. *Public Administration, 78*(3), 485–512.

Bate, P., & Robert, G. (2002). Knowledge management and communities of practice in the private sector: Lessons for modernizing the National Health Service in England and Wales. *Public Administration, 80*(4), 643–663.

Beech, N. (2011). Liminality and the practices of identity reconstruction. *Human Relations, 64*(2), 285–302.

Bensaou, B. M., Galunic, C., & Jonczyk-Sédès, C. (2014). Players and purists: Networking strategies and agency of service professionals. *Organization Science, 25*(1), 29–56.

Bevan, G., & Hood, C. (2006). What's measured is what matters: Targets and gaming in the English public health care system. *Public Administration, 84*(3), 517–538.

Bevan, G., Karanikolos, M., Exley, J., Nolte, E., Connolly, S., & Mays, N. (2014). *The four health systems of the United Kingdom: How do they compare?* London: Health Foundation & Nuffield Trust.

Blackler, F. (1995). Knowledge, knowledge work and organizations: An overview and interpretation. *Organization Studies, 16*(6), 1021–1046.

Boaden, R., Marchington, M., Hyde, P., Harris, C., Sparrow, P., & Pass, S. (2008). *The process of engagement and alignment: Improving health through HRM.* London: CIPD.

Boland, R., & Tenkasi, R. (1995). Perspective making and perspective taking in communities of knowing. *Organization Science, 6*(4), 350–372.

Bolton, S. C. (2005). 'Making up' managers. *Work, Employment and Society, 19*(1), 5–23.

Braithwaite, J. (2010). Between-group behaviour in health care: Gaps, edges, boundaries, disconnections, weak ties, spaces and holes: A systematic review. *BMC Health Services Research, 10,* 330–330.

Braithwaite, J. (2015). Bridging gaps to promote networked care between teams and groups in health delivery systems: A systematic review of non-health literature. *BMJ Open, 5*(9), 1–12.

Bresnen, M. (1995). All things to all people? Perceptions, attributions and constructions of leadership. *Leadership Quarterly, 6*(4), 495–513.

Bresnen, M., Hodgson, D., Bailey, S., Hyde, P., & Hassard, J. (2014). Being a manager, becoming a professional? A case study and interview-based exploration of the use of management knowledge across communities of practice in health-care organizations. *Health Services Delivery Research, 2*(14), 1–166.

Bresnen, M., Hyde, P., Hodgson, D., Bailey, S., & Hassard, J. (2015). Leadership talk: From managerialism to leaderism in healthcare after the crash. *Leadership, 11*(4), 451–470.

Brocklehurst, M., Grey, C., & Sturdy, A. (2009). Management: The work that dares not speak its name. *Management Learning, 41*(1), 7–19.

Brooks, I. (1999). Managerialist professionalism: The destruction of a non-conforming subculture. *British Journal of Management, 10*(1), 41–52.

Brown, A. (2015). Identities and identity work in organizations. *International Journal of Management Reviews, 17*, 20–40.

Brown, J., & Duguid, P. (2001). Knowledge and organization: A social-practice perspective. *Organization Science, 12*(2), 198–213.

Bryman, A. E. (1986). *Leadership and organizations.* London: Routledge & Kegan Paul.

Buchanan, D. (2013). Pure plays and hybrids: Acute trusts management profile and capacity. *Journal of Health Services Research & Policy, 18*(2), 90–97.

Buchanan, D., Addicot, R., Fitzgerald, L., Ferlie, E., & Baeza, J. (2007). Nobody in charge: Distributed change agency in healthcare. *Human Relations, 60*(7), 1065–1090.

Buchanan, D., Denyer, D., Jaina, J., Kelliher, C., Moore, C., Parry, E., & Pilbeam, C. (2013). How do they manage? A qualitative study of the realities of middle and front-line management work in healthcare. *Health Services and Delivery Research, 1*(4), 1–248.

Buchanan, D., & Fitzgerald, L. (2011). New lock, new stock, new barrel, same gun: The accessorized bureaucracy of health care. In S. Clegg, M. Harris, & H. Hopfl (Eds.), *Managing modernity: Beyond bureaucracy?* (pp. 56–80). Oxford: Oxford University Press.

Burgess, N., & Currie, G. (2013). The knowledge brokering role of the hybrid middle level manager: The case of healthcare. *British Journal of Management, 24*, S132–S142.

Burgess, N., Strauss, G., Currie, G., & Wood, G. (2015). Organizational ambidexterity and the hybrid middle manager: The case of patient safety in UK hospitals. *Human Resource Management, 54*(S1), S87–S109.

Burrell, G., & Morgan, G. (1979). *Sociological paradigms and organizational analysis.* London: Heinemann.

Burt, R. (1992). *Structural holes.* Cambridge, MA: Harvard University Press.

Buttigieg, S., Rathert, C., & von Eiff, W. (Eds.). (2015). *International best practices in healthcare management.* Bingley: Emerald.

Campbell, D. (2014, 9 December). NHS bill for management advisers doubles to £640m. *The Guardian,* www.theguardian.com/society/2014/dec/2009/nhs-management-consultants-bill-doubles-2640m.

Carlile, P. (2002). A pragmatic view of knowledge and boundaries: Boundary objects in new product development. *Organization Science, 13*(4), 442–455.

Carlile, P. (2004). Transferring, translating, and transforming: An integrative framework for managing knowledge across boundaries. *Organization Science, 15*(5), 555–568.

Carroll, B., & Levy, L. (2008). Defaulting to management: Leadership defined by what it is not. *Organization, 15*(1), 75–96.

Casciaro, T., Gino, F., & Kouchaki, M. (2014). The contaminating effects of building instrumental ties: How networking can make us feel dirty. *Administrative Science Quarterly, 59*(4), 705–735.

Cascio, W. (2002). *Responsible restructuring: Creative and profitable alternatives to layoffs.* San Francisco, CA: Berrett-Koehler.

Cascio, W. (2005). Strategies for responsible restructuring. *Academy of Management Executive, 16*(3), 80–91.

Castells, M. (1996). *The rise of the network society: Vol 1. The information age.* Oxford: Blackwell.

Chambers, N., & Walshe, K. (2010). Healthcare reform and leadership. In S. Brookes & K. Grint (Eds.), *The new public leadership challenge* (pp. 33–53). Basingstoke: Palgrave MacMillan.

Clarence, E., & Painter, C. (1998). Public services under new labour: Collaborative discourses and local networking. *Public Policy and Administration, 13,* 8–22.

Clark, T., & Salaman, G. (1998). Telling tales: Management gurus' narratives and the construction of managerial identity. *Journal of Management Studies, 35*(2), 137–161.

Clarke, C., Brown, A., & Hope Hailey, V. (2009). Working identities? Antagonistic discursive resources and managerial identity. *Human Relations, 62*(3), 323–352.

Clegg, S., & Palmer, G. (1996). *The politics of management knowledge.* London: Sage Publications.

Cohen, W., & Levinthal, D. (1990). Absorptive capacity: A new perspective on learning and innovation. *Administrative Science Quarterly, 35*(1), 128–152.

Coleman, J. (1988). Social capital in the creation of human capital. *American Journal of Sociology, 94*(Supplement), S95–S120.

Collinson, D. L. (2003). Identities and insecurities: Selves at work. *Organization, 10*(3), 527–547.

Contu, A., & Willmott, H. (2003). Re-embedding situatedness: The importance of power relations in learning theory. *Organization Science, 14*(3), 283–296.

Cook, S., & Brown, J. (1999). Bridging epistemologies: The generative dance between organizational knowledge and organizational knowing. *Organization Science, 10*(4), 381–400.

Cooksey, D. (2006). *A review of UK health research funding.* London: Stationary Office.

Coyle-Shapiro, J., & Parzefall, M. (2008). Psychological contracts. In C. Cooper & J. Barling (Eds.), *The Sage handbook of organizational behaviour* (pp. 17–34). London: Sage Publications.

Creed, W. E. D., Dejordy, R., & Lok, J. (2010). Being the change: Resolving institutional contradiction through identity work. *Academy of Management Journal, 53*(6), 1336–1364.

Croft, C., Currie, G., & Lockett, A. (2015). Broken 'two-way windows'? An exploration of professional hybrids. *Public Administration, 93*(2), 380–394.

Currie, G. (1997). Contested terrain: The incomplete closure of managerialism in the health service. *Health Manpower Management, 23*(4), 123–132.

Currie, G. (2006). Reluctant but resourceful middle managers: The case of nurses in the NHS. *Journal of Nursing Management, 14,* 5–12.

Currie, G., Finn, R., & Martin, G. (2008). Accounting for the 'dark side' of new organizational forms: The case of healthcare professionals. *Human Relations, 61*(4), 539–564.

Currie, G., Finn, R., & Martin, G. (2010). Role transition and the interaction of relational and social identity: New nursing roles in the English NHS. *Organization Studies, 31*(7), 941–961.

Currie, G., & Procter, S. (2005). The antecedents of middle managers' strategic contribution: The case of a professional bureaucracy. *Journal of Management Studies, 42*(7), 1325–1356.

Currie, G., & Suhomlinova, O. (2006). The impact of institutional forces upon knowledge sharing in the UK NHS: The triumph of professional power and the inconsistency of policy. *Public Administration, 84*(1), 1–30.

Currie, G., & White, L. (2012). Inter-professional barriers and knowledge brokering in an organizational context: The case of healthcare. *Organization Studies, 33*(10), 1333–1361.

Czarniawska, B., & Joerges, B. (1996). Travels of ideas. In B. Czarniawska & G. Sevón (Eds.), *Translating organizational change* (pp. 13–48). Berlin: de Gruyter.

Czarniawska, B., & Sevón, G. (Eds.). (1996). *Translating organizational change.* Berlin: de Gruyter.

Czarniawska-Joerges, B. (1990). Merchants of meaning: Management consulting in the Swedish public sector. In B. Turner (Ed.), *Organizational symbolism* (pp. 139–150). New York: De Gruyter.

Czarniawska-Joerges, B. (1994). Narratives of individual and organizational identities. In S. Deetz (Ed.), *Communication yearbook* (pp. 193–221). Newbury Park, CA: Sage Publications.

Davies, H., & Harrison, S. (2003). Trends in doctor-manager relationships. *British Medical Journal, 326,* 646–649.

Dayan, M. (2014). *The Francis report: One year on.* London: Nuffield Trust.

DDRB. (2016). *Written evidence from the health department for England.* London: Department of Health.

de Janasz, S. C., & Forret, M. L. (2008). Learning the art of networking: A critical skill for enhancing social capital and career success. *Journal of Management Education, 32*(5), 629–650.

Delbridge, R. (1998). *Life on the line in contemporary manufacturing.* Oxford: Oxford University Press.

Dellve, L., & Wikström, E. (2009). Managing complex workplace stress in health care organizations: Leaders' perceived legitimacy conflicts. *Journal of Nursing Management, 17*(8), 931–941.

Denis, J. L., Langley, A., & Rouleau, L. (2010). The practice of leadership in the messy world of organizations. *Leadership, 6*(1), 67–88.

Department of Health. (1990). *NHS and community care act.* London: The Stationery Office.

Department of Health. (1997). *The new NHS: Modern, dependable.* London: The Stationery Office.

Department of Health. (2000). *NHS plan: A plan for investment.* London: The Stationery Office.

Department of Health. (2008). *High quality care for all (NHS next stage review final report): Darzi report.* London: The Stationery Office.

Department of Health. (2010). *Equity and excellence: Liberating the NHS.* London: The Stationery Office.

Dopson, S. (1994). Management: The one disease consultants did not think existed. *Journal of Management in Medicine, 8*(3), 326–336.

Dopson, S., & Fitzgerald, L. (2006). The role of the middle manager in the implementation of evidence-based health care. *Journal of Nursing Management, 14,* 43–51.

Dopson, S., Fitzgerald, L., & Ferlie, E. (2008). Understanding change and innovation in healthcare settings: Reconceptualizing the active role of context. *Journal of Change Management, 8*(3–4), 213–231.

Down, S., & Reveley, J. (2009). Between narration and interaction: Situating first-line supervisor identity work. *Human Relations, 62*(3), 379–401.

Drucker, P. (1974). *Management: Tasks, responsibilities, practices.* London: Heinemann.

Eccles, M., Armstrong, D., Baker, R., Cleary, K., Davies, H., Davies, S., . . . Sibbald, B. (2009). An implementation science research agenda. *Implementation Science, 4*(18), 1–7.

Edwards, N. (2002). Clinical networks. *British Medical Journal, 324,* 63.

Eisenhardt, K., & Graebner, M. (2007). Theory building from cases: Opportunities and challenges. *Academy of Management Journal, 50*(1), 25–32.

Engwall, L., & Kipping, M. (2013). Management consulting: Dynamics, debates, and directions. *International Journal of Strategic Communication, 7*(2), 84–98.

Exworthy, M., Macfarlane, F., & Willmott, M. (2009). *NHS management: 60 years in transition.* London: Nuffield Trust.

Exworthy, M., Powell, M., & Mohan, J. (1999). The NHS: Quasi-market, quasi-hierarchy and quasi-network? *Public Money and Management, 19*(4), 15–22.

Ezzamel, M., Morris, J., & Smith, J. (2005). *Accounting for new organizational forms: The case of subcontracting and outsourcing.* London: CIMA.

Ferlie, E. (2016). *Analysing health care organizations: A personal anthology.* London: Routledge.

Ferlie, E., Crilly, T., & Jashapara, A. (2012). Knowledge mobilization in healthcare: A critical review. *Social Science & Medicine, 74*(8), 1297–1304.

Ferlie, E., Fitzgerald, L., McGivern, G., Dopson, S., & Bennett, C. (2013). *Making wicked problems governable? The case of managed networks in health care.* Oxford: Oxford University Press.

Ferlie, E., Fitzgerald, L., McGivern, G., Dopson, S., & Exworthy, M. (2010). *Networks in health care: A comparative study of their management, impact and performance.* London: National Institute for Health Research.

Ferlie, E., Fitzgerald, L., Wood, M., & Hawkins, C. (2005). The non-spread of innovations: The mediating role of professionals. *Academy of Management Journal, 48*(1), 117–134.

Ferlie, E., Ledger, J., Dopson, S., Fischer, M. D., Fitzgerald, L., McGivern, G., & Bennett, C. (2015). The political economy of management knowledge: Management texts in English healthcare organizations. *Public Administration, 94,* 185–203.

Ferlie, E., McGivern, G., & FitzGerald, L. (2012). A new mode of organizing in health care? Governmentality and managed networks in cancer services in England. *Social Science & Medicine, 74*(3), 340–347.

Ferlie, E., & Pettigrew, A. (1996). Managing through networks: Some issues and implications for the NHS. *British Journal of Management, 7*(1), 581–599.

Fischer, M. D., Dopson, S., Fitzgerald, L., Bennett, C., Ferlie, E., Ledger, J., & McGivern, G. (2015). Knowledge leadership: Mobilizing management research by becoming the knowledge object. *Human Relations, 69*(7), 1563–1585.

Fitzgerald, L. (2002). Interlocking interactions, the diffusion of innovations in healthcare. *Human Relations, 55*(12), 1429–1449.

Fitzgerald, L., & Ferlie, E. (2000). Professionals: Back to the future. *Human Relations, 53,* 713–739.

Flynn, R., Williams, G., & Pickard, S. (1996). *Markets and networks: Contracting in community health services.* Buckingham: Open University Press.

Ford, J. (2010). Studying leadership critically: A psychosocial lens on leadership identities. *Leadership, 6*(1), 47–65.

Ford, J., & Harding, N. (2007). Move over management: We are all leaders now. *Management Learning, 38*(5), 475–498.

Foucault, M. (1977). *Discipline and punish: The birth of the prison* (A. Sheridan, Trans.). Harmondsworth: Penguin.

Foucault, M. (1980). *Power/knowledge: Selected interviews and other writings, 1972–1977* (C. Gordon, Ed.). Brighton, Sussex: Harvester Press.

Fournier, V., & Grey, C. (2000). At the critical moment: Conditions and prospects for critical management studies. *Human Relations, 53*(1), 7–32.

Francis, R. (2013). *Report of the Mid Staffordshire NHS foundation trust public inquiry.* London: Stationary Office.

Friedson, E. (1970). *Profession of medicine.* New York: Dodd, Mead.

Fulop, L., & Mark, A. (2013). Leading in healthcare—foregrounding context. *Leadership, 9*(2), 151–161.

Fulop, N., Walters, R., 6, P., & Spurgeon, P. (2012). Implementing changes to hospital services: Factors influencing the process and 'results' of reconfiguration. *Health Policy, 104*(2), 128–135.

Gabbay, J., & Le May, A. (2004). Evidence-based guidelines or collectively constructed mindlines? Ethnographic study of knowledge management in primary care. *British Medical Journal, 329,* 1013–1018.

Gabriel, Y., Gray, D., & Goregaokar, H. (2010). Temporary derailment or end of the line? Managers coping with unemployment at 50. *Organization Studies, 31*(12), 1687–1712.

Gardner, W., Avolio, B., & Walumbwa, F. (Eds.). (2005). *Authentic leadership theory and practice: Origins, effects, and development.* San Diego, CA: Elsevier.

Garfinkel, H. (1984). *Studies in ethnomethodology.* Cambridge: Polity Press.

Garsten, C. (1999). Betwixt and between: Temporary employees as liminal subjects in flexible organizations. *Organization Studies, 20*(4), 601–617.

Gherardi, S. (2000). Practice-based theorizing on learning and knowing in organizations. *Organization, 7*(2), 211–223.

Gherardi, S. (2001). From organizational learning to practice-based knowing. *Human Relations, 54*(1), 131–139.

Gherardi, S. (2006). *Organizational knowledge: The texture of work-place learning.* Oxford: Blackwell.

Gherardi, S., & Nicolini, D. (2000). To transfer is to transform: The circulation of safety knowledge. *Organization, 7*(2), 329–348.

Giddens, A. (1991). *Modernity and self-identity: Self and society in the late modern age.* Cambridge: Polity.

Goldsmith, S., & Eggers, W. (2004). *Governing by network: The new shape of the public sector.* Washington, DC: Brookings.

Gouldner, A. W. (1958). Cosmopolitans and locals: Toward an analysis of latent social roles – ii. *Administrative Science Quarterly, 2*(4), 444–480.

Gourlay, S. (2006). Conceptualizing knowledge creation: A critique of Nonaka's theory. *Journal of Management Studies, 43*(7), 1415–1436.

Grabher, G., & Ibert, O. (2006). Bad company? The ambiguity of personal knowledge networks. *Journal of Economic Geography, 6*(3), 251–271.

Granovetter, M. (1973). The strength of weak ties. *The American Journal of Sociology, 78*(6), 1360–1380.

Grant, R. (1996). Toward a knowledge-based theory of the firm. *Strategic Management Journal, 17*(Winter), 109–122.

Greenhalgh, T. (2010a). *Diffusion, spread and sustainability of innovations in health service delivery and organization.* Paper presented at the 'The spread and sustainability of CLAHRC ways of working,' Leeds Marriott Hotel, UK.

Greenhalgh, T. (2010b). What is this knowledge that we seek to 'exchange'? *The Milbank Quarterly, 88*(4), 492–499.

Greenwood, R., Oliver, C., Suddaby, R., & Sahlin, K. (2008). *The Sage handbook of organizational institutionalism.* London: Sage Publications.

Greenwood, R., Suddaby, R., & Hinings, C. R. (2002). Theorizing change: The role of professional associations in the transformation of institutionalized fields. *Academy of Management Journal, 45*(1), 58–80.

Grey, C. (1997). Management as a technical practice: Professionalization or responsibilization? *Systems Practice, 10*(6), 703–725.

Grey, C. (1999). 'We are all managers now'; 'we always were': On the development and demise of management. *Journal of Management Studies, 36*(5), 561–585.

Griffiths, F., Cave, J., Boardman, F., Ren, J., Pawlikowska, T., Ball, R., . . . Cohen, A. (2012). Social networks—the future for health care delivery. *Social Science & Medicine, 75*(12), 2233–2241.

Griffiths, R. (1983). *Report of the NHS management inquiry.* London: Department of Health and Social Security.

Grint, K. (1994). Reengineering history: Social resonances and business process reengineering. *Organization, 1*(1), 179–201.

Grint, K. (2005). Problems, problems, problems: The social construction of 'leadership'. *Human Relations, 58*(11), 1467–1494.

Grint, K. (Ed.). (1997). *Leadership: Classical, contemporary and critical approaches.* Oxford: Oxford University Press.

Gronn, P. (2002). Distributed leadership as a unit of analysis. *The Leadership Quarterly, 13*(4), 423–451.

Hales, C. P. (1986). What do managers do? A critical review of the evidence. *Journal of Management Studies, 23*(1), 88–115.

Ham, C., Heenan, D., Longley, M., & Steel, D. (2013). *Integrated care in Northern Ireland, Scotland and Wales: Lessons for England.* London: The King's Fund.

Hammer, M., & Champy, J. (1993). *Reengineering the corporation: A manifesto for business revolution.* London: Nicholas Brealey Publishing.

Handy, C. (2009). *Gods of management* (5th ed.). London: Souvenir.

Hansen, M. T. (2002). Knowledge networks: Explaining effective knowledge sharing in multiunit companies. *Organization Science, 13*(3), 232–248.

Harris, R., & Holt, R. (2013). Interacting institutional logics in general dental practice. *Social Science & Medicine, 94*, 63–70.

Harrison, R., & Miller, S. (1999). The contribution of clinical directors to the strategic capability of the organization. *British Journal of Management, 10*, 23–39.

Harrison, S. (1999). Clinical autonomy and UK health policy: Past and future. In M. Exworthy & S. Halford (Eds.), *Professionals and the new managerialism in the public sector*, 50–64. Buckingham: Open University Press.

Harrison, S., & McDonald, R. (2008). *The politics of healthcare in Britain*. London: Sage Publications.

Harrison, S., & Wood, B. (1999). Designing health service organization in the UK, 1968 to 1998: From blueprint to bright idea and 'manipulated emergence'. *Public Administration, 77*(4), 751–768.

Hartley, J., & Benington, J. (2006). Copy and paste, or graft and transplant? Knowledge sharing through inter-organizational networks. *Public Money & Management, 26*(2), 101–108.

Hassard, J., McCann, L., & Morris, J. (2009). *Managing in the modern corporation*. Cambridge: Cambridge University Press.

Heebels, B., Atzema, O., & van Aalst, I. (2013). Social networks and cultural mediators: The multiplexity of personal ties in publishing. *Industry and Innovation, 20*(8), 701–718.

Hodgson, D. (2002). Know your customer: Marketing, governmentality and the 'new consumer' of financial services. *Management Decision, 40*(4), 318–328.

Hood, C. (2006). Gaming in target world: The targets approach to managing British public services. *Public Administration Review, 66*(4), 515–521.

Huczynski, A. (1993). *Management gurus: What makes them and how to become one*. New York: Routledge.

Huy, Q. (2001). In praise of middle managers. *Harvard Business Review, 79*(8), 72–79.

Huy, Q. (2002). Emotional balancing of organizational continuity and radical change: The contribution of middle managers. *Administrative Science Quarterly, 47*(1), 31–69.

Hyde, P. (2010). Changing relationships between health service managers: Confrontation, collusion and collaboration. In J. Braithwaite, P. Hyde, & C. Pope (Eds.), *Culture and climate in health care organizations* (pp. 7–20). Basingstoke: Palgrave MacMillan.

Hyde, P., & Davies, H. (2004). Service design, culture and performance: Collusion and co-production in health care. *Human Relations, 57*(11), 1407–1426.

Hyde, P., & Exworthy, M. (2016). Setting the workers free? Managers in the (once again) reformed NHS. In M. Exworthy, R. Mannion, & M. Powell (Eds.), *Dismantling the NHS? Evaluating the effect of health reforms* (pp. 257–278). Bristol: Policy Press.

Hyde, P., Granter, E., Hassard, J., & McCann, L. (2016). *Deconstructing the welfare state: Managing healthcare in the age of reform*. London: Routledge.

Hyde, P., Granter, E., Hassard, J., McCann, L., & Morris, J. (2013). *Roles and behaviours of junior managers: Managing new organizational forms of healthcare. Final report*. London: NIHR Service Delivery and Organization Programme.

Hyde, P., Granter, E., McCann, L., Hassard, J., Dickenson, H., & Mannion, R. (Eds.). (2012). The lost health service tribe: In search of middle managers. In *The reform of health care: Shaping, adapting and resisting policy developments* (pp. 7–20). Basingstoke: Palgrave Macmillan.

Hyde, P., & McBride, A. (2011). The healthcare workforce. In K. Walshe & J. Smith (Eds.), *Healthcare management* (pp. 337–353). Maidenhead: Open University Press.

Hyde, P., & Thomas, A. (2002). Organizational defences revisited: Systems and contexts. *Journal of Managerial Psychology, 17*(5), 408–421.

Ibarra, H. H. (1999). Provisional selves: Experimenting with image and identity in professional adaptation. *Administrative Science Quarterly, 44*(4), 764–791.

Ibarra, H. H., & Barbulescu, R. (2010). Identity as narrative: Prevalence, effectiveness, and consequences of narrative identity work in macro work role transitions. *Academy of Management Review, 35*(1), 135–154.

Iedema, R., Degeling, J., Braithwaite, J., & White, L. (2004). It's an interesting conversation I'm hearing: The doctor as manager. *Organization Studies, 25*(1), 15–33.

Jackson, B. G. (1996). Re-engineering the sense of self: The manager and the management guru. *Journal of Management Studies, 33*(5), 571–590.

Järventie-Thesleff, R., & Tienari, J. (2016). Roles as mediators in identity work. *Organization Studies, 37*(2), 237–265.

Khurana, R. (2002). The curse of the superstar CEO. *Harvard Business Review, September,* 1–10.

Khurana, R. (2010). *From higher aims to hired hands: The social transformation of American business schools and the unfulfilled promise of management as a profession.* Princeton: Princeton University Press.

Kickert, W., Klijn, E., & Koppenjan, J. (1997). *Managing complex networks.* London: Sage Publications.

Kings Fund. (2011). *The future of leadership and management in the NHS: No more heroes.* London: The King's Fund.

Kippist, L., & Fitzgerald, A. (2009). Organizational professional conflict and hybrid clinician managers. *Journal of Health Organization and Management, 23*(6), 642–655.

Kirkpatrick, I. (1999). Markets, bureaucracy and public management: The worst of both worlds? Public services without markets or bureaucracy. *Public Money & Management, 19*(4), 7–14.

Kirkpatrick, I., Ackroyd, S., & Walker, R. (2005). *The new managerialism and public service professions.* London: Palgrave.

Klein, R. (2010). *The new politics of the NHS: From creation to reinvention.* Oxford: Radcliffe Publishing.

Knights, D., & McCabe, D. (2003). Governing through teamwork: Reconstituting subjectivity in a call centre. *Journal of Management Studies, 40*(7), 1587–1619.

Knorr-Cetina, K. (1999). *Epistemic cultures: How the sciences make knowledge.* Cambridge, MA: Harvard University Press.

Kotter, J. P. (1982). What effective general managers really do. *Harvard Business Review, 60*(6), 156–167.

Kotter, J. P. (1990). *A force for change: How leadership differs from management.* New York: Free Press.

Kreiner, G. E., Ashforth, B. E., & Sluss, D. M. (2006). Identity dynamics in occupational dirty work: Integrating social identity and system justification perspectives. *Organization Science, 17*(5), 619–636.

Lafond, S. (2015). *Current NHS spending in England.* London: Health Foundation.

Larson, M. S. (1977). *The rise of professionalism: A sociological analysis.* Berkeley: University of California Press.

Lave, J., & Wenger, E. (1991). *Situated learning: Legitimate peripheral participation.* Cambridge: Cambridge University Press.

Lawrence, T., & Suddaby, R. (2006). Institutions and institutional work. In S. Clegg, C. Hardy, T. Lawrence, & W. Nord (Eds.), *Handbook of organization studies* (pp. 215–254). London: Sage Publications.

Learmonth, M. (2005). Doing things with words: The case of 'management' and 'administration'. *Public Administration, 83*(3), 617–637.

Learmonth, M., & Harding, N. (2006). Evidence-based management: The very idea. *Public Administration, 84*(2), 245–266.

Learmonth, M., & Humphreys, M. (2012). Autoethnography and academic identity: Glimpsing business school doppelgangers. *Organization, 19*(1), 99–117.

Le Grand, J. (1999). Competition, co-operation or control? Tales from the British National Health Service. *Health Affairs, 18*, 27–99.

Lindblom, C. (1959). The science of 'muddling through'. *Public Administration Review, 19*(2), 79–88.

Lindkvist, L. (2005). Knowledge communities and knowledge collectivities: A typology of knowledge work in groups. *Journal of Management Studies, 42*(6), 1189–1210.

Llewellyn, S. (2001). Two-way windows: Clinicians as medical managers. *Organization Studies, 22*(4), 593–623.

Lloyd, J., Schneider, J., Scales, K., Bailey, S., & Jones, R. (2011). In-group identity as an obstacle to effective multidisciplinary teamworking: Findings from an ethnographic study of healthcare assistants in dementia care. *Journal of Interprofessional Care, 25*(5), 345–351.

Lockett, A., Currie, G., Finn, R., Martin, G., & Waring, J. (2013). The influence of social position on sense-making about organizational change. *Academy of Management Journal, 57*(4), 1102–1129.

MacIntosh, R., Beech, N., & Martin, G. (2012). Dialogues and dialectics: Limits to clinician-manager interaction in healthcare organizations. *Social Science & Medicine, 74*, 332–339.

Marchington, M., Grimshaw, D., Rubery, J., & Willmott, H. (2005). *Fragmenting work: Blurring organizational boundaries and disordering hierarchies.* Oxford: Oxford University Press.

Marsh, D., & Rhodes, R. (1992). Policy communities and issue networks. In D. Marsh & R. Rhodes (Eds.), *Policy networks in British government* (pp. 249–268). Oxford: Oxford University Press.

Martin, G. P., & Learmonth, M. (2012). A critical account of the rise and spread of 'leadership': The case of UK healthcare. *Social Science and Medicine, 74*(3), 281–288.

McCann, L., Hassard, J. S., Granter, E., & Hyde, P. J. (2015). Casting the lean spell: The promotion, dilution and erosion of lean management in the NHS. *Human Relations, 68*(10), 1557–1577.

McCann, L., Morris, J., & Hassard, J. (2008). Normalized intensity: The new labour process of middle management. *Journal of Management Studies, 45*(2), 343–371.

McCartney, S., Berman Brown, R., & Bell, L. (1993). Professionals in health care: Perceptions of managers. *Journal of Management in Medicine, 7*(5), 48–55.

McConville, T. (2006). Devolved HRM responsibilities, middle-managers and role dissonance. *Personnel Review, 35*(6), 637–653.

McDonald, R. (2014). Leadership and leadership development in healthcare settings—a simplistic solution to complex problems? *International Journal of Health Policy and Management, 3*(5), 227–229.

McGivern, G., Currie, G., Ferlie, E., Fitzgerald, L., & Waring, J. (2015). Hybrid manager-professionals' identity work: The maintenance and hybridization of medical professionalism in managerial contexts. *Public Administration, 93*(2), 412–432.

McGivern, G., & Ferlie, E. (2007). Playing tick-box games: Interrelating defences in professional appraisal. *Human Relations, 60*(9), 1361–1385.

McGivern, G., Lambrianou, A., Ferlie, E., & Cowie, M. (2009). Enacting evidence into clinical practice: The case of coronary heart disease. *Public Money & Management, 29*(5), 307–312.

McKee, L., Ferlie, E., & Hyde, P. (Eds.). (2008). *Organizing and reorganizing: Power and change in health care organizations.* London: Palgrave MacMillan.

McNulty, T. (2002). Reengineering as knowledge management: A case of change in UK healthcare. *Management Learning, 33*(4), 439–458.

McNulty, T., & Ferlie, E. (2002). *Reengineering health care: The complexities of organizational transformation.* Oxford: Oxford University Press.

Merali, F. (2003). NHS managers' views of their culture and their public image: The implications for NHS reforms. *The International Journal of Public Sector Management, 16*(7), 549–563.

Miles, R. E., & Snow, C. C. (1986). Network organizations: New concepts for new forms. *California Management Review, 28*(3), 62–73.

Miller, J. H. (2014). Professionalism interrupted? Professionalism's challenges to local knowledge in New Zealand counselling. *Current Sociology, 62*(1), 100–113.

Mintzberg, H. (1973). *The nature of managerial work.* New York: Harper and Row.

Mintzberg, H. (1979). *The structuring of organizations.* Englewood Cliffs, NJ: Prentice-Hall.

Mol, A. (2008). *The logic of care: Health and the problem of patient choice.* London: Routledge.

Morrell, K., & Learmonth, M. (2015). Against evidence-based management for management learning. *Academy of Management Learning and Education, 14*(4), 520–533.

Morris, J., & Farrell, C. (2007). The 'post-bureaucratic' public sector organization: New organizational forms and HRM in ten UK public sector organizations. *International Journal of Human Resource Management, 18*(9), 1575–1588.

Murphy, R. (1988). *Social closure: The theory of monopolization and exclusion.* Oxford; New York: Clarendon Press; Oxford University Press.

Musson, G., & Duberley, J. (2007). Change or be exchanged: The discourse of participation and the management of identity. *Journal of Management Studies, 44*(1), 164–185.

Nahapiet, J., & Ghoshal, S. (1998). Social capital, intellectual capital, and the organizational advantage. *Academy of Management Review, 23*(2), 242–266.

National Audit Office. (2012). *Healthcare across the UK: A comparison of the NHS in England, Scotland, Wales and Northern Ireland.* London: Stationary Office.

Newell, S., Edelman, L., Scarbrough, H., Swan, J., & Bresnen, M. (2003). 'Best practice' development and transfer in the NHS: The importance of process as well as product knowledge. *Health Services Management Research, 16*, 1–12.

Newell, S., Robertson, M., Scarbrough, H., & Swan, J. (2009). *Managing knowledge work and innovation*. Basingstoke: Palgrave Macmillan.

Newman, J. (2001). *Modernizing governance*. London: Sage Publications.

NHS England. (2014). *Five year forward view*. London: NHS England.

NHS Information Centre. (2010). *NHS hospital and community services non-medical staff England 1999–2009*. London: The NHS Information Centre.

NHS Information Centre. (2012). *NHS workforce: Summary of staff in the NHS: Results from September 2011 census*. London: The NHS Information Centre.

Nicolini, D. (2011). Practice as the site of knowing: Insights from the field of telemedicine. *Organization Science, 22*(3), 602–620.

Nicolini, D., Gheradi, S., & Yanow, D. (Eds.). (2003). *Knowing in organizations: A practice-based approach*. Armonk, NY: ME Sharpe.

Nicolini, D., Powell, P., Conville, P., & Martinez-Solano, L. (2008). Managing knowledge in the healthcare sector: A review. *International Journal of Management Reviews, 10*(3), 245–263.

Nicolson, P., Rowland, E., Lokman, P., Fox, R., Gabriel, Y., & Heffernan, K. (2011). *Leadership and better patient care: Managing in the NHS. Final report*. London: NIHR NETSCC Health Services and Delivery Research.

Nonaka, I. (1994). A dynamic theory of organizational knowledge creation. *Organization Science, 5*(1), 14–37.

Nonaka, I., & Takeuchi, I. (1995). *The knowledge creating organization*. Oxford: Oxford University Press.

Noordegraaf, M. (2011a). Remaking professionals? How associations and professional education connect professionalism and organizations. *Current Sociology, 59*(4), 465–488.

Noordegraaf, M. (2011b). Risky business: How professionals and professional fields (must) deal with organizational issues. *Organization Studies, 32*(10), 1349–1371.

Noordegraaf, M. (2015). Hybrid professionalism and beyond: (New) forms of public professionalism in changing organizational and societal contexts. *Journal of Professions and Organization, 2*(2), 187–206.

Noordegraaf, M., & Van Der Meulen, M. (2008). Professional power play: Organizing management in health care. *Public Administration, 86*(4), 1055–1069.

Oborn, E., Barrett, M., & Racko, G. (2013). Knowledge translation in healthcare. *Journal of Health Organization and Management, 27*(4), 412–431.

OECD. (2002). *Measuring up: Improving health system performance in OECD countries*. Paris: Organization for Economic Co-Operation and Development.

O'Reilly, D., & Reed, M. (2011). The grit in the oyster: Professionalism, managerialism and leaderism as discourses of UK public services modernization. *Organization Studies, 32*(8), 1079–1101.

Orlikowski, W. (2002). Knowing in practice: Enacting a collective capability in distributed organizing. *Organization Science, 13*(3), 249–273.

Orr, J. (1996). *Talking about machines: An ethnography of a modern job*. Ithaca, NY: ILR/Cornell University Press.

Osborne, D., & Gaebler, T. (1993). *Reinventing government: How the entrepreneurial spirit is transforming the public sector*. London: Penguin.

Ouchi, W. G. (1991). Markets, bureaucracies and clans. In G. Thompson, J. Frances, R. Levacic, & J. Mitchell (Eds.), *Markets, hierarchies, networks: The co-ordination of social life* (pp. 442–458). London: Sage Publications.

Owen-Smith, J., Riccaboni, M., Pammolli, F., & Powell, W. (2002). A comparison of us and European university-industry relations in the life sciences. *Management Science, 48*(1), 24–43.

Paton, S., & Hodgson, D. (2016). Project managers on the edge: Liminality and identity in the management of technical work. *New Technology Work and Employment, 31*(1), 26–40.

Perri, P., Goodwin, N., Peck, E., & Freeman, T. (2006). *Managing networks of twenty first century organizations.* Basingstoke: Palgrave Macmillan.

Peters, T., & Waterman, D. (1982). *In search of excellence.* New York: Harper and Row.

Pfeffer, J., & Sutton, R. (2006). *Hard facts, dangerous half-truths and total non-sense: Profiting from evidence-based management.* Boston, MA: Harvard Business School Press.

Polanyi, M. (1966). *The tacit dimension.* Garden City, NY: Doubleday.

Pollitt, C. (2013). The evolving narratives of public management reform. *Public Management Review, 15*(6), 899–922.

Powell, M. (1999). New labour and the 'third way' in the British NHS. *International Journal of Health Services, 29*, 353–370.

Powell, M., Durose, J., Duberley, J., Exworthy, M., Fewtrell, C., MacFarlane, F., & Moss, P. (2012). *Talent management in the NHS managerial workforce. Final report.* London: NIHR NETSCC Health Services and Delivery Research.

Powell, T. (1995). Total quality management as competitive advantage: A review and empirical study. *Strategic Management Journal, 16*(1), 15–37.

Powell, W. W. (1990). Neither market nor hierarchy: Network forms of organization. *Research in Organizational Behaviour, 12*, 295–336.

Powell, W. W., & DiMaggio, P. (Eds.). (1991). *The new institutionalism in organizational analysis.* Chicago: University of Chicago Press.

Preston, D., & Loan-Clarke, J. (2000). The NHS manager: A view from the bridge. *Journal of Management in Medicine, 14*(2), 100–108.

Putnam, R. (2001). *Bowling alone: The collapse and revival of American community.* New York: Simon and Schuster.

Radnor, Z. J., Holweg, M., & Waring, J. (2012). Lean in healthcare: The unfilled promise? *Social Science & Medicine, 74*(3), 364–371.

Raelin, J. A. (1985). The basis for the professional's resistance to managerial control. *Human Resource Management, 24*(2), 147–175.

Reay, T., & Hinings, C. R. (2005). The recomposition of an organizational field: Healthcare in Alberta. *Organization Studies, 26*(3), 351–384.

Reed, M., & Anthony, P. (1992). Professionalizing management and managing professionalization: British management in the 1980s. *Journal of Management Studies, 29*(5), 591–613.

Reeves, A., McKee, M., Basu, S., & Stuckler, D. (2014). The political economy of austerity and healthcare: Cross-national analysis of expenditure changes in 27 European nations 1995–2011. *Health Policy, 115*(1), 1–8.

Reynolds, L., Attaran, A., Hervey, T., & McKee, M. (2012). Competition-based reform of the National Health Service in England: A one-way street? *International Journal of Health Services, 42*(2), 213–217.

Reynolds, M. (1998). Reflection and critical reflection in management learning. *Management Learning, 29*(2), 183–200.

Roberts, J. (2006). Limits to communities of practice. *Journal of Management Studies, 43*(3), 623–639.

Robertson, M., Swan, J., & Newell, S. (1996). The role of networks in the diffusion of technological innovation. *Journal of Management Studies, 33*(3), 333–359.

Rousseau, D. (2006). Presidential address: Is there such a thing as 'evidence-based management'? *Academy of Management Review, 31*(2), 256–269.

Røvik, K. (2002). The secrets of winners: Management ideas that flow. In K. Sahlin-Andersson & L. Engwall (Eds.), *The expansion of management knowledge* (pp. 113–144). Stanford, CA: Stanford Business Books.

Sahlin-Andersson, K., & Engwall, L. (2002). Carriers, flows and sources of management knowledge. In K. Sahlin-Andersson & L. Engwall (Eds.), *The expansion of management knowledge* (pp. 3–32). Stanford, CA: Stanford Business Books.

Scarbrough, H., D'Andreta, D., Evans, S., Marabelli, M., Newell, S., Powell, J., & Swan, J. (2014). Networked innovation in the health sector: Comparative qualitative study of the role of collaborations for leadership in applied health research and care in translating research into practice. *Health Services and Delivery Research, 2*(13), 1–158.

Scarbrough, H., Swan, J., Laurent, S., Bresnen, M., Edelman, L., & Newell, S. (2004). Project-based learning and the role of learning boundaries. *Organization Studies, 25*(9), 1579–1600.

Senge, P. (1993). *The fifth discipline*. London: Century Hutchinson.

Sheaff, R., Marshall, M., Rogers, A., Roland, M., Sibbald, B., & Pickard, S. (2004). Governmentality by network in English primary healthcare. *Social Policy & Administration, 38*(1), 89–103.

Silverman, D. (1970). *The theory of organizations*. London: Heinemann.

Spender, J. C. (1996). Making knowledge the basis of a dynamic theory of the firm. *Strategic Management Journal, 17*, 45–62.

Spurgeon, P., Clark, J., & Ham, C. (2011). *Medical leadership: From the dark side to centre stage*. London: Radcliffe.

Stewart, P., Richardson, M., Danford, A., Murphy, K., Richardson, T., & Wass, V. (2009). *We sell our time no more: Workers' struggles against lean production in the British car industry*. London: Pluto Press.

Stewart, R. (1976). *Contrasts in management*. Maidenhead: McGraw-Hill.

Stewart, R. (1983). Managerial behaviour: How research has changed the traditional picture. In M. J. Earl (Ed.), *Perspectives on management* (pp. 82–98). London: Oxford University Press.

Strauss, A., & Corbin, J. (1990). *Basics of qualitative research: Grounded theory procedure and techniques*. Newbury Park, CA: Sage Publications.

Street, A., & Grasic, K. (2015, 2 April). Fact check: Are there more NHS doctors and nurses than before the coalition? *The Conversation*, https://theconversation.com/fact-check-are-there-more-nhs-doctors-and-nurses-than-before-the-coalition-39607 (accessed 3.12.15).

Stuckler, D., Basu, S., Suhrcke, M., Coutts, A., & McKee, M. (2009). The public health effect of economic crises and alternative policy responses in Europe: An empirical analysis. *The Lancet, 374*(9686), 315–323.

Sturdy, A. (2011). Consultancy's consequences? A critical assessment of management consultancy's impact on management. *British Journal of Management, 22*(3), 517–530.

Sturdy, A., Handley, K., Clark, T., & Fincham, R. (2009). *Management consultancy: Boundaries and knowledge in action*. Oxford: Oxford University Press.

Suddaby, R., & Viale, T. (2011). Professionals and field-level change: Institutional work and the professional project. *Current Sociology, 59*(4), 423–442.

Sullivan, H., & Skelcher, C. (2002). *Working across boundaries—collaboration in public services.* Basingstoke: Palgrave Macmillan.

Sveningsson, S., & Alvesson, M. (2003). Managing managerial identities: Organizational fragmentation, discourse and identity struggle. *Human Relations, 56*(10), 1163–1193.

Swan, J., Bresnen, M., Newell, S., & Robertson, M. (2007). The object of knowledge: The role of objects in biomedical innovation. *Human Relations, 60*(12), 1809–1837.

Swan, J., Clarke, A., Nicolini, D., Powell, J., & Roginski, C. (2012). *Evidence in management decisions: Advancing knowledge utilization in healthcare management. Final report.* London: NIHR Service Delivery and Organization Programme.

Swan, J., Goussevskaia, A., Newell, S., Robertson, M., Bresnen, M., & Obembe, A. (2007). Modes of organizing biomedical innovation in the UK and US and the role of integrative and relational capabilities. *Research Policy, 36*, 529–547.

Swan, J., Scarbrough, H., & Robertson, M. (2002). The construction of 'communities of practice' in the management of innovation. *Management Learning, 33*(4), 477–496.

Szulanski, G. (1996). Exploring internal stickiness: Impediments to the transfer of best practice within the firm. *Strategic Management Journal, 17*, 27–43.

Tansley, C., & Tietze, S. (2013). Rites of passage through talent management progression stages: An identity work perspective. *International Journal of Human Resource Management, 24*(9), 1799–1815.

Tempest, S., & Starkey, K. (2004). The effects of liminality on individual and organizational learning. *Organization Studies, 25*(4), 507–527.

Thomas, R., & Linstead, A. (2002). Losing the plot? Middle managers and identity. *Organization, 9*(1), 71–93.

Thompson, G. (2003). *Between hierarchies and markets—the logic and limit of network forms of organization.* Oxford: Oxford University Press.

Thompson, G., Frances, J., Levacic, R., & Mitchell, J. (Eds.). (1991). *Markets, hierarchies, networks: The co-ordination of social life.* London: Sage Publications.

Thrift, N. (2005). *Knowing capitalism.* London: Sage Publications.

Tomlinson, M., O'Reilly, D., & Wallace, M. (2013). Developing leaders as symbolic violence: Reproducing public service leadership through the (misrecognized) development of leaders' capitals'. *Management Learning, 44*(1), 81–97.

Tsoukas, H. (1996). The firm as a distributed knowledge system: A constructionist approach. *Strategic Management Journal, 17*(Winter), 11–25.

Tsoukas, H. (2005). *Complex knowledge: Studies in organizational epistemology.* Oxford: Oxford University Press.

Uzzi, B. (1997). Social structure and competition in inter-firm networks: The paradox of embeddedness. *Administrative Science Quarterly, 42*(1), 35–67.

von Knorring, M., Alexanderson, K., & Eliasson, A. (2016). Healthcare managers' construction of the manager role in relation to the medical profession. *Journal of Health Organization and Management, 39*(3), 421–440.

Wallace, M., & Tomlinson, M. (2010). Contextualizing leader dynamics: How public service leaders endeavour to build influence. *Leadership, 6*(1), 21–45.

Walshe, K., & Rundall, T. (2001). Evidence-based management: From theory to practice in health care. *The Milbank Quarterly, 79*(3), 429–457.

Walshe, K., & Smith, J. (Eds.). (2016). *Healthcare management*. Maidenhead: Open University Press.

Ward, V., Smith, S., House, A., & Hamer, S. (2012). Exploring knowledge exchange: A useful framework for practice and policy. *Social Science & Medicine, 74*(3), 297–304.

Waring, J., & Currie, G. (2009). Managing expert knowledge: Organizational challenges and managerial futures for the UK medical profession. *Organization Studies, 30*(7), 755–778.

Waring, J. J., & Bishop, S. (2010). Lean healthcare: Rhetoric, ritual and resistance. *Social Science and Medicine, 71*(7), 1332–1340.

Watson, T. J. (1994). *In search of management: Culture, chaos and control in managerial work*. London: Thompson Business Press.

Watson, T. J. (2008). Managing identity: Identity work, personal predicaments and structural circumstances. *Organization, 15*(1), 121–143.

Watson, T. J. (2009). Narrative, life story and manager identity: A case study in autobiographical identity work. *Human Relations, 62*(3), 425–452.

Watson, T. J., & Harris, P. (1999). *The emergent manager*. London; Thousand Oaks, CA: Sage Publications.

Weick, K. (1995). *Sensemaking in organizations*. Thousand Oaks, CA: Sage Publications.

Wenger, E. (1998). *Communities of practice: Learning, meaning, and identity*. Cambridge, UK: Cambridge University Press.

Wenger, E. (2000). Communities of practice and social learning systems. *Organization, 7*(2), 225–246.

Wenger, E., McDermott, R., & Snyder, W. (2002). *Cultivating communities of practice: A guide to managing knowledge*. Boston, MA: Harvard Business School Press.

Western, S. (2008). *Leadership: A critical text*. London: Sage Publications.

Whitehead, M., Hanratty, B., & Popay, J. (2010). NHS reform: Untried remedies for misdiagnosed problems? *The Lancet, 6763*(10), 231–237.

WHO. (2000). *The world health report 2000: Health systems: Improving performance*. Geneva: World Health Organization.

WHO. (2006). *Working together for health*. Geneva: World Health Organization.

Willem, A., & Buelens, M. (2006). Knowledge sharing in public sector organizations: The effect of organizational characteristics on interdepartmental knowledge sharing. *Journal of Public Administration Research and Theory, 17*(4), 581–606.

Williams, K., Haslam, C., Johal, S., & Williams, J. (1994). *Cars: Analysis, history, cases*. Oxford: Berghahn Books.

Willmott, H. (1993). Strength is ignorance; slavery is freedom: Managing culture in modern organizations. *Journal of Management Studies, 30*(4), 515–552.

Womack, J., Jones, D., & Roos, D. (1990). *The machine that changed the world*. New York: Rawson Associates.

Wu, Y. C. (2010). An exploration of substitutes for leadership: Problems and prospects. *Social Behaviour and Personality, 38*(5), 583–596.

Yin, R. (1984). *Case study research: Design and methods*. Beverly Hills, CA: Sage Publications.

Yin, R. (2003). *Case study research: Design and methods*. London: Sage Publications.

Zaleznik, A. (1977). Managers and leaders: Are they different? *Harvard Business Review, 55*(3), 67–78.

Zbaracki, M. (1998). The rhetoric and reality of total quality management. *Administrative Science Quarterly, 43*(3), 602–636.

Zollo, M., & Winter, S. (2002). Deliberate learning and the evolution of dynamic capabilities. *Organization Science, 13*(3), 339–351.

Index

accidental managers 90–4, 162–3
Acute Trust 32; accidental managers
91–4; age distribution 36; aspiring
managers 88–9; becoming
managers at 162–4; characteristics
of 32; clinical backgrounds and
qualifications 85; comparison of
trusts 32, 41; data collection 40;
description of 42–5; experience
and management knowledge
118–21, 123; gender distribution
36; general managers at 159; levels
of formal training 37; management
and leadership 70–3; management
educational qualifications
113–15; management training
and development 123, 125, 127;
managers by group 35; managing
clinical-managerial divide 63–5, 160;
networking in 137, 139–40, 143–6,
148; networks in 135, 170–1; non-
clinical educational qualifications 86;
pure play managers 98–9; reluctant
managers 94–7; years spent in 36
allied health professionals (AHPs) 78,
84, 150, 179
Aspiring Directors 123
aspiring managers 21, 64, 88–90, 99,
162–3
Athena programmes 19, 123, 141, 163

Bevan, Nye 21
Breaking Through 18–19, 123

career: development 5–6, 26, 36, 39;
development programmes 12, 18,
21, 125–6; and hybrid managers
82–4, 86–7, 99–100, 162–4; and
identity 79–82; narratives 81–2, 162;
networking for 137, 142–5, 148,
169–70; trajectories 57, 66, 78–9,
162–4, 179
Care Quality Commission (CQC) 16,
116, 175
Care Trust 32–3; accidental managers
91, 93–4; age distribution 36;
aspiring managers 88–9; becoming
managers at 162–4; characteristics
of 32; clinical backgrounds and
qualifications 85; comparison of
trusts 32, 41; data collection 40;
description of 45–8; experience and
management knowledge 118–19,
122–3; gender distribution 36; levels
of formal training 37; management
and leadership 71, 73–6; management
educational qualifications 113–14;
management training and development
124, 126–7; managers by group 35;
managing clinical-managerial divide
65–6, 160; networking in 137, 140–3,
145, 147–8; networks in 135, 170–1;
non-clinical educational qualifications
86; reluctant managers 96; years
spent in 36
case study trusts 41–51; Acute Trust
32, 41–5; Care Trust 32–3, 41, 45–8;
comparison of 32, 41; Specialist
Trust 32–3, 41, 49–51; *see also*
Acute Trust; Care Trust; Specialist
Trust
Castells, Manuel 131
Choice and Partnership Approach 117
Clinical Commissioning Groups
(CCGs) 15, 45, 134
clinical experience: influence on
management 109–13, 128;
management knowledge and 165–8

clinical-managerial divide: hybridity in healthcare 162–4; managing professionals 62–8

clinical managers 78; becoming 162–4; clinical backgrounds and qualifications 85; gender distribution by trust 36; levels of training 38; management training and development 123, 127; managerial cohort 34; network contacts of 135; networking of 142–3, 169; non-clinical educational qualifications 86; responsibilities of 58; sample by trust 35

coaching: counselling and 148; informal 141; mentoring and 120–1, 126, 168

codified systems: management knowledge 103–4, 113–16

Commission for Health Improvement (CHI) 14

Community Health and Standards Act (2003) 12

community of practice 26–7; healthcare management as 27–8, 173–5; and power 28, 108

comparative case study method: adoption 31–3; analytical generalizability 31

competitive tensions: networking challenge 152–3

consultants 35, 43, 50, 124; bridging clinical-managerial divide 63–7; management 17, 29, 103–4, 111; nurses as 89

Darzi Review (2008) 12, 15

data: coding and analysis 40–1; collection by interviews and observation methods 38–40

differentiation 55, 179

discourse 28, 79, 108; clinical 83, 106, 111, 140; financial 112, 128; and identity 79, 81–4; leaderism 21–2, 29, 68, 161; managerial 4, 62–3, 103–4

diversity: managerial, in healthcare 158–9

educational qualifications: influence on management knowledge 113–16

Elizabeth Garratt Anderson Programme 21

Equity and Excellence: Liberating the NHS (white paper) 11, 15

estates management 34, 127, 164

evidence-based management (EBMgt) 3, 106, 165

evidence-based medicine (EBM) 3, 165

finance 47–8, 177; emphasis on 112–13, 166; functional manager 34, 167, 173; managerial work 58–9, 62, 160; NHS 15–16; professional network 139; specialist area 113, 115, 127, 164; use of public 105

financial managers 6, 33, 164, 167

Five Year Forward View (NHS England) 15

Foundation Trust *see* NHS Foundation Trust

Francis Report (2013) 16

front-line staffing 17

functional managers: becoming 162–4; clinical backgrounds and qualifications 85; gender distribution by trust 36; levels of training 38; management knowledge of 167; management training and development 123–4, 126–7; managerial cohort 34; network contacts of 135; networking of 139–41, 143–5, 147–8, 169; non-clinical educational qualifications 86; responsibilities of 58, 61–2; sample by trust 35

Gateway to Leadership 18–19, 123

General Electric 20

general managers 6, 33–4, 78; becoming 162–4; clinical backgrounds and qualifications 85; gender distribution by trust 36; influence on management knowledge 110–12; levels of training 38; management training and development 123–5, 127; managerial cohort 34; network contacts of 135; networking of 139–40, 142–6, 148, 169–70; non-clinical educational qualifications 86; responsibilities of 58–61, 159; sample by trust 35

Graduate Management Training Scheme (GMTS) 18–19, 97–9, 123, 126, 139–40, 170

'hard' skills: technical 59

Health and Social Care Act (2012) 11–12, 15, 17, 20, 22–3, 157

204 *Index*

healthcare: managing delivery of
2–4; sector 10–11; understanding
networks in 131–3; *see also* National
Health Service (NHS)
Healthcare Leadership Model 21
healthcare management 7–8; as
community of practice 27–8, 173–5;
diversity in 158–9; future research
directions 180–1; institutional
barriers 105–6; institutional
reporting requirements and 116–8;
knowledge 104–7; perspectives on
practice 25–30; professionalization
of 178–9; prospects for professional
cadre in 177–80; research on 7–8
healthcare managers *see* managers
healthcare organizations: differentiation
in 55, 179; hybrid managers in 82–4;
integration of 45–8; management of
1–2; managing 10–11; rationalization
of 62, 92, 178
HR (human resource management)
123, 126; functional manager 34,
167, 173; managerial work 59, 160;
professional network 134, 139;
specialist area 113, 115, 127, 164,
166
hybridization: concept of 179; identity
work and 81–2, 99–100; work in
healthcare 62–3, 78–9
hybrid managers 9, 78, 100n1;
accidental managers 90–4; aspiring
managers 88–90; becoming 162–4;
in healthcare organizations 82–4;
incidental hybrids 83; pure play
managers 97–9; reluctant managers
94–7; two-way space of 83; willing
hybrids 83, 89; *see also* managers,
becoming

IAPT (Improving Access to
Psychological Therapies) 117
identity: healthcare managers
57–8; managerial careers 79–82;
ontological security 80; processes
of 26–8
identity work 57, 79–82, 84, 179;
see also identity
influence: networking for 137, 145–6,
148
information sharing: networking
challenge 150–2
initiatives: NHS management and
leadership 18–22

Inspiring Leaders (Department of
Health) 19
institutional work 80, 92
integration 45–8
intensification 3, 17, 43, 55, 149;
see also normalized intensity
interpersonal relationships: manager
and employee 59–60
interviews: data collection 38–40
isolation: networking challenge 154–5
IT (information technology) 34, 59,
113, 127, 167

knowledge 9; collectivity 175;
differences in knowing and
networking 179–80; information
sharing 150–2; management 4–7,
165–8; mobilization 2, 23, 30, 101–2,
106–8, 128, 175–7; networking for
137–40, 148; problems mobilizing,
and networks 175–7; stickiness
122–3; translation 5, 26, 29, 105–7,
113–16, 165–6; *see also* management
knowledge
knowledge and learning: healthcare
management 25–30

leaderism: discourse of 21–2, 29, 68,
161
leadership: concept of 5, 68–9, 74–6;
management and 68–76, 160–1;
management-leadership distinction
in NHS 174; portrayal of 70
Leadership Delivery Partners 22
leadership development: initiatives at
NHS 18–22
Leadership Qualities Framework 19, 21
lean production principles: knowledge
of 166–7
learning: problems mobilizing
knowledge and networks 175–7
legitimacy: clinical 168; of managers
54, 68, 79, 84, 97–8, 104–6; of
management knowledge 116, 140,
175–6
legitimate peripheral participation 27

management: concepts and practices
103–4; consequences at NHS 16–18;
discourse 4, 62–3, 103–4; diversity
in 6; fads and fashions 29, 104;
healthcare 7–8; initiatives for change
at NHS 18–22; knowing, networking
and practicing 4–7; leadership

and 68–76, 160–1; management-leadership distinction in NHS 174; portrayal of 70; theory and practice of work 55–8

management knowledge 26, 28–30; ambiguity of 102–4; clinical and specialist practices influencing 109–13, 128; clinical experience in 165–8; codified, tools and techniques 103–4, 113–16; de-professionalization of managers 177–8; experiential learning 118–23; of functional managers 167; healthcare challenges 101–2; in healthcare context 104–7; healthcare managers 1–2; institutional reporting requirements and 116–18; from knowledge to knowing 107–9; lean production principles in 166–7; legitimacy 116, 140, 175–6; managers' orientations to types of 109–28; networking relationships 130; problems mobilizing knowledge and networks 175–7; search for best practice 116–18; training and development 123–8

managerial cohorts: clinical backgrounds and qualifications 85; definition and identification 33–5; non-clinical educational qualifications 86; *see also* clinical managers; functional managers; general managers

managerialism 29, 106, 132, 166, 177

managers: backgrounds and experiences 84–7; bridging clinical-managerial divide 62–8; consequences at NHS 16–18; content and context of work 159–62; de-professionalization of 178; identities and careers of 79–82, 159–62; legitimacy 54, 68, 79, 84, 97–8, 104–6; management and leadership 68–76, 160–1; nature of managerial work and practice 53–5; networking of 168–72; problems mobilizing knowledge and networks 175–7; roles, responsibilities and skills of 58–62; theory and practice of work by 55–8; *see also* managers, becoming

managers, becoming: accidental managers 90–4, 162–3; aspiring managers 88–90, 162–3; changing managerial identity 82–4; clinical backgrounds and qualifications 85;

hybrid managers in healthcare 82–4; managers' perspectives on 87–99; pure play managers 97–9; reluctant managers 94–7, 162–3; *see also* hybrid managers

market experts 21

mentoring: management knowledge 120–1; networking 144, 147–8; relationships 143, 148

middle management 3, 35, 73, 94, 96, 166: challenges of 110, 127; defining 6; delayering of in healthcare 54–5, 67; in NHS 7, 29, 101; responsibilities of 33

Mid Staffordshire NHS Foundation Trust 16, 23

mind-lines 108

mobilization: of knowledge 2, 23, 30, 101–2, 106–8, 128, 175–7; of networks 175–7

Modernization Agenda 19

Monitor 16, 116; Acute Trust 42–3; Specialist Trust 49–50

multiplex networking 146–9

Myers-Briggs indicator: personality assessment 124–5

muddling through 119

National Health Service (NHS) 3, 7, 10; charting management changes in 12; consequences for managers and management 16–18; importance of clinicians within 161–2; initiatives for management change and leadership development 18–22; management 4; management and leadership training programmes 18; management-leadership distinction in 174; managing clinical-managerial divide 63–8; managing healthcare organizations of 10–11; middle managers 7; network concept in 131–2, 155–6; networking for career 142, 144; reforming and restructuring the 12–16; research context at 157–8; typology of networks 134; wage bill for 11

National Institute for Clinical Excellence (NICE) 14, 16, 23n3, 116

National Institute for Health and Clinical Excellence (NICE) 23, 24n3

National Voices 21

networked manager 153–4

networking 9, 130–1; for career
142–5; challenges to 149–55;
differences in knowing and 179–80;
for influence 145–6; for knowledge
138–40; knowledge transfer 108–9;
management 4–7; managers 168–72;
motives of 137; multiplex 146–9;
from networks to 136–49; peripheral
awareness and passive 139; problem-
solving and active 139; processes
of 26; purposes and motivations in
170–1; for support 140–2; tensions
and dilemmas in 175–7; ties 121,
123, 133, 168, 176
networks 8; concept of 5, 177;
dimensions of 134; diversity by trust
type 170–1; from, to networking
136–49; knowledge sharing 30;
locating in practice 133, 135;
networks of practice 132; problems
mobilizing knowledge and 175–7;
relationships 130; typology of 134;
understanding healthcare 131–3
The New NHS: Modern, Dependable
(white paper) 14
NHS and Community Care Act (1990)
12–13
NHS Foundation Trust 14, 16; Acute
Trust 32, 41–5; Care Trust 32–3, 41,
45–8; search for best practice 116;
Specialist Trust 32–3, 41, 49–51;
types of 32
NHS Leadership Academy 18–20, 182;
executive/senior leadership programme
18, 21; foundation programme 18,
20; mid-career programme 18, 21;
primary tasks 20; website 4*n*4,
24*n*6–8
NHS Leadership Council 18–19
NHS Management Inquiry (Griffiths)
13
NHS Plan (Department of Health) 14
NHS Training Authority 13
Nicholson, Sir David 15
Nicholson Challenge 15
normalized intensity 17, 120; *see also*
intensification

observation methods: data collection
38–40
ontological security: identity work 80
*The Operating Framework for the
NHS in England 2008/09* 19

payment by results 14, 17
peripheral awareness: networking as
139
personality assessment: Myers-Briggs
124–5
power 5, 28, 75–6, 108; clinical 62,
66, 83–4, 106, 161–2, 165, 175; in
communities of practice 28, 108; of
finance 128; in networks 135
practice: management work 55–8;
managing healthcare 4–7;
recommendations for 181–3
problem-solving: networking as 139
professional bureaucracy 2, 62, 106
professional identity: concept of 5;
of managers 79–82, 159–62
professional intransigence 62
professionalization: concept of 5,
8; literature on 28; healthcare
management 55, 62, 163, 177–9;
of NHS managers 19–20
professionals: bridging clinical-
managerial divide 62–8
project management (PM) 59, 114
protectionism: networking challenge
151
providers 11, 13–16, 41, 132
purchasers 13, 32–3, 132
pure play managers 82, 88; ambitions
and opportunities 97–9; healthcare
164

Quality, Innovation, Productivity and
Prevention (QIPP) 17

rationalization: organizational 62, 92,
178
rationalization: psychological 90, 93,
97; *see also* sense-making
reforming: National Health Service
(NHS) 12–16
Registered General Nurse (RGN) 85
Registered Mental Nurse (RMN) 85
reluctant managers: 94–7, 162–3
research: age distribution by trust 36;
coding and analysing data 40–1;
collecting data by interviews and
observation 38–40; comparative case
study method 31–3; developing an
approach 30–41; future directions
180–1; gender distribution by
trust and group 36; healthcare
management 7–8, 25–30; identifying

managerial cohorts 33–5; levels of formal training by management group 38; levels of formal training by trust 37; managerial experience 37–8; managers by group and by trust 35; sample characteristics 35–8; years spent in post, trust and NHS 36
restructuring: National Health Service (NHS) 12–16
The Rise of the Network Society (Castells) 131

Seacole, Mary 20
sense-making 79–80, 84, 160, 179; *see also* rationalization
single loop learning 122
situated learning 27, 168, 178; *see also* communities of practice
social connectedness 136
socialization: networking as 153–4
social learning: management knowledge 120–3
'soft' skills: personal and relational 59
specialist experience: influence on management 109–13
Specialist Trust 33; accidental managers 91–4; age distribution 36; aspiring managers 89–90; becoming managers at 162–4; characteristics of 32; clinical backgrounds and qualifications 85, 87; comparison of trusts 32, 41; data collection 40; description of 49–51; experience and management knowledge

119, 121–2; gender distribution 36; levels of formal training 37; management and leadership 72–3, 76; management educational qualifications 113; management training and development 124, 127; managers at 159; managers by group 35; managing clinical-managerial divide 63, 66–8, 160; networking in 137, 139–40, 142–4; networks in 170–1; non-clinical educational qualifications 86; pure play managers 98; reluctant managers 96; years spent in 36
State Registered Nurse (SRN) 85
sticky knowledge 122–3
stress 95–6, 149
subsidiarity: principle of 19–20
superleader: concept of 73
support: networking for 137, 140–2, 148

theory: management work 55–8
training and development: management 123–8
training programmes: NHS management and leadership 18
translation gap 104–5

vision 60, 91, 103; of aspiring managers 88; developing the 21, 160; of leadership 22, 77; management and leadership 68, 70–4

Working for Patients (white paper) 13

Printed in the United States
by Baker & Taylor Publisher Services

Printed in the United States
by Baker & Taylor Publisher Services